D1249028

THE LITTLE GRANDMOTHER
OF THE RUSSIAN REVOLUTION

Catherine Breshkovsky

The
Little Grandmother
of the
Russian Revolution

REMINISCENCES AND LETTERS OF
CATHERINE BRESHKOVSKY

Breshko-Breshkovskaia, Ekaterina

EDITED BY
ALICE STONE BLACKWELL

BOSTON
LITTLE, BROWN, AND COMPANY
1918

Copyright, 1917,

BY LITTLE, BROWN, AND COMPANY.

———

All rights reserved

Published, November, 1917
Reprinted, December, 1917 (twice)
January, 1918

920
B842b
97258

Norwood Press
Set up and electrotyped by J. S. Cushing Co., Norwood, Mass., U.S.A.

PREFACE

THE material in this book is drawn mainly from three sources. Madame Breshkovsky, while in New York, gave Doctor Abraham Cahan an account of her childhood and youth. He wrote out her reminiscences, and published them in his paper, the *Jewish Daily Forward*, in instalments, running from October 23, 1904, to January 18, 1905.

This account, translated from the Yiddish, and somewhat condensed, is here printed in English for the first time. It brings the narrative down to her first arrest. Through an interpreter, she gave a description of her early prison experiences and an outline of her later life to Ernest Poole, who published it in the *Outlook*. To the *Outlook* I am indebted also for her letters written in prison to her son. Her experiences after she was sent to Siberia for the second time are told in her own correspondence.

Her full name, in Russian, is Ekaterina Constantinovna Breshko-Breshkovskaya. I have used the shortened form of it which she herself used in this country.

ALICE STONE BLACKWELL.

3 MONADNOCK STREET,
DORCHESTER, MASS.

THE LITTLE GRANDMOTHER OF THE RUSSIAN REVOLUTION

CHAPTER I

THE Russian revolution is one of the great events of modern history. While it seemed to come with surprising suddenness, it was really the fruit of the labors and sacrifices of thousands of Russia's noblest men and women. Preëminent among these stands out the figure of Catherine Breshkovsky, known to millions by the affectionate name of Baboushka, the "Dear Little Grandmother" of the revolution.

She was born in 1844, on an estate in the district of Vitebsk, in Little Russia. She was fortunate in her parents. Whenever she speaks of them, her face lights up. "I had wonderful parents," she says. "If there is anything good in me, I owe it all to them." Her father, Constantine Mikhailovitch Verigo, was the son of a Polish aristocrat. Her mother, Olga Ivanovna Goremykina, came of a noble family of Great Russia. Catherine is therefore three fourths Russian and one fourth Polish.

Constantine Verigo was a handsome, elegant man, of majestic presence, with a large head, a high forehead, and blue eyes twinkling with good nature.

Even when his brow grew cloudy and his manner stern, the children were never afraid of him.

Neither her father nor her mother ever made an enemy. Her father was frank and open-hearted, with a hot temper that revolted against injustice. He often told the other landowners just what he thought of their pretences and their brutal treatment of their subordinates; but these outbursts were never laid up against him. He was universally respected and liked. His chief pleasure was to sit alone and read the works of liberal writers.

Her mother was not so handsome as her father, but had an intelligent and amiable face, exquisite manners, and irreproachable tact. She had attended school at the well-known Smolin Convent in Petrograd, and was a woman of culture. She was sincerely religious. She cared little for the pomps and ceremonies of the Greek Church, but brought her children up on the gospels, and on beautiful stories of holy men and women.

The mother was very careful in her behavior towards others, regardful of appearances and of "good form." If a truth were painful, she delicately concealed it. Over and over again she said to her children, "The best thing in life is the golden mean." She constantly admonished them that nothing was so harmful as excess. If a child failed to read her Bible, the mother would reprove her; and if the child then read the Bible too assiduously, the mother would reprove her again, and repeat that excess of any kind was fraught with danger. This was drummed into the children's ears so often that they dreaded to hear it. Nevertheless this polished lady was genuinely tender and warm-hearted. She was always well dressed, and took care that her children too should be neatly clad. On week days and Sundays alike, everybody wore clean clothes; no one needed to make any change when company was expected.

The home life of the family was rarely ruffled by unruly tempers or hasty words. The children were never whipped. If they misbehaved, their mother lectured them for hours, gently inculcating "the golden mean." Not a word of profanity was ever heard. Catherine's elder sister Natalie, when about eighteen, was a guest for a short time in a musician's family. On her return home she reported with much excitement that he had used in his talk such shocking vulgarisms as "Bah!" and "Piff!"

When Catherine was four years old, her father bought a large estate in the district of Tchernigov. There her childhood was passed.

She had a quick temper as a child. At three years old, she once got so angry that she struck her mother in the eye with a stick. In the end her mother's training enabled her to conquer this fault.

In her childhood she was always distressed about her innumerable "sins." "I would sin and straightway repent it," she said. "My heart was continually rent with grief over my misdeeds." What were the four-year-old girl's offenses? She would speak Russian when ordered to speak French, or she would sulk and pout when told to be "nice" to her brother and sister, or perhaps, later, she might refuse to learn her grammar lesson, which she hated. Her mother would sermonize her till Katya's little heart "softened like butter", and the tears streamed down her cheeks.

She would go to bed full of good resolutions, but when the next day came, again she would speak Russian when bidden to speak French.

When the children went out to walk, Katya used to keep apart from the others. She loved solitude. She had a passion for scrutinizing things and meditating over them, as her father did. This was one of her chief "sins." Governesses found the child quite unmanageable in this particular. She would persistently disappear from the rest of the group, and have to be hunted for with excitement and anxiety, until she was finally discovered and driven back to the fold. One German governess was so vexed by her habit of suddenly vanishing that she exclaimed, "Katya is a spider!"

Her mother could not understand this eccentric child. What added to her concern was that the little girl's neck was slightly crooked. "*Malheureuse enfant!*" she would sigh, with a mournful shake of the head. And Katya, hearing it, would wonder, "What are they bothering about?" Her crooked neck never troubled her. She was wholly indifferent as to her looks.

She used to run off to the meadows and watch the cows grazing, and then go to the huts of the serfs, and mingle with the peasant children and their mothers, studying their life, and entering into every peasant woman's troubles.

From earliest childhood she was vividly impressed by the sharp contrast between the condition of her father's hundreds of serfs and that of her own family. Sometimes she would seize a little peasant boy by the hand and hurry him into her beautiful home, leading him through the exquisitely furnished rooms till she found her mother sitting in the parlor, reading or knitting. Then she would beg her mother to look at the poor little fellow, whose legs were so skinny, his stomach so big, his face so dirty and hollow, and his clothing nothing but rags. To her mother this seemed natural. The unnatural thing was for a rich little girl to drag a dirty peasant child into her mother's parlor.

Her mother had taught her to be kind and courteous to the servants, and she loved to pass her time with them; but whenever her mother found her among them, she drew her away, saying, "Katya, this is no place for you."

She wrote in after years: "We lived in a large house, richly decorated and handsomely furnished, surrounded by beautiful parks and gardens. It was always open to receive visits from other families of the nobility who were scattered about the district where we lived, and to guests from other parts of the empire, especially during the great fêtes which were given several times a year. Their carriages filled the court-yard, their servants of every degree crowded the corridors and anterooms, and ladies in elegant toilets and men in full dress surrounded the enormous tables, which groaned beneath the weight of the festal meats, prepared by cooks who had served their apprenticeship in St. Petersburg, Warsaw, and even Paris. The Russian nobility loved luxury, and they knew how to secure admirable service. Orchestras, troops of actors and singers were found in the homes of the Russian gentry. Yet all these actors and musicians, as well as the cooks, valets and nurses, were Russian peasants, transformed by the will of their masters that they might make a brave show, a little court, in imitation of that of the Czar.

"But the life of the manor-house was not the only one to attract the attention of a child with vivid imagination, warm heart and active mind. Scattered about my father's estate, as about every other landed proprietor's dwelling, were so-called villages, long streets of miserable huts where lived great robust creatures clad in coarse garments, uncombed, almost unwashed, who, if they saw their master or any of his family coming, would hastily pull off their head covering and bow almost to the ground. These were the peasants who tilled the soil. Rising before the sun, they could not go to bed till late at night, for they had to pass all their time at work in the fields, the meadows, the woods, the granaries, the stables, the parks, the pastures. They worked everywhere and always. They were scolded, they were whipped, they were exiled to Siberia, at the whim of their master, for the least fault. Their wives and daughters were taken to serve the master or his sons as mistresses; their children were carried off without their consent to be trained as servants or to serve in the house. The men would come to the master begging bread for which their families were famishing; the women would come weeping, demanding their children of whom they had been robbed. How many times, stupefied and shocked, I have been the witness of such humiliating, degrading, excruciating things! How many times I have thrown myself at my father's feet to implore pardon for a so-called culprit, whose only fault, perhaps, was to have fallen asleep while herding the sheep! How many times I have been indignant to see how hundreds of peasants would be kept waiting in the court-yard, bare-headed and shivering with cold, waiting for the master to appear, who, after making them wait all day, would send them off without a word, so taken up was he with gambling at cards with other lords, who in their turn were making their coachmen wait on the carriage box till their hands were frozen!

"These things tormented my childish mind, and pursued me even into my bed, where I would lie awake for hours, unable to sleep for thinking of all the horrors about me.

"I had wide opportunity to observe the life of the peasantry, for they came in groups to discuss every event relating to their communal life with my father, and during such hours I was always at his side, that I might hear what the peasants had to say. There were questions about the fields, the pastures, the woods, the building of cabins, the taxes they must pay, the roads to be built, the marshes to be drained. Then there were questions about recruiting; for in those days it was only the peasants who gave their sons to the Russian army. Child as I was, I could not understand why these honest folk should bear the entire burden of work and of taxes. I saw that my father, good though he was, put much more heart into looking after his own interests than the interests of his serfs, and I was shocked at the inequality between the rich and the poor.

"Often I escaped from home and went alone to the neighboring villages to visit the huts of our peasants; and there I would see old men lying on the straw,

friendless and famished, while all through the long
summer days the entire population strong enough to
work was in the fields, where they would have to toil
till the night fell. The little children, dirty, emaci-
ated, would be quarreling in the mud or dust, eating
from the same dish with the dogs, and even the pigs.
Every Sunday I would see the peasants going into
our church, praying with fervor, pouring out their
tears, and giving their last kopek in the name of God
that there might be a better life in the next world,
since that was their only hope of happiness.

"From the age of eight, how to find justice was the
question that troubled me."

Yet the Verigos treated their serfs with much more
consideration than most Russian landowners. Her
father never had a serf flogged. Their serfs appreciated
the difference, and constantly boasted of it. "We
belong to the Verigos!" they would say with pride.
When Katya, in conversation with the neighbors,
referred to the contrast between the condition of her
father's serfs and theirs, she would be cut short with
the retort, "Well, your estate is a republic!" Yet
even among the Verigos there was not a really warm
and friendly feeling toward the peasants, except on
Katya's part.

The selfish desire to grab everything, which often
shows itself in children at one stage of their development, was unknown to Katya. Her tendency was to
give away everything that came into her hands. If
she were given some crisp delicacy, fresh from the
oven, she would immediately present it to one of the
servants. If she got a new toy, she passed it on to
some peasant child before the day was out. Often

she came home without her cloak or without her dress, having given it away to some shivering, half-clad creature. Rebuked by her mother, she answered, "Mamma, you read to us from the gospel that if any one has two garments he should give one to the poor. Why are you angry if I do just what you read to us?"

Katya cared little for dolls or playthings, but was very fond of living creatures. She longed for a kitten or a calf. At five years old she begged her mother to give her the entire charge of a young calf. At first her mother would not hear of it. Finally she yielded in part. The children were taken to the barnyard and told that each might choose a calf. They were then brought into the house and instructed to work the names of their pets upon cloth collars, and afterwards they were allowed to adorn the calves with the collars. Their mother thought this was quite enough, and forbade the children to go near the calves any more.

Katya was not satisfied. She yearned to have a little calf of her own, that she could take care of and make a companion. One day as she wandered through the fields, she came upon a thick branch broken from a tree, with twigs growing in such a way as to give it a rough resemblance to an animal. Her heart beat with joy. Here at last was her calf! She propped it up against the tree, and hurried to the house for provisions. She set food before it in one dish and milk in another. Three times a day she fed it, visiting it secretly, and weaving around it all sorts of fancies.

But one day when she was with her governess and

the other children, she was seized with an irresistible wish to visit her calf. Half unconsciously, she led them towards it. As soon as they caught sight of it, they all exclaimed, "Ah, Katya's calf! It is Katya's calf!" Katya felt abashed. Her illusion was shattered, and her wooden calf gave her no further pleasure.

She was always dreaming of helping some one. After the loss of her calf, this dream absorbed her whole being.

She was more interested in people than in anything else. When the family made journeys in their coach, she often caught sight of Jews, and she was moved to great curiosity by their singularities. She looked with awe upon these people who spoke a strange language, wore outlandish clothes, and ate food prepared according to peculiar rules.

Once she saw a group of men with shaven heads and bare feet, laden with heavy chains, driven along the street, under guard. She was much impressed by the sorrowful sight, and asked her mother who they were.

"They are unfortunate people — lost people, who have taken the wrong path in life," her mother answered. But the response did not dispel the mystery. She was constantly asking questions to which she got no answer.

Her chief concern, however, was for the great class of peasants. Her dream was to help them and make them happy. She imagined herself the mistress of a vast estate, where all the unfortunate serfs in the world might live, wearing beautiful clothes, having plenty to eat, and passing their days free from care.

On quiet summer afternoons she would lie down with the tall grass all around her, and look up into the sky, with its flocks of fleecy clouds. In the distance there was a hill over which a coach occasionally passed. Every cloud that drifted by seemed to bear the form of some definite object — a tree, a giant, a city, hills and valleys — whatever she had heard or read about. Against these clouds as a background she built her castles in the air.

She had heard of America, and how Columbus and his companions went there in search of gold, and found treasure in abundance; and she planned to go to California, and there heap up fortunes to bring back with her for the serfs. She would buy vast tracts of land — there they were, in the clouds, mostly islands — and there the peasants should live and cultivate the fertile soil. As she gazed into the many-colored clouds, she saw the very world that she hoped to create.

Katya talked freely of her plans about California, and when her family made fun of them, she answered naïvely, "But many people have brought gold from that land!"

CHAPTER II

THE estate of the Verigos was an oasis in the desert. Among the families that they visited, Katya saw very different scenes.

A neighbor and relative of the Verigos was Madame Shiria, a widow with an idiot son. She had the disposal of his immense fortune, and squandered it recklessly. Other relatives tried to have a guardian appointed for him. It was the government's custom to let all matters be decided by the nobility rather than by experts. Instead of having a commission of doctors determine whether the young man was mentally deficient, the authorities decreed that the question should be settled by his acquaintances. Then on every side there were disputes, one person crying, "Fedia is an idiot!" and another protesting, "Fedia is not an idiot!" The line of cleavage was between those who expected to inherit something from Fedia's estate and those who hoped to get a handsome present from Fedia's mother. Madame Shiria hired a young man to personate her son, and placed him in a notary's office as proof that he was quite able to manage his own affairs. Meanwhile she continued to squander his property. She lived like a queen. During a single winter in Berlin she spent two hundred thousand rubles. She was a woman of rare beauty, and captivated the heart of the

German Emperor; but she filled honest little Katya
with disgust.

Once during a grand ball at Madame Shiria's, Katya
ran from room to room, looking and listening, as was
her custom. The band was playing, couples were
dancing, and laughter and merrymaking reigned
supreme. At last Katya reached the outer room. In
the shadow of the doorway stood a sorrowful figure with
bowed head. It was a serf waiting to see Madame
Shiria. He had been waiting there all day in the same
attitude. He was in tatters, and through the rents in
his rags his limbs looked like those of a skeleton. At
last Madame Shiria's silken train was heard sweeping
along the polished floor, and she appeared. The
starving peasant trembled, and a faint light of hope
flickered in his eyes. She asked in a chilling tone,
"What do you want here?" He threw himself at her
feet, and broke into a storm of sobs.

"My lady, God bless you! Have pity on me. My
cow is dead. Help me, I beg of you!"

Madame Shiria stepped back with disdain. "How
do these things concern me? Go to my steward.
Go."

The serf had already been to the steward, who had
sent him to the lady. Katya and her sisters pleaded
for the unfortunate man, but he was put out of the
house, and Madame Shiria went back to her ballroom.
Katya's heart felt as if it were weighed down by a
heavy stone.

Another neighbor was fat Duke Baratov, whose
"god was his belly." Poor himself, he had married a
rich countess, and built a luxurious palace with his
wife's money. He kept an orchestra, and gave magnifi-

cent banquets and balls. On every holiday a fortune
was spent on the champagne alone. And all this
fountain of squandered wealth flowed from a source
buried in muddy huts and squalid poverty — from the
meek and oppressed peasants. Their last penny,
their last bit of cloth, cheese, butter, and bread went
into his storehouse, while they were starving. He
plundered not only the peasants but the merchants.
If a merchant came to buy wheat, the Duke would
exact a large deposit in advance, promising prompt
delivery of the wheat in return. Then he would sell
the same wheat over and over again to half a dozen
other merchants, taking a deposit from each, and, of
course, failing to deliver the grain. The merchants had
no redress against a nobleman. The Duke was a frequent visitor at Madame Shiria's, where a circle of the
more worthless nobility used to gather. Katya knew
this group. She often heard their behavior discussed
and condemned in her own home.

Another nobleman was a kleptomaniac, to put it
delicately. Wherever he went, his friends had to
keep an eye on their silver spoons and candlesticks.

There were a few nobles of a better type. Constantine Verigo liked Nicholas Kovalik—the father of that
Kovalik who afterwards became a leader in the revolutionary movement of the seventies. Young Kovalik's mother and Katya's mother had been schoolmates.
The friendship between the two families was so close
that, although their estates lay far apart, visits were
frequent; and the simplicity and sincerity of the
Kovaliks made a lasting impression on Katya.

When the nobles of the better sort got together, she
noticed that they often discussed certain matters in

subdued tones and behind closed doors. Sometimes one would read aloud an article not wholly favorable to the Czar, or recite a poem by Pushkin or Chamikon. Those were the days of the terrible Czar Nicholas. Nobody dared to say a word against him in public, but the nobles condemned him in secret. Then came the Crimean War, and the great siege of Sebastopol; and those same nobles freely offered the Czar regiments of serfs gathered from their estates. Thousands of peasants wearing red girdles and red hatbands were torn from their families, armed with guns and axes, and sent forth to do or die, in the name of God and the Czar. These contradictions between men's thoughts and their actions grated on the young girl's feelings, and made her wonder.

Another acquaintance of the Verigos was a Duchess Galitzin, living on a grand estate near Lugovetz in the Starodubov district, in a palace that an emperor might have envied. She was a member of the highest aristocracy, as intimate with the Czar's family as with her own. When Katya was still very young, the Duchess invited Constantine Verigo to take charge of her vast estate as her steward, and Verigo, having but little to do, consented.

He rode to Lugovetz, taking his family with him. Katya now had a chance to see what was considered the highest society; and when they afterwards went to Petrograd, she found herself among the very flower of the aristocracy. The old Duchess had ladies in waiting of various degrees, and innumerable servants and attendants, all graded and classified. Before any one entered her august presence, it was necessary to go through a long series of scrutinies and cross-examinations. The only rebel against these ceremonies was little Katya. She objected to bowing before the Duchess as before a goddess. Her mother told her that the Duchess was her elder in years, and demanded reverence; but Katya felt that the old lady preferred submission to reverence, and fear to love.

The mother had brought the children up on the Bible and religious stories; but in the Duchess's library they found material of every kind. There were pictures of foreign countries, landscapes and love scenes, romances and books of history and travel. At nine years old Katya had read the whole of Karanzin's "History of Russia", in several volumes. She read books of travel with eagerness, and remembered the details so well that once, years after, when she talked about foreign countries with the captain of a ship, he felt sure that she must have actually visited the places she described. Her practical mind led her also to devour discussions of the market price of wheat, of land, etc., and to study her father's business records and letters. She did not care for fiction. What interested her was real life.

As she learned more, she grew more and more heartsick over the way the peasants were treated. When she was but ten years old, her indignation against the flogging of the serfs broke out in such hot words that her old peasant nurse begged her to speak low.

"My father helped me to think," she says. "He was a man of broad, liberal ideas. We read together many books of science and travel. Social science absorbed me. By sixteen I had read much of Voltaire, Rousseau, and Diderot, and I knew the French Revolution by heart. I spoke French from babyhood, and my German governess had taught me German; and at that time the world's best thought was not garbled by the Russian censorship.

"Fired by such ideas, I saw the poor, degraded slaves around me, and longed to set them free. At first I believed that freedom could be reached without a radical change of government. No revolutionary spirit had yet been kindled. It was the first great era of the Liberals. The emancipation of the serfs was soon to take place; so too the introduction of trial by jury; and these promised reforms sent a social impulse sweeping through Russia. I was thrilled by the glad news. Filled with young enthusiasm, I opened a little school near our estate.

"I found the peasant an abject, ignorant creature, who did not understand even the meagre rights he already had. He could think only of his mud hut and his plot of ground. As for the government, he knew only that in peace he must pay money; in war, lives. The new rumors had kindled his old heart-deep hope of freedom. The twenty peasants in my school, like the millions in Russia, suspected that the proclamation had been hidden, and often went to the landowners demanding their freedom. At last the manifesto emancipating the serfs arrived."

This was in 1861, when Catherine was seventeen. It was an era of hope and enthusiasm among the Russian Liberals. But in some respects emancipation made the lot of the peasants worse instead of better. Under the old régime, each serf, besides cultivating his master's estates, had had a plot of ground on which he raised food for his own family. He had supposed that this plot of ground would still belong to him. He soon found his mistake.

"The peasant was free. No longer bound to the land, his landlord ordered him off. He was shown a little strip of the poorest soil, there to be free and starve. He was bewildered; he could not imagine himself without his old plot of land. For centuries past, an estate had always been described as containing so many 'souls.' It was sold for so much per 'soul.' The 'soul' and the plot had always gone together. So the peasant had thought that his soul and his plot would be freed together. In dull but growing rage, he refused to leave his plot of land for the wretched strip. 'Masters,' he cried, 'how can I nourish my little ones through a Russian winter? Such land means death.' This cry rose all over Russia.

"The government appointed in every district an 'arbiter' to persuade the peasants. The arbiter failed. Then troops were quartered in their huts, families were starved, old people were beaten by drunkards, daughters were raped. The peasants grew more wild, and then began the flogging. In a village near ours, where they refused to leave their plots, they were driven into line on the village street; every tenth man was called out and flogged with the knout; some died. Two weeks later, as they still held out, every fifth man was flogged. The poor ignorant creatures still held desperately to what they thought their rights; again the line, and now every man was dragged forward to the flogging. This process went on for five years all over Russia, until at last, bleeding and exhausted, the peasants gave in.

"I heard heartrending stories in my little school-house, and many more through my father, the arbiter of our district. The peasants thronged to our house day and night. Many were carried in, crippled by the knout. Sobbing wives told of husbands killed before their eyes. Often the poor wretches literally grovelled, clasping my father's knees, begging him to read the manifesto again and find it was a mistake, beseeching him to search for help in that mysterious region, the law court. From such interviews he came to me worn and haggard.

"I now saw how ineffectual were my attempts; I felt that tremendous economic and political changes must be made; but I was still a Liberal, and thought only of reform, not of revolution. To seek guidance, to find out what older heads were thinking, I went at nineteen with my mother and sister to St. Petersburg. Into our compartment on the train came a handsome young prince returning from official duties in Siberia. For hours he discussed with me the problems that were rushing upon us. His words thrilled like fire. Our excited voices rose steadily higher, until my mother begged me, as my nurse had done before, to speak low. That young prince was Peter Kropotkin."

In Petrograd, Catherine joined the central group of Liberals, men and women of noble birth and university training; doctors, lawyers, journalists, novelists, poets, scientists. Since higher education for women was strictly forbidden, they had already become law-breakers by opening classes for women in the natural and political sciences. All these classes she attended.

Her mother fell ill and had to go home. She wanted to take Catherine with her; but the young girl objected. She longed for independence; she believed it to be a duty to earn her own living. Many of the younger nobility had come to the same conviction. Prince

Kropotkin, in his "Memoirs of a Revolutionist", quotes the words of the Russian poet, Nekrasof, "The bread that has been made by slaves is bitter." He adds:

"The young generation actually refused to eat that bread, and to enjoy the riches that had been accumulated in their fathers' houses by means of servile labor, whether the laborers were actual serfs, or slaves of the present industrial system.

"All Russia read with astonishment, in the indictment produced in court against Karakózoff and his friends, that these young men, owners of considerable fortunes, used to live three or four in a room, never spending more than five dollars apiece a month for all their needs, and giving their fortunes to start coöperative associations, coöperative workshops (where they themselves worked), and the like. Five years later, thousands and thousands of the Russian youth — the best part of it — were doing the same. During the years 1860–1865, in almost every wealthy family a bitter struggle was going on between the fathers, who wanted to maintain the old traditions, and the sons and daughters, who defended their right to dispose of their lives according to their own ideals. Young men left the military service, the counter, the shop, and flocked to the university towns. Girls bred in the most aristocratic families rushed penniless to St. Petersburg, Moscow, and Kiev, eager to learn a profession. . . . After hard and bitter struggles, many of them won personal freedom. Now they wanted to utilize it, not for their own personal enjoyment, but to carry to the people the knowledge that had emancipated them."

Catherine compromised with her mother by entering

a nobleman's household as governess to his children.
It was useful work, and it enabled her to stay in the
city. She held this position for two years and a half,
and was well treated, her character commanding both
affection and respect. Meanwhile she studied the
working of the zemstvo. Every institution that was a
beginning of representative government, however imperfect, was holy in the eyes of the Russian "intellectuals."

Her father finally insisted upon her returning home.
He promised that she should be independent, and live
on her own earnings. He helped her to open a board-
ing school for girls, and through the influence of her
relatives she obtained many pupils, daughters of rich
parents, who paid for their instruction. Her father
also built her a cottage where she taught the peasant
children free. All that she earned above her livelihood
she devoted to helping the peasants. She would buy
a cow for one, a horse for another, doing her utmost
to relieve the misery around her. "I now drew closer
to the people," she says. "I began to realize the dull
memory every peasant has of flogging and toil from
time immemorial. I felt their subconscious but heart-
deep longing for freedom."

Three years later, at the age of twenty-five, she
married a liberal, broad-minded young nobleman, with
a good education and a good heart. He was active
in the district zemstvo, and took a sincere interest in
the peasants. He was glad to help Catherine in her
good work, and they established a coöperative bank
and a peasants' agricultural school. Several of the
younger landowners became interested, and they met
together frequently.

Catherine, however, felt the need of doing something more radical. In quest of more light and more helpers, she went to Kiev, where one of her sisters was nursing a husband lying at the point of death. Catherine attended the funeral, and comforted the widow. Just then she got a letter from Kovalik, the friend of her childhood, announcing that he and several others who were profoundly dissatisfied with the state of things in Russia were going to America to found a colony where everybody would work with their hands as well as their brains — a sort of Brook Farm. He invited her to join them. She replied:

"Never. How can we leave Russia now, when there is so much of importance to be done here, that is hardly even begun? In America they are better off without us than the people in Russia are with us."

Meanwhile she looked about her in Kiev for recruits to the cause of progress. She knew no one in the city, but she determined to search for "good people." The university students had established a lunch room where meals could be had for six rubles a month. Any outsider could eat there at the same price. Catherine paid for a month's board in advance, and came every day, to eat and observe. The room occupied the whole ground floor of an old wooden building. The tables were long rough-hewn fixtures, with tablecloths not over clean. At each corner stood piles of thick, heavy white plates, and at meal times these would be dropped along in a row with a great clatter, amid the din made by the students, talking, discussing, and waxing hot in argument, seemingly much more interested in feeding their minds than their stomachs. Catherine was wearing her old-fashioned Atlas fur, with its short sleeves, sable collar, and satin hood — a garb long out of style; but neither she nor the students cared about fashion. Dinner was served from one to five P.M., and she ate leisurely, meanwhile watching the students' faces, listening to their talk, and trying to judge of their characters. After a while she wrote on slips of paper her name and the address of the hotel where she and her sister were staying, and the next day at dinner time she distributed the slips to the students who had made the most favorable impression upon her, saying, "Come to see me, and let us talk things over."

Five students came the same evening. They were frank, sympathetic young men, students not only of books but of life. She came to the point at once. "Why are you doing nothing," she said, "when the great mass of the people in Russia are starving, with the yoke on their necks and the wolf at the door? Why are you idlers? Why do you use the academic to screen your eyes from the real?"

All gave the same answer: "We are idlers; but what is to be done? How can we make things better?" Some of them were acquainted with revolutionists: but they were not sure whether they wanted to become revolutionists themselves or not.

No immediate answer could be given to their question, "What is to be done?" But they began to cultivate a closer acquaintance with the revolutionists, and introduced Catherine to them.

Soon she was summoned home. Then she and her husband and their little circle of Liberals made a vigorous effort to secure better treatment for the peasants through political action.

She says: "It is a poor patriot that will not thoroughly try his government before he rises against it. We searched the laws and edicts; we found certain scant and long-neglected peasants' rights of local suffrage; and then we began showing the peasants how to use these rights that they already had."

Catherine proved an effective speaker at the meetings they held among the peasants. She had a clear, strong voice; she could talk to the people in words that they understood; and she exercised the power that always emanates from a great personality and a great heart.

The peasants flocked to the local elections, and began electing men of liberal views as judges, arbiters, and other officials. One of Catherine's brothers was chosen as a judge, and so was her friend Kovalik, whose plan of starting a colony in America had encountered many difficulties and had been indefinitely postponed. While he was on a visit to the Verigos, Catherine persuaded him to become a candidate. As a resident of another province he was disqualified; but Constantine Verigo made a nominal lease of his estate to Kovalik, and thus rendered him eligible. He was a man of marked ability, and a natural leader. The other judges elected him as their chief; and in three months he cleared up an accumulation of eight hundred cases that had clogged the docket for years. He and the other Liberal officials decided all cases with strict justice to the peasants, and defended their legal rights against the oppression of the nobility. But when the more despotic landowners were ousted from the positions that they had made a source of graft, they denounced the little group of Liberals to the Minister of the Interior as a band of conspirators against the government. In less than a year, Kovalik was turned out of his judgeship on a technicality; Constantine Verigo was deposed from office, as a dangerous man; several of their friends were exiled to Siberia without trial; Catherine and her husband were put under police surveillance, and the school and the bank that they had opened for the peasants were closed.

A rigid inquiry was also instituted as to the kind of addresses that Catherine had been making to the peasants, and the Governor of the province himself asked Constantine Verigo for an explanation. Verigo said that his daughter had felt it her duty to expound the new laws to the peasants, so that they might have a clearer understanding of their rights. The Governor answered dryly, "We want no apostles here." He intimated bluntly to Verigo that the less he and his household meddled with peasant questions the better it would be for them, and for the peasants too.

This experience convinced Catherine of the necessity of a change in the existing form of government, before any serious improvement could be brought about. All over Russia the attempts made by liberal-minded men and women to educate and elevate the peasants by peaceful means were meeting with the same fate. Punished as criminals for teaching the peasants their legal rights, they learned to see the autocratic government as it really was, a vast system of corruption, watching jealously through spies and secret police to keep its peasant victims from being taught anything that could make them think or act like men.

To try to overthrow the autocracy was to face imprisonment, torture, exile, and death. Catherine was twenty-six years old. Her husband, like herself, had a whole life before him. She felt that it was only fair to put the matter frankly before him. She asked him if he was ready to expose himself to these tremendous consequences. He answered that he was not. "I am," she said; and she started out upon the undertaking without him.

She secured letters of introduction to such noblemen as had shown a wish to improve the condition of the peasants, and traveled about the country visiting their estates, and studying whatever they had done in the way of starting schools, coöperative workshops, and the like. She tried to impress upon them that the fundamental need was for the peasants to own the land; but she could not make the nobles see it. She also found that the heavy hand of the government was always ready to shut down upon even their mildest efforts at improvement. She came home feeling that she had gained nothing but experience and an added knowledge of life.

By this time the spirit of revolution was fairly awake. A Liberal named Nechayev had gathered together a group of revolutionists. They were discovered and arrested, and their trial in 1871 was the first great event in the long struggle for freedom. The procession of political exiles along the Great Siberian Road had begun. Meanwhile their revolutionary documents had been published, and were read by thousands of Liberals throughout Russia.

Catherine went to Kiev, and joined a revolutionary group.

CHAPTER III

THE revolutionists at this time were divided into Lavrists and Bakuninites, according as they favored the program of Peter Lavrov or Michael Bakunin. The Lavrists believed that the peasants must be gradually educated for freedom and revolution. The Bakuninites believed in organizing the peasants for revolution as promptly as possible. They held that they would soon be ripe for revolt, because of the prevailing misery. "Hunger is the most efficient teacher," they said. "Tell the peasant why he is hungry, and show him how he can feed himself, and he will learn quite readily."

Lavrov and Bakunin, who were then living in Switzerland as political refugees, were good friends despite their difference of view, and so were most of their followers. It was a difference of method only; their aim was the same. Both Lavrists and Bakuninites felt that the nobles had been living in wealth and ease for centuries on the labor of the peasants; that it was only through oppression and robbery of the peasants that they were able to pass their time in luxury and amusement; and the younger generation looked upon it as their duty to make reparation to the peasants, so far as possible, and to give their lives to bring them freedom and happiness.

Catherine, like most of those who had lived close to the peasants, was a Bakuninite. In Kiev she soon gathered around her a group of young men and women who loved and admired her. Among these her special friend was Maria Kalyenkina, a girl who later became famous for her courage and her faith in the revolution. She had been a village school-teacher. Under the influence of Nekrasof's songs of the peasants, she became an ardent revolutionist, and went to Kiev to absorb the most advanced revolutionary ideas of the day. She entered a school for midwives, and there met Catherine's sister Olga. Thus she became acquainted with Catherine, who was nine years older than "little Masha", but found in her a kindred spirit. Masha was quiet, sweet-tempered, industrious, and daring beyond all others in a crisis. She talked little, and did much. A secret entrusted to her was as safe as in the grave. She was a pretty girl, of rather frail physique, with a remarkably fair skin and yellow hair. She took no sentimental interest in the young men, though many of them took a sentimental interest in her. When Catherine commented upon her indifference to men, she answered, "I love the movement." To this day her old friend speaks with enthusiasm of this sweet girl, gentle as a lamb, yet brave as a lioness.

From a smouldering hotbed of revolution, Kiev had now become a seething volcano. It was full of young enthusiasts who were determined to do or die. The movement "To the people!" which had been sweeping all over Russia was at its height in Kiev. Russian young men and women were studying at Swiss universities, and drinking in republican ideas. Many young Russians also made pilgrimages to Switzerland to visit Lavrov and Bakunin, and came back full of revolutionary zeal. The Russian government became alarmed, and issued an order that all Russian students in Switzerland must return by a certain date, or they would not be allowed to cross the frontier from Switzerland into Russia. The Russian students, however, used to stay as long as they liked, and then come back by way of Austria, getting across the Austrian frontier with comparative ease; and Kiev was their first stopping place. The revolutionists "made in Switzerland" were smuggled into Russia by way of Kiev.

The movement "To the people!" had changed in character. After the emancipation of the serfs, thousands of young men and women from the richer classes had asked themselves how they could be most useful to "the masses", and decided that the only way was to go and settle among the poor, and live as they did. Prince Kropotkin says:

"Young men went into the villages as doctors, doctors' helpers, teachers, village scribes, even as agricultural laborers, blacksmiths, wood-cutters, and so on, and tried to live there in close contact with the peasants. Girls passed teachers' examinations, learned midwifery or nursing, and went by the hundred into the villages, devoting themselves entirely to the poorest part of the population.

"These people went without any ideal of social reconstruction in their minds, or any thought of revolution. They simply wanted to teach the mass of the peasants to read, to interest them in other things, to give them medical help, and in any way to aid in raising them from their darkness and misery; and at the same time to learn what were *their* popular ideals of a better social life."

This movement was entirely legal, and was carried

on openly. But it was frowned upon by the government, and the would-be helpers of the peasants were ruthlessly suppressed. Then most of them became revolutionists. The experience of Catherine and her friends in this respect was typical.

Thereupon great numbers, including many of the nobility, disguised themselves as peasants, and lived and worked side by side with the poorest of the people, secretly preparing them for revolution. They felt that in this way they could get a better understanding of peasant conditions, since those who wear the shoe know where it pinches. They also felt that it would be unworthy to live in ease and comfort themselves while urging the peasants to face the greatest dangers and sacrifices. "We shall have the right to agitate among them when we are of them," said Catherine. Moreover, this was the only way to overcome the peasants' timid distrust. Victimized for so many centuries, the ex-serfs were as much afraid of the revolutionists as they were of the government. The peasant was almost like a dumb animal. If he cherished any thoughts of revolt, he hardly dared tell them to any one, and he certainly would never confide them to a nobleman.

Before entering upon the active revolutionary work which would take her away from home for good, and which was almost sure to end in exile or death, Catherine made a round of farewell visits among her relatives and friends. First she went to bid good-bye to her elder sister Natalie, who lived in the district of Novo-Aleksandriya, in the province of Kovno. From there she went to Lugovetz for a last interview with her parents and her husband. It was a sad and memorable meeting. Three years before, when Catherine's school had been suppressed and her father dismissed from office, she had told her husband that she was ready to lay down her life for the cause. The time had now come when she was to make the sacrifice. Her husband was overcome with grief. He begged her to give up her intention, and go with him to their estate in the province of Moghilev. He was a man of noble character, but he lacked the iron determination needed to face the terrible consequences of working for freedom under the shadow of the Czar. Her family pleaded a still stronger argument; they reminded her that she was soon to become a mother. On the one side was a life of domestic love, amid wealth, luxury, and splendor; on the other, prison and exile. Many would have said that duty bade her stay. She was profoundly convinced that the call of the greatest and gravest duty bade her go. Thus believing, she was resolute. With an aching heart, she bade them all farewell. She never saw any of them again. Her husband died soon after she was sent to Siberia; and before she returned, her parents also had passed away.

In Kiev, Catherine lived with her widowed sister Olga and her young friend, Masha Kalyenkina. Around these three as a nucleus there grew up a circle that became known as "the commune." It was the revolutionary center of Kiev, and a powerful influence in the awakening of Russia.

They had to earn a living while carrying on their revolutionary work. Catherine cut out little squares of paper, and wrote on each her name and address, with the announcement that she was ready to give expert instruction in such and such subjects. She took her stand on the corner of a street where there was an academy for young ladies, and gave her cards to the girls as they came out of school. Her friends laughed at this homely way of soliciting work, but it proved successful. So many mothers and aunts and elderly cousins of the schoolgirls applied for lessons that she had to turn many away. She earned on an average one hundred and forty rubles a month. This was ample for the needs of the modest household. She was busy all day and half the night, and always went to bed thoroughly tired; yet she found her health better than when she had been a lady of leisure. She had a strong constitution, and seemed to thrive on hard and continuous work.

The discussions between the Lavrists and Bakuninites were still going on, and sometimes waxed very warm. One night when Catherine was about to go to bed, more weary than usual, she received a call from Axelrod, the leader of the Lavrists in Kiev. His appearance at that unusual hour in a camp of strong Bakuninites was a surprise.

"You must come to an important meeting," he said. "We have here two delegates sent from Peter Lavrov, and two more from Odessa, and we are to talk over some very important matters."

Axelrod had faith in her breadth of mind. Although she belonged to the opposite faction, he knew that she placed her love for the peasants above all party lines.

He led her through dark side streets and deserted alleys to an unfinished building without a roof. In one of its rooms seven men were waiting. Catherine was the only woman.

She was especially impressed by one of the group.

He was very young, with blushing cheeks, and spoke in the most respectful manner to those present, because all of them were his elders. Axelrod introduced him with a ring of delight in his voice. "Katya," he said, "this young man is a peasant. He was once a serf, and used to ride as a footman behind his master's coach."

To revolutionists, in those days, nothing was holier or dearer than a peasant — especially a peasant who seemed to realize their ideals. For was not this young man educated, and full of advanced ideas, and eager to aid in spreading liberty and light? Axelrod was proud to introduce him.

The nobleman who owned this young serf had noticed that the boy was exceptionally bright, and had given him an education. When he came to Kiev as a delegate, he was a student at the University of Odessa. He seemed modest and plain, and took only a humble part in the discussion. No one could guess then that seven or eight years later he would become the most conspicuous revolutionary figure in Russia. His name was Andrei Zhelyabov. When the Czar Alexander II, after emancipating the serfs and giving the nation hopes of further great reforms, backslid in his later life and became a ruthless reactionary, it was Andrei Zhelyabov who organized and carried through the conspiracy that resulted in his assassination.

In the unfinished building in Kiev, the discussion turned on the old topic, how best to help the peasants. As usual, there were some who believed in cautious and deliberate approaches, and others who favored quick action. The delegates from Lavrov soared to higher and higher regions, and the delegates from

Odessa tried bravely but unsuccessfully to follow them. As the talk grew more and more philosophical and abstruse, Axelrod and Catherine lost all interest in it, and both fell fast asleep.

Catherine was determined to go out and work among the peasants; but she was advised to wait a little while until some further degree of organization should have been effected among them. Efforts to this end were being made throughout the country, stimulated from Petrograd by Kovalik and others of like views. The opponents of the Bakuninites called them, half mockingly, "flame-seekers", because they sought out those villages where a longing for freedom was already smouldering in the peasants' hearts, and tried to fan it into flame. Catherine was a "flame-seeker."

In "the commune" life was carried on simply, without ceremony or affectation. Plain living and high thinking were the order of the day. Catherine and her friends lived on the poorest fare, while their minds were busy with the greatest questions, all centering about the problem of the peasants.

On the outside, the homes of members of "the commune" differed little from other houses; but inside it was like a different world. There were many large rooms, and each looked like a workshop. In one were carpenters' tools, with noblemen working as apprentices to the trade; in another students were learning shoe-making; in yet another etchers were preparing metal seals to stamp false passports.

There was a general office where letters and telegrams were received, all in cipher. Here young men and women could be seen discussing political and economic questions. Some were dressed as peasants, others, not yet wholly hardened to discomfort, were wearing a sort of compromise costume, while a third group, newcomers, were arrayed in the costliest finery of fashion. It was a noteworthy gathering of the different grades of radicals in their fortress, making preparations for an attack upon their colossal foe. A barefooted man in peasant garb might be seen talking with a man dressed in the height of style, the second listening to the first attentively and even deferentially, because of his wider knowledge and experience of peasant conditions.

The whole community was absorbed in the study of the peasant. They would get together in the sitting room and sing folksongs, or tell stories of the peasants illustrating their simplicity and good nature, or their dullness and superstition. There was much laughter. The members of the community were merry and full of hope.

One day Leventhal came into the group with his bride, the daughter of Doctor Kominer. Both were barefooted, poorly clad, pale and exhausted. They had been working all day with the bricklayers, helping to put up a big building, carrying heavy pails of water, and stamping the lime into a paste with their feet. They were worn out, and their limbs felt sore and distorted.

"It is no joke, trying to agitate for freedom among men who toil so miserably," they said. "Both they and we are all tired out. They are used up, they cannot listen without falling asleep; and we are ill, we cannot muster strength enough to stand up and talk."

This was the typical argument of those who advocated beginning with minor reforms, improving the condition of the workers so that they could get rest after their day's labor. There was a common Russian adage, "An empty stomach makes a poor student." Then, too, the revolutionists argued, how could they have the heart to try to spur up a tired, hungry, worn-out man to action, and inspire him with a fighting spirit?

To "the commune" came also Vera Pavlovna, who was nominally married to an officer. Such marriages were frequent in those days. A girl living in the country, who was in sympathy with the revolution, would wish to go to the city in order to work for it, or simply in order to study. Her conservative parents would refuse their sanction, and without it she could not get a passport. Then some chivalrous man in sympathy with the revolution — perhaps an officer, sometimes even a nobleman — would offer to marry her, with a private understanding between them that the union was to be merely nominal. With the marriage, the father's legal authority over the girl passed to her husband. With his consent, she could take out a passport, and go wherever she pleased. He made no claim on her, and often they parted after the wedding, never to meet again.

Vera Pavlovna with others went to work in some large gardens belonging to monks of the Orthodox Greek Church. There they came in contact with peasants, and tried to influence them. As the monks were often more tyrannical even than the nobles, there was cause enough for discontent; but when Vera and her friends tried to stir the peasants to action, they answered, calmly: "We do not care anything about the monks. We are planting and gathering these gardens for God."

Meanwhile a cousin of Catherine's, a woman of

enlightenment and benevolence, invited her to visit her estate at Goryany, in the district of Vitebsk, and to make it a center for her humanitarian activities. Catherine made the visit, and was pleased with the work that her cousin had done among the peasants. Before giving a definite answer, she went to Petrograd to get in touch with the leading workers for freedom there. She found much revolutionary sentiment fermenting throughout the city. She mentioned her cousin's plan to Kovalik. He answered, "Katinka, you have done enough of this social reform work. It is high time for you to plunge into the thick of battle. Why don't you join the ranks?"

He meant that she ought to take a peasant's pack upon her broad shoulders, and go out to sow the seeds of revolution in the hearts of the people. He scorned half-way measures of mere benevolence.

In Petrograd as in Kiev, Catherine soon became the center of a circle to whom she was a shining light. Her strong, simple character, her winning smile, her dauntless courage, her frank, vigorous, and pointed conversation, were admired wherever the "intellectuals" of Petrograd came together.

In her rooms she held gatherings of young people who met to discuss the burning questions of the day, to decide what ought to be done, and to plan for putting their ardent thoughts into ardent deeds. Many of them were destined to become famous in the revolutionary movement.

While Catherine was in Petrograd, her son was born. After recovering from her confinement, she returned to Kiev, and joined her brother's wife, Vera, of whom she was very fond. It had been agreed that

Vera and her husband should undertake the care of Catherine's child, and they had promised to treat him as if he were their own. Vera was living in "the commune." Catherine found her ill, and nursed her tenderly till she got better.

A great grief befell Catherine at this time. Her sister Olga died of brain fever, calling in her delirium upon Catherine, whom she had loved better than any one else.

"Women have always loved me. I am proud of it," said Catherine, in speaking of the strong friendship that existed between her and her sisters, her sister-in-law, and other women.

Her sister-in-law stayed in Kiev for some time after her recovery. Finally her husband came to take her home. Catherine then had the anguish of parting with her child. The scene is still vivid in her memory. Outside stood the coach, drawn by two restless horses that snorted and pawed the ground. Vera and her husband were seated in the coach. Catherine came out to them with the baby in her arms. She gave the child to Vera. For a moment or two there was dead silence. Then Catherine burst into tears, weeping and sobbing like an inconsolable child. Vera cried, "Katya, Katya! what is the matter with you?" But the mother wept on. Vera gave her a hasty kiss on the forehead, and the coach drove rapidly away, rattling over the stones.

Catherine stood dazed and bewildered. Her eyes were fixed upon the turning wheels of the coach, and when they disappeared in the distance, she still gazed after them. It was a bright spring day, but a cold autumn seemed to have settled down upon her. She felt forlorn and deserted. She says:

"My heart felt torn into a thousand pieces. My feet were lame, my arms stiff. I could not move from the spot. I thought of the warning that had been given me when I first spoke of my wish to work for the peasants. While I was still a girl, they said, 'Wait! You will get married, and that will tie you down. Your young blood will be calmed; your running brook will become a quiet lake.' And the time came when I was married, and I was conscious of no change in my spirit. I felt for the people's cause as strongly as ever — even more strongly. And then friends told me, 'Just wait, you will have an estate of your own to care for, and that will take up all your time and thoughts.' But my husband and I bought an estate, and no such result followed; for I could never let one tiny estate outweigh the vast plains of all Russia. My spirit and my convictions remained the same. And with time came new counsel from friends. Now they argued: 'Yes, you have remained unchanged by husband and home, but you will succumb to the command of Nature. With the birth of a child will come the death of your revolutionary ideals. The wings you have used for soaring high in the air among the clouds you will now use to shelter your little one.' And I gave birth to a little one. I felt that in that boy my youth was buried, and that when he was taken from my body, the fire of my spirit had gone out with him. But it was not so. The conflict between my love for the child and my love for the revolution and for the freedom of Russia robbed me of many a night's sleep. I knew that I could not be a mother and still be a revolutionist. Those were not two tasks to which it was possible to give a divided attention. Either the one or the other must absorb one's whole being, one's entire devotion. So I gave my child to Vera and my brother, to be brought up as their own.

"I was not the only one called upon to make such a sacrifice. Among the women in the struggle for Russian freedom there were many who chose to be fighters for justice rather than mothers of the victims of tyranny."

CHAPTER IV

CATHERINE now made all her preparations to start out as a missionary of revolution among the peasants. She invited two comrades to go with her, Masha Kalyenkina and Yakov Stephanovitch.

Stephanovitch was one of the most sincere among the young revolutionists. He was a boy of twenty, tall and broad, with an open, honest face, and lips so thick that he was often called "the White Negro." He was very silent. He was the son of an intelligent priest, who was an inspector over thirty schools, and who had secured positions for many revolutionists as teachers.

Stephanovitch had fitted himself to be a shoemaker and cobbler. Masha had gone among the dye-workers and painters and learned their trade. Then she taught it to Catherine. This was an itinerant trade, and hence well suited to revolutionists.

One bright morning in July, 1874, the three set out together from "the commune." Interested eyes watched them from every window, as they passed down the narrow street. All three were dressed as peasants, and carried packs on their backs, containing a few coarse garments and the tools of their respective trades. They were provided with false passports. Catherine's passport described her as forty years of age, though she was only thirty. A skilful arrangement of her hair beneath a peasant woman's shawl gave her the appearance of added years. She wore enormous bark shoes, a shirt of thick canvas, a skirt of coarse sacking, and a black jacket with a loose red belt. She had used acid on her face and hands. The two women carried boards for painting and dyeing. The party passed as three cousins from the province of Orlov in Great Russia.

It was a beautiful day. Catherine and her companions were very happy. Their hearts were overflowing with good will towards all mankind, and in their love for the oppressed they found a sort of religious joy.

They made their way to a port on the Dnieper River where a boat was about to start for the city of Tcherkass. It was full of laborers and peasants, who were talking and eating. The three travelers pulled out of their wallets bread, dried fish, and cider, and began to eat and drink with the rest. Some of the peasants asked them where they came from and whither they were bound. They answered, "We come from Orlov, and we are looking for work. We have heard that in such and such a town there is need of workers in our line."

There was nothing strange in this. Since the emancipation of the serfs, swarms of destitute peasants who had lost their land had been wandering all over Russia looking for work. This explanation also made it needless for them to try to imitate the peasant speech of the province. The dialect of Great Russia was so different from that of Little Russia that the peasants could not tell whether they were speaking like educated

persons or like peasants. Catherine and Masha had
the soft hands of women who had never done heavy
manual labor; but when Catherine explained that
they had been the servants of a wealthy nobleman, it
was assumed that they had been employed in some
of the lighter tasks. As for Stephanovitch, his hands
were already callous with hard work.

At Tcherkass, as they trudged up the sandy hill
from the landing, little Masha found herself unequal
to the weight of her heavy pack. It bowed her down
more and more. Her friends wanted to relieve her.
At first she rejected their help with indignation, saying, "What sort of a peasant woman am I, if I cannot
carry a load?" At last she had to succumb, and let
the others divide part of her burden between them.

Presently they came to a statue of the great Russian
poet, Shevchenko. They were curious to find out
how much the peasants knew about this man, who had
been one of the best friends of their cause. Some had
never heard of him; others thought he had been some
mighty man revered by the nobility. This was all
they could learn.

When they reached the heart of the city they felt
as if everybody were looking at them; but they were
soon reassured. Nobody took any notice of them.
They walked till they were tired, then sat down on a
little rocky eminence, and shared a loaf of bread.

They passed through the city, to the last row of low
wooden houses, and out into the open country. On
one side the vast plains stretched away without end;
on the other the forest seemed to frown down upon
them. Sometimes a coach rattled by, covering them
with clouds of dust. Sometimes the road was swampy.

The two women found it hard work, tramping under a heavy pack. After a while they had to sit down to rest their aching feet. Stephanovitch was used to walking for miles in the mud and dust, and he scorned their daintiness.

"Come, now, you have had enough of sitting!" he said, standing in front of them. They were exhausted; but they knew they must reach the next village before dusk if they were to find shelter in any peasant hut. The peasants were suspicious of strangers, and would not take in anybody who came after dark. They rose and trudged on.

About six o'clock they arrived at the village of Byelozerye. Thoroughly tired, they sat down in a cottage porch. Passing peasants asked them where they came from and where they were going. They answered as before, that they came from the province of Orlov, and were looking for work. Soon the district clerk appeared, and demanded, with a haughty gesture, "Have you your passports?" With inward misgivings, but with unmoved faces, they pulled their false passports out of their blouses. Stephanovitch asked where they could get a night's lodging. The clerk did not condescend to answer. With the same haughty air, he glanced over the passports, and handed them back without a word. They folded them up reverently — a peasant looks upon a passport as something almost sacred — and put them back in their breasts. All breathed more freely when the functionary had gone.

They were still at a loss for a lodging. "We must go to a tavern," said Stephanovitch. "We shall find more people there." But it was the middle of the

week, and the inn was almost deserted. Only the
Jewish host sat behind the counter, and a tall, ragged,
tipsy peasant was sprawling over a table. He had
been a soldier in the Crimean War, and his great delight
was to tell boastful and fantastic stories about it.

"None of our soldiers could talk with the Turks,"
he began. "But I talked with them as easily as I do
with you. I would meet a Turk and say to him,
'Chaldi, Maldi!' and he would reply straight to the
point, 'Maldi, Chaldi', and in this way we would
keep on through a long conversation."

At first the travelers were amused, but they soon
grew tired. They urged the boaster to direct them
to a lodging, but he stood in the middle of the room
and kept on declaiming his stories. Finally Stephanovitch treated him to several glasses of whisky, and
then he remembered that a friend of his, a widower,
had a room to let; but it was at the other end of the
village. He offered to escort them, but they assured
him they could find the way.

Trudging along with their packs, they laughed.
"Maldi, Chaldi!" said Catherine. "Chaldi, Maldi!"
answered Stephanovitch. Masha, walking slightly
bent under her burden, smiled in silence.

It was a typical little Russian village, a row of small
white houses, and between every two houses a well.
After many inquiries they found the place. The widower agreed to rent them the house, but he warned
them that it was too filthy for them to sleep in it that
night. An old woman, a relative of his, generously
invited them to spend the night with her, and prepared some food for them. She gave each a barley
bun, as big as a man's fist. The remembrance of their

flavor fills Catherine with horror to this day. They ate some cakes, and then began to nibble at the agonizing slippery buns. They tried hard to swallow them, but it seemed a physical impossibility. Then they thought of the great men who had sprung from the peasantry, and who had been brought up on such fare; and that helped them to get it down.

During the meal they talked with their hostess, and described their hardships while looking for work.

"Well, well, no need to worry," she answered. "The girls will come to you to have their kerchiefs painted, and their boots, too. You will have plenty to do."

After the ordeal of breakfast, the three travelers went to look at their new home. The walls were rotten and tottering, the floors broken and carpeted with vermin, and on every side there were rat-holes, hung with cobwebs. They stood helpless in the midst of the dirt. Perhaps they let a momentary thought stray to the soft featherbeds and the pots of roses and morning glories in the chambers of the homes that they had left. Their hostess remarked, in the most matter-of-fact way: "You had better get some fresh, warm manure from the fields and mix it with lime. That makes a good wash for the floor. Then you can take some fresh hay and arrange the beds."

Mixing the lime and manure was considered strictly a woman's job, and Stephanovitch could not help. Catherine and Masha set to work courageously; but the task of kneading lime and steaming manure into a paste to varnish a worm-eaten floor was altogether new to the two delicately bred ladies. They were

overcome with nausea. Stephanovitch smiled, with
his arms folded behind him.

"Woman's work!" he sang out heartlessly.

"Why don't you help? It's so hard to talk, you
know!" answered Catherine mockingly.

"That's a good one!" retorted Stephanovitch.
"Why, I should be the laughingstock of the peasants
and their wives!"

Finally it was done. The house was cleaned as far
as possible, the travelers' packs were lugged across
from their lodging place, fresh straw was spread, and
all arrangements were made for the night's rest. But
there was to be no sleep for Catherine and Masha.
As soon as they blew out their tallow candles, armies
of bugs and insects swarmed out of hiding and attacked
them. It seemed impossible that the house could
have held so many. Stephanovitch slept as peasants
can, even under such circumstances; but the two
women could not rest for a moment. They kept up
a constant fight with the invaders. They rolled from
side to side; they shifted from their beds to the floor;
but the attacking legions followed them, and were
reinforced by armies of mice. With the break of
dawn the tormentors retired. The humming and
buzzing and squeaking died away, and the weary women
got a few hours' repose.

Then they started out to ply their trade. Masha
painted a handkerchief as a sample of what she could
do, and Catherine polished a boot for the same purpose. Stephanovitch set up a little shoe shop in one
part of the house. They gradually attracted cus-
tomers. They entered into familiar talk with them,
and inquired into the particulars of their condition,

asking how much land had been given to each peasant, etc., etc.

They found that the emancipation of the serfs had made very little change in this district, because it consisted of crown lands, and there was no private land to be had. These peasants had been serfs not of the nobles, but of the Czar, and were rather proud of the fact. They were no better off for it, however. Indeed, they were at a special disadvantage, because they had no forests, and so had to buy their fuel. Naturally, they stole wood, and were mercilessly punished for it. But they never thought of finding fault with the Czar; they would rather have found fault with Nature's unequal distribution of forests. The Czar was the father of all the peasants. If anybody was to blame, it was the officials. They had ordered the forests to be burned. Surely the Czar never knew of that!

The "flame-seekers" found no smouldering rebellion here. But they heard that in the town of Smyela there were some energetic young men who were in the habit of standing up against the nobles. "There are live doings in Smyela," gossip reported. The three apostles tightened their red Cossack belts and set out for Smyela.

At Smyela most of the people worked in the sugar factories. A Count Babrinski had received a large grant of unused land. He sent for thousands of peasants from the estates in Great Russia, and had them plant sugar beets and build refineries, so that he could ship the sugar direct from his land to market. The town was made up of his two or three thousand laborers. The peasants who had lived there from child-

hood, and were now married, occupied several blocks
of small wooden huts. The unmarried hands, and
those who came from other districts to work, dug themselves holes in the hillside, where they lived rent
free. Anyone could scoop himself out a burrow and
floor it with boards; and the hills were dotted with
these burrows, where men, women, and children were
huddled together, without regard to sex or social rela-
tionship. Many of the young girls bore illegitimate
children. They wore their hair in small braids, hoping
in this way to pass for legitimate wives; but the married women in the cottages nicknamed them "braiders",
and looked upon them and their children with scorn.

The human rabbit warrens on the hill were close
to the sugar refineries, and the sugar refineries were
close to the Count's magnificent palace. One glance
could take in the extremes of poverty and wealth;
and the breeze brought the mouldy stench of the hill
holes, mingled with the fragrance of the Count's
gardens and kitchen.

The three wandering idealists found a tiny cabin
in which an old man lived close by the cottage of his
married son, and persuaded him to rent it to them.
He was tall, broad-shouldered, and erect, despite his
eighty years, with a flowing beard, and a bright,
energetic face. In his youth he had been shipped
to Smyela, along with many other young men, to work
on Count Babrinski's estate. The pioneer labor on
the land was very hard, and the peasants were flogged
almost to death. So ruthless was the Count's treatment that they made up their minds to combine
against him. The old man recalled, with a flash in
his eye, how he had led them. But soldiers were sent

against them, and they were put down after a few volleys of grapeshot and many floggings. He, as the leader, had been so beaten that he was confined to his bed for weeks. Since then there had been no rebellion.

This old man had many talks with Catherine and her friends, and showed them much kindness, supplying them with many small conveniences; but he knew that they were poor, and he refused all their invitations to dine with them. Finally Catherine got around the difficulty by inviting him to come over for a talk, and then offering him a share of the dinner casually, as a sort of secondary phase of the discussion. He would wax enthusiastic over the work to be done against the oppression of the nobles.

"We must fight or die," Catherine and her friends would say to him. "We must be silent and ready, not silent and helpless."

"Ah, if I were only in my teens again!" he would sigh. "But winter lies thick on me, and I am stiff and old. We need youth for that."

They got acquainted with a younger peasant named Ivan, and tried to indoctrinate him.

"What made you leave Orlov?" he asked.

"We could not get any ground to till. When we were freed from serfdom, we were freed from the land, too — that is, we were free to leave."

"Well, that's nothing new," said Ivan. "We have had the same trouble right here. Why, there isn't even any pasture land for the cows, or any plots for gardens. We have to buy everything we need; and we have to pay for it, too."

Under serfdom, the peasants had been able to supply most of their wants from the soil.

"The time has come now when we must all work," went on Ivan. "From the tiniest tot to the oldest man — men, women, and children; we all have our price: the men at forty kopeks a day, the women at twenty-five, and the kiddies at ten."

But when Catherine tried to show him that they must join hands against the government, he answered:

"It can't be. The Czar knows nothing of all these things that his officials and subordinates do. They are all rascals, and they keep it from him, for fear of being punished if he knew. Why, do you think the Czar is a fool? Do you think he does not know that without land the peasant cannot live?"

Catherine insisted that the Czar was no better than the nobles, and that he was in league with them.

Ivan answered: "How can it pay the Czar to be on the side of the nobles when they are only a handful and the peasants are millions? Besides, who pays all the taxes? Who serves in the army? Who feeds the nation? The peasant, and only the peasant."

"What you say is very true," answered Catherine, "but for all that, the Czar is the peasants' enemy. Who is the Czar? He himself is a nobleman. He feasts and drinks with the nobles about him. They are his friends and advisers. What he says, they do, and what they want, he says."

But Ivan persisted: "The Czar is good to his peasants. They are his children. Everything that is bad comes from the barons and the lords."

To the Russian peasants, the Czar was a deity. It was easier for them to believe the most fantastic fables than to give up their faith in the "good Little Father." They were firmly convinced that the book of laws issued by the Czar when serfdom was abolished had been intercepted by some conscienceless officials, who had torn out of it several pages full of blessings for the peasants, and had interpolated a long list of oppressive laws that the Czar never meant or knew anything about. Their hope was that some day some peasant might discover the original pages in his haystack or pigpen.

But Catherine persisted:

"You say the Czar is the peasants' friend. Well, how about the army? To whom does that belong? Is it not the Czar's?"

"It is."

"And who commands the army and tells it what to do? Is not that the Czar's business?"

"It is."

"Then why do the soldiers flog and shoot you? Why do they murder you and your children in cold blood when you organize clubs? Because it is the Czar who tells them to do it. They take orders only from him."

Ivan wrinkled his forehead. He murmured: "Really, it is strange. I can't say. Maybe false reports are circulated about us, and reach the Czar's ear. You know how deceitful those officials are. They pour poison into his ear. God bless him, what can he do? He doesn't know."

After a good deal of talk, Ivan became convinced that they would have to fight, and fight hard, to set things right.

"Are there others who have such ideas?" asked Catherine.

"Well, yes," he replied guardedly. "How have you found it in other places?"

"Oh, there are many everywhere who understand the truth, and they are ready to organize and join in the movement against the oppressors. The Czar is seated on the peak, far too high for you to reach him. But the mountain rests on your shoulders: and if you walk away, the whole burden will fall, and the peak, which was formerly high above your head, will lie in the mud beneath your feet."

Ivan wrinkled his brows again. He was thinking.

After repeated conversations with the revolutionists, he said: "Well, we will talk it over. If there is to be an uprising, we must all stand together. The separate groups all over the country must unite. You seem to travel everywhere. Talk it over with the people in many other villages. Perhaps they will help us."

"Why, do you suppose that I am the only one?" said Catherine. "Hundreds and hundreds of men and women all over Russia at this moment are talking to the peasants as I talk to you. The wrongs that we children of the soil have to suffer are too great. We are broken and ruined under them. And why must we endure them? Many are going about saying these things. They are even distributing books and pamphlets about our sorrows. Just see, I have such a booklet here."

She pulled out from her blouse "Moses and his Four Brothers", a pamphlet that the revolutionists used to distribute in the villages. It was a story containing a concise exposition of the principles of freedom, and a criticism of the Russian autocracy, sugar-coated over with romance. She began to read this aloud to Ivan and his wife. Both were deeply impressed. Ivan exclaimed with enthusiasm:

"Those are golden words! They speak what we feel."

"That is not enough," said Catherine. "One feels much, and one says much. But does one always do enough? You must make me acquainted with others."

"Yes, you are right. There are friends and neighbors with whom you ought to talk. They too feel a great deal. I will bring you and them together." And he added, excitedly, "You will bring along the original pages that were torn out of the book of laws?"

It was agreed that the first meeting of the factory hands should be held in Ivan's house. Meanwhile Catherine tried to get in touch with some peasants less gentle and phlegmatic than he. She heard of two brothers in the sugar refinery who were noted for their pugnacity and grit. They had been leaders in all the struggles for better pay. She went to the house of one of them. It was evening, but he had not yet come home. She found his wife in great fear and anxiety because of the disappearance of their hog. She knew what her husband would do to her if the animal was lost through her lack of watchfulness. Catherine tried to comfort her. Bursting into tears, the poor woman seized her hand and covered it with kisses. It was an unheard-of thing for one peasant woman to kiss the hand of another, and Catherine was greatly taken aback. She was afraid the woman had penetrated her disguise. But the unusual act was only due to gratitude for the unaccustomed sympathy. The wife's terror did not give Catherine a very favorable idea of the husband; nevertheless, she wished to await his return, but the wife urged her to go, not wanting her to witness a painful scene.

The next day Catherine saw the man, and talked to him about the many wrongs of the factory workers. "It is strange," she said, "that when your wages are cut down a few kopeks a day you make a terrible outcry and fight desperately against it; but when the nobles take away your land and all your rights, you are as meek as cattle."

"What can we do?" he asked. "If the crowd holds back and only one man steps forward, what do you expect him to accomplish? The crowd disowns him and the oppressors give him a flogging and send him to Siberia."

The same idea had been expressed to Catherine again and again. She tried the brother, but found no encouragement. He was immensely proud of the factory, although he lived as miserably as the rest of its two thousand hands. "Where will you find such another factory?" he boasted. "Where is there one that employs so many workers, and turns out so much sugar?"

At last the Sunday appointed for the meeting came. About forty peasants filed slowly into Ivan's house. They sat on chairs, tables, window sills, and bedsteads.

Ivan began: "My brothers, the 'original papers' are among us. The good and noble writings which the lawless nobles and officials tore out of the statutes are now here, and are going to be read to us."

There was dead silence. The peasants were all ears. Catherine was almost as breathless as they. Her heart throbbed with joy over the fulfilment of her long cherished hope. For the first time, she was to address a gathering of peasants in a peasant's home — not students, not educated men and women, but the children of the soil, the crude, rough foundations of the Russian nation. She said to them:

"I have no miraculous papers, stolen from law books; but I have other valuable papers, which, although not written by the Czar, are nevertheless full of sympathy and interest for the peasants. These works are by very good people — indeed, by the best people in Russia. They are all written about you — about the wrongs you have suffered in silence and resignation, about the outrages committed upon you, and about your rights as human beings."

"But who will read these things to us?" asked the peasants. None of them could read.

"Oh, she — 'Auntie,'" answered Ivan.

"What! Can she read?"

"Read! Why, she reads very well," exclaimed Ivan.

She began to read. There was a complete hush. The peasants drank in every word; the motion of their mouths imitated every syllable uttered by the reader. She read in a clear, strong, pleasant voice, and with beaming eyes. The peasants were fascinated and almost hypnotized. At the close, many shouted:

"God! What noble words!" "What golden words!" "What truth!"

Catherine's face shone. This was one of the supreme moments of her life.

"Well," she said, "what is to come of it? We must do something. We cannot remain indifferent to this horrid injustice all around us."

At these words the audience awakened from their trance. An elderly peasant answered:

"You are right. Your words are golden words. But how can we organize for a revolt? If we alone were to take arms against the power of the government, we should be flogged, ruined. The soldiers would be sent against us, and that would be the end of it. But if many other villages joined us, then perhaps —"

"And I think," another peasant interrupted, "that we had better wait till the Czar learns about our miserable condition, and the atrocities committed by the nobles. Then he will avenge us."

Catherine told him that he was utterly mistaken; that the Czar was no better than the nobles, perhaps even worse; and that to look to the Czar for help was like seeking salvation at the hands of the devil. Uproar followed; not another intelligible word was spoken. The peasants were completely confounded. To hear the Czar and the devil named in one breath was too much for them. Catherine withdrew from the meeting, excited and a little disturbed.

The facts leaked out and reached the authorities. Stephanovitch was warned that he must vanish. He did so. A young man brought the same warning to Catherine and Masha, with a sum of money. He urged them to start at once for Tcherkass, where Stephanovitch would rejoin them. Then he too disappeared. The two women told the peasants that they had had an offer of work in another district, and must leave at once. Every one was sorry to have them go. Even their aged host's daughter-in-law, a shrew that scolded and cursed continually, shed tears at their departure. The old man himself was deeply moved. He said to Catherine:

"I lived happily with my wife for many years, but that which I have felt toward you I have felt toward no other woman. You are one in a thousand. May God help you in all that you undertake!"

CHAPTER V

MASHA returned to Kiev. Catherine stayed for a time in Tcherkass. As she wandered about the town, looking for new recruits, she came one day upon a group of working people seated on a stone wall near the river, where they were employed about the landing. Several women were cooking the midday meal in a large pot mounted on three bricks. This was a communal group, that worked and ate together. If any member was ill, his part of the food was sent home to him. Communal clubs of this kind had their origin in the most ancient customs and traditions of Russia. Coöperative colonies and other community undertakings existed and flourished in large numbers throughout the country. The revolutionists took a great interest in them. They believed that if the workers could act in concert to provide for their material wants, they could learn to fight in concert to secure a free government.

Catherine was pleased to come upon this example of folk brotherhood. She greeted the laborers, and they responded cordially. Handing her a spoon, they urged her to sit down and share their meal.

"Where do you come from?" they asked.

"From Orlov. I am waiting for my nephew. When he arrives, we shall go together to look for work."

"What is doing in your neighborhood?" they said.

"What should there be doing? There is no land for the peasants."

"Ah!" they exclaimed in chorus, "the old story — no land."

Catherine turned the conversation to a village that was much talked about at the time, where the peasants, driven desperate by the oppression of the nobles, had appointed delegates to go and complain to the Czar.

"Ah, delegates!" exclaimed one of the workers, with a gesture of despair. "What good does it do to send delegates? They were thrown into jail, and are rotting there to this day."

"But what do you think of the Czar's not even allowing his children, the peasants, to come to him with their complaints?" said Catherine.

"The Czar is not to blame," was the prompt reply. "You think he knows that we come to him, and so arrests us. But the nobles and the officials do not even let us get near him."

"What a fine Czar," said Catherine, "not to know when his peasants want to see him, or not to be able to let them come to him! There are millions and millions of peasants, and only a handful of nobles, yet he never sees the peasants, and he always sees the nobles. Do you call that justice? Be honest with yourselves — is that fair?"

A confusion of voices arose. The younger laborers sided with Catherine, but the older ones all defended the Czar.

"Who freed us from serfdom?" said one old man. "Was it not the Czar? Have you so soon forgotten a noble deed of bounty?"

Catherine had many talks with laborers and peasants in Tcherkass. She had given away all her literature, but she soon learned to speak to them so that their hearts were like wax in her hands. She was as good a listener as she was a talker. Her love and sympathy made each of them feel as if he were opening his heart to a mother. They told her all their troubles. When it was time to go, they could hardly tear themselves away. They would go to the door, hesitate, and turn back to ask about something they had forgotten; walk lingeringly to the door again, go out, and then send somebody back to ask just one more question of the strange, wonderful peasant woman.

When Stephanovitch arrived, Catherine and he took boat down the Dnieper River to the district of Yelizavetgrad, in the province of Kherson. Here there were many Dissenters, known as Evangelists. They had undergone much persecution from the government, but had resisted so stoutly that now they were tacitly permitted to pray as they pleased. Not knowing where their head center was, the two revolutionists said to some of the passengers on the boat:

"People talk of a new sort of religion in these parts. Do you know what it is all about?"

Some of the peasants looked shocked, others shrugged and smiled. Some were too frightened to take any notice of the question. One answered, laughing:

"Why, do you want to join this new faith?"

They discussed the Dissenters with everybody who was willing to talk about them, in order to find out how they were generally regarded.

One peasant said: "These Evangelists are certainly in league with the devil and his imps; for if you put a three-ruble piece on the doorsill of an Evangelist's cottage, the next day you will find a hundred-ruble piece in place of it."

These stories grew out of the fact that no Evangelist touched liquor, or squandered his earnings; and no stranger was ever turned away from the door. The priests of the Orthodox Greek Church denounced these heretics, and warned the people to have nothing to do with them; but the peasants found them humble, courteous, hospitable, and helpful, always doing good. They could not reconcile what they heard in church with what they saw in daily life.

The two "flame-seekers" stopped at the village of Lyubomirka. Here the opponents of the State Church had gained a large following, because they had an able local leader, Ivan Ryobashapka. He was not only a man of strong character, but a diplomatist. He was a carpenter, and he had presented the chief of police with a handsomely-carved bureau and the police inspector with a beautiful cabinet. In Lyubomirka the Evangelists were looked upon leniently by the police, while everywhere else they were flogged. When the two revolutionists arrived, Ryobashapka was away, but was expected back in a few days.

To disarm suspicion, they took up their quarters with a very orthodox peasant. They rented the cabin adjoining his cottage, and there Stephanovitch set out his shoemaker's tools and Catherine her dyestuffs and paintbrushes. They questioned their host and his wife about the Evangelists, and were told that they had a terrible reputation, which it was hard even for such children of the devil to live up to; in fact, their outward behavior was fairly good, but of course that did not matter, since the village priest declared that their religion was horrible.

"Do any of these dreadful people live near here?" asked Catherine.

"Why, there is one of them only next door; and what an Evangelist he is! His eyes sparkle and burn. You cannot look in his eyes without feeling that the devil is there. He is one of the leaders, too. He can talk about his religion for hours. He likes it better than food or work. But what sort of religion can they have, without a church, and without the sanction of the Czar? Imagine people sitting and singing and praying within bare walls, and with no sacred candles!"

Not wishing to be seen going along the road to visit Stephan, the Evangelist, Catherine climbed over the fence into his ground. He stopped work, and leaned on his hoe, looking at her with his brilliant eyes.

"Good day, brother," she said.

"Good day, sister," he replied.

Catherine sat down on a pile of hay, and began to sew on a shirt that she had brought with her.

"I do not want to disturb you," she said. "Finish your work, and then we will talk."

He dropped his hoe, saying, "It is easy enough to let this work wait, but we should never let the word of God wait a moment."

Leading her into the house, he proceeded to expound the doctrines of the reformed religion with fervor. How could she endure the absurdities of the Greek Church, the false pomps and ceremonies of the blinded image-worshippers? Why not embrace the pure, the noble, the only true faith? His face shone with earnestness. A strange feeling stole over Catherine. Two apostles of two different movements were standing face to face, each bent upon converting the other.

"How do you know that I have not already embraced the doctrines of Evangelism?" she said.

"Of course, I do not know," he answered, "but something seems to tell me you are not yet a complete Evangelist."

"I realize fully," said Catherine, "that the faith of the Orthodox Greek Church is false in many respects, and that it needs to be rooted out of the country. But that is not the only evil in Russia that needs to be rooted out. The government that fosters the Greek Church is depraved, too. The writings of the holy fathers, which declare the country's ruler to be the anointed of God, ought to be destroyed as imbecile. We go a step further than you Evangelists. We oppose not merely the false doctrines in the State Church, but falsehood and evil wherever and whenever it shows itself. We oppose it in the laws that men make for their brothers; we oppose it in the daily life of every man, woman, and child. Do you believe that it is wrong to worship the image of God, but right to worship the image of the Czar?"

"What are you saying, sister?" asked the Evangelist, in surprise. "Does not the gospel say expressly that we should render unto Cæsar the things that are Cæsar's and unto God the things that are God's?"

In reply, Catherine quoted several other texts which entirely demolished the interpretation that the Evangelist had put upon that one. Having been brought up on the Bible, she was fortified with a great array of revolutionary passages of Scripture. To every evil which could be traced to the Czar, she applied a quotation from Holy Writ. "How can God have anointed a ruler who does everything that God condemns? Does God encourage misery and poverty among his children on earth? Does He encourage oppression and murder? Well, but that is just what the Czar does encourage!"

Whenever Catherine waxed eloquent, the Evangelist would meditate for a while, and then say dreamily: "Who knows? Perhaps, if one of us Evangelists could come into the Czar's presence, he would tell the Czar everything, and then everything would change for the better. The trouble is that he is always surrounded by unscrupulous nobles and officials. Ah, if one of our members could only approach him!"

Catherine told the Evangelist that her nephew was deeply interested in these subjects, and she would bring him over to have a talk about them if Stephan would arrange to have some other Evangelists present. To this he gladly agreed.

Catherine introduced Stephanovitch to Stephan, and they argued for hours, Stephanovitch bringing forward many texts to prove the need of a revolution. Then Catherine began to chat with the Evangelist about his family. He told her he had been married twice, and had two children by his first wife.

"That is the source of all my troubles," he said. "There is continual quarreling between the stepmother and her stepchildren."

"What do you do about it?"

"Well, what would you expect? The world has found a cure for such cases, hasn't it?" He smiled — not a pleasant smile. "Sometimes I have to give the children a thrashing to keep them within bounds, and sometimes my wife gets it. Then things quiet down, all right."

Catherine knew that most peasants beat their wives, but in the case of a deeply religious Evangelist she had hoped to find a higher type of family life.

"What!" she exclaimed. "A man of your intelligence do such an unmanly thing? Would it not be much better to quiet your wife and children by talking to them?"

Just then a slender young peasant woman came in, with a child in her arms, and an older boy and girl hanging to her dress. There was a weary, melancholy look in her deep sunken eyes. Catherine had a talk with her, while Stephanovitch engaged the husband in another discussion.

"Sister, my heart is full to bursting," said the frail little woman. "When we come together to pray, they all bow their heads and murmur their thoughts and wishes to God, but my heart is heavy and I am dumb. I cannot pray, for my conscience is not clear, and I feel dreadful misgivings. In the Holy Book it says that we should all love one another; but what kind of love have we here? The children vex and torment me, my husband beats me, and I am ignored and trampled upon. Nobody ever pays the slightest heed to my wishes. I sometimes feel that I have no place here; and so I cannot honestly pray to thank God."

The poor woman wept bitterly, stifling her sobs for fear they might reach her husband's ear. Catherine could hardly keep back her own tears.

The meeting at the Evangelist's house was held the

next night. The room was packed. There were
many men, and some women and children. None of
the men were young. Some had interesting faces;
there was something there beside the careworn wrinkles
of the peasant; there was a faint glow of enthusiasm
in their eyes. All wore their holiday garments of white
linen freshly washed and pressed, with green belts;
and the women had on brilliantly dyed shawls. A
kerosene lamp hung from the ceiling. They sang
psalms and hymns with a German rhythm. The
harmony was poor, for the Russian peasants were still
unaccustomed to the musical genius of the German
Protestants whose religion they had adopted; but
they struggled through the lines heroically, making
up in enthusiasm what they lacked in skill.

Then a peasant rose and prayed, his eyes fixed upon
the wall in the left-hand corner of the room, where
the sacred images and pictures are found in the houses
of peasants belonging to the Greek Church. Here
they had been replaced by a strip of bright-colored wall
paper and several flower vases. He called upon God,
asking the cause of man's debasement, and how this
sinful creature could ascend into the light of heaven.
Meanwhile the other peasants shook their heads with
rhythmic piety, their lips faintly murmuring tender
supplications, their eyes all fixed upon the many-colored
wall paper in the left corner. Then a woman arose.
She prayed that sin might be swept from the earth,
and that Evangelism might come into its own in every
part of the land. She mourned over the frailty of
mankind, with her eyes fixed on the spot where the
picture of the Madonna used to hang; and the eyes
of the whole assembly gazed in the same direction.

Then Stephan said: "Brothers and sisters, we have here two guests who wish to become familiar with our creed and our manner of praying. They are inclined towards the Evangelistic faith, but they are still uncertain upon several points, and they want to inform themselves by asking us some questions."

Catherine then took the floor. She said: "It is written in the Holy Book that faith without works is dead. Where there is true religion, there must be action. If so, then, when the Holy Scriptures tell us to help the downtrodden and oppressed, we must do more than merely repeat the words after them. We must practice what we preach. We must really help those who are suffering."

"Well, well, that is certain," assented several peasants.

"But I know of many villages where the peasants are on the verge of absolute starvation — where the old people never eat bread and the babies never get milk. They need not only religion, but food. They are so hungry that they cannot even think about religion."

She went on to describe the dire poverty she had seen in other districts she had visited — places where peasants ate the bran that here was thrown to the cattle; places where women and children were mercilessly flogged for the slightest neglect of their work. Her pictures were so vivid and gripping that the women melted into tears, and the men bowed their heads in sorrow. One short peasant with fiery red hair broke into shouts; he wanted to go out at once to feed the starving people from the bursting granaries of the wealthy nobles.

"And why have we all this suffering around us?" continued Catherine. "Because the peasants, since their emancipation from serfdom, have been given no land; because they have been ruthlessly robbed of all their possessions and of all their rights, not only in regard to religion, but in all social, political, and economic matters."

The Evangelists were wholly under the spell of Catherine's magnetic personality. They shouted approval, and declared they would avenge the wrongs of their brethren. There was enthusiastic confusion.

Suddenly the door opened. On the threshold stood a remarkably handsome man. His face was domineering, his bearing martial, his dress almost splendid. He held a Bible in his hand.

"Ah! Here is Brother Peter!" cried the peasants.

Peter was the right-hand man of the absent Ryobashapka. He had received a hint that it would be well for him to attend the meeting, as the Evangelists would need a man who could hold his own in argument.

He marched with a self-confident air to the middle of the room, took a good look at the two strangers, and sat down to listen. Stephanovitch began an address, quoting from the Scriptures, but was interrupted by Peter with the text, "Render unto Cæsar the things that are Cæsar's." Stephanovitch responded with such a shower of revolutionary texts that Peter was soon confounded and put to silence. Then Catherine again described the miserable condition of the peasants in different parts of Russia. She told of peasants who never baked, and sometimes were driven to eat grass; of whole villages suffering from a contagious eye-trouble, because the people lived in burrows; of peasants who spent the whole summer picking crumbs and other bits of food out of the barrels, and lived during the winter on what they had been able to save of the food thus collected. They were as gaunt as skeletons, yet they were exploited, and taxed, and forced to serve in the army. She told of the thousands and thousands who wandered from place to place in search of work, destitute and starving, till they found their last bed in a ditch, and no one knew when or where they died; and all because the peasants had been deprived of the land that was rightfully their own.

The listeners wept and groaned in heartfelt sympathy.

"Well," said Catherine, "can you know of all this that is going on around you, and not care?"

"No, no! Never!" cried the little peasant with the red hair.

"We must do something," exclaimed others.

Then Catherine and Stephanovitch explained that there was a great revolutionary organization, with branches all over Russia, which was planning to win justice for the wronged and bleeding children of the soil. The revolutionists, they said, were also preachers of a religion, and one of its maxims was, "No stone shall be left unturned until life in this world is started on an honest basis." "Brothers and sisters," said Catherine, "will you join us in this movement for justice and equality?"

The peasants hesitated. Then they answered, "We are all in full sympathy with you, but we cannot decide upon anything till our eldest brother, Ryobashapka, is here to advise us."

"And have you no wills of your own — no minds of your own?" said Catherine.

"It is wiser to wait for him," they insisted. "He attends to all our affairs, and he once traveled all the way to St. Petersburg in our cause."

The peasants parted with the revolutionists in a very friendly spirit. Peter tried to slip away unnoticed, but Catherine insisted upon shaking hands with him. The audience left one by one, so as not to attract attention. Then Stephan took Catherine and her nephew into his back yard, silenced his dog with a kick, and helped them over the fence, so that no one might know they had been visiting the heretics.

The next morning their host asked them if they had yet met his neighbor Stephan. Catherine said that they had, and that he seemed to be a fairly good sort of peasant, only that his religion was not quite what it ought to be. She and Stephanovitch spent the day studying the Scriptures, in preparation for the evening meeting. They drew their ammunition especially from the Epistles.

In the evening a still larger gathering of Evangelists met in Stephan's house. Peter was there, Bible in hand, ready to renew the fight. He held out somewhat longer than before, but he was finally discomfited, and took shelter behind the little red-headed man, who was absorbed in admiration of Catherine.

Stephanovitch spoke about the early trials of the Apostles, telling how they had opposed autocratic rulers, and had refused to recognize the divine right of kings, or the sacredness of their laws and edicts. The peasants waxed still more enthusiastic, and were all ready to join the revolutionary movement, if only Ryobashapka approved. Catherine had misgivings about their blind trust in this "elder brother." She feared also that Ryobashapka would be influenced against her and Stephanovitch in advance, by Brother Peter, whose pride had been wounded by his defeat in argument.

The next evening they found the peasants restless and full of expectation. "To-day we shall come to a decision," said Stephan. "Our oldest and wisest brother has just got back. He will soon be here." The peasants kept stealing glances at the door. At last it opened, to admit a powerful, broad-shouldered giant, ruddy and well fed, with a high forehead and piercing eyes. He gazed at the two visitors in silence for a few moments, then marched through the crowd straight up to them, and thundered, "Where do you come from?"

"From Orlov."

"Why are you wandering about? Why don't you settle down somewhere?"

"We have no land. We are looking for work."

"Where are your passports? Have you passports?"

Catherine and Stephanovitch rose, and began slowly to pull out their passports, but the look of mingled scorn and pity that Catherine cast upon the arrogant carpenter made him blush to his ears. It was the business of the government alone to demand passports; and it did not become an Evangelist to help the persecuting government in making its inquisitions. But Ryobashapka represented that he only wanted to make sure they were not tramps. God knew who might be prowling about among respectable people!

"Well, now, why do you come to us?" he asked, after looking at the passports.

"We are truth-seekers," they answered, "and we heard that you people here have discovered and uphold the true faith."

"Well, that wouldn't be so bad; but I understand that you are agitating for a rebellion against the Czar."

"We simply believe that the oppressed should defend themselves against their oppressors."

Ryobashapka defended obedience to the Czar from the gospels. His arguments were soon demolished, but this only made him more bitter. "If I did not understand the teachings of my religion and practice them," he said, "I should turn you over to the police this minute."

"There would be nothing new in that," answered Catherine, with a shade of mockery in her tone. "The Czar has plenty of spies and informers."

Confusion followed. Many of the Evangelists were displeased with Ryobashapka's roughness.

"Why bully them so?" they said. "They mean well. They are seekers after the truth."

"They have the people's welfare at heart," said the little man with the red head.

"What is all this excitement about?" asked the carpenter, frowning. "I said I had a right to turn them over to the police, but that, being an honest Evangelist, I shall not avail myself of the right. There is nothing harsh about that."

This calmed the disturbance. The two revolutionists then reminded the peasants that the government did not permit a true interpretation of the Bible, and that the people suffered severely in consequence.

"Here you are," they said, "trying to live according to your own convictions, and you are continually molested and persecuted." Catherine described the sufferings of others who tried to live according to their ideals, and how they were all arrested, or flogged, or sent to Siberia. "Do you think a Czar who permits such things is pleasing to God?" she said.

"What are you driving at?" cried Ryobashapka. "Do you mean to tell me that if the officials will not permit an honest interpretation of the Bible, they will permit rebellion and an honest form of government? Perhaps, if you went to prison for a year or two, as I have done, you would learn a thing or two. I know what I have gone through to get our right of free worship for this congregation, and I don't fancy the idea of going through it again. We have been flogged and persecuted, we have been thrown into prison and had our property confiscated and our rights taken away, over and over again; and now, when our burden has grown somewhat lighter, and we are about to be able to enjoy our newly won liberties in peace, I certainly don't see why we should join in a most desperate undertaking, which will ruin everything for us. We have had enough of persecution. We have no particular fancy for Siberia, or the fortress of St. Peter and St. Paul."

He made a long and telling speech, and carried all the peasants with him. The two revolutionists retired, completely routed.

They would not leave town at once, for that would have seemed like flight. They stayed long enough to allay suspicion. When Catherine went to bid Stephan good-by, he said, in a voice of deep emotion:

"I cannot express what I feel, but I know that the first time I set eyes upon you, when you came over the fence into my yard, something was lighted up in my heart. When I heard you attack the Czar and his degenerate court, I wondered, thinking, 'Perhaps this woman is the Czar's own daughter, for is it not written somewhere that "the doom of the house of kings shall be sounded by one of their own household"?'"

Stephan invited her to come to his house that night with her "nephew." He treated them with every mark of consideration, and when they started to leave the town, he sent his little daughter to show them the way, so that they might not have to inquire of strangers. The barefooted child ran ahead of them through the darkness, leading them through winding paths to a hill on the outskirts of the town. There she pointed out the road, made them a pretty curtsy, and vanished like a little fairy of the night.

CHAPTER VI

THE two "flame-seekers" next went to Zlatopol. They found in the market place many Roumanian women, with heads so wrapped up that only their eyes could be seen. Just as they arrived, a policeman snatched a paper ruble from one woman's hand, and made off with it. The woman screamed, and Stephanovitch, who always fired up at the sight of injustice, started after the policeman. Catherine hung on to his coat with all her might.

"You child!" she said. "Do you want to ruin everything by starting a riot here?"

In Zlatopol she had a large supply of revolutionary literature printed, and spent some time distributing her pamphlets and holding meetings among the peasants. Then she traveled on, going from village to village.

"I did my organizing by night," she said, in telling of her experiences. "You desire a picture? A low room with mud floor and walls. Rafters just over your head, and still higher, thatch. The room was packed with men, women, and children. Two big fellows sat up on the high brick stove, with their dangling feet knocking occasional applause. These people had been gathered by my host, a brave peasant whom I had picked out, and he in turn had chosen only those whom Siberia could not terrify. I reminded them of their floggings; I pointed to those who were crippled for life; to women whose husbands had died under the lash; and when I asked if men were to be forever flogged, they would cry out so fiercely that the three or four cattle in the next room would bellow and have to be quieted. Again I would ask what chance their babies had of living, and in reply some peasant woman would tell how her baby had died the winter before. Why? I asked. Because they had only the most wretched bits of land. To be free and live, the people must own the land! From my cloak I would bring a book of fables written to teach our principles and stir the love of freedom. And then, far into the night, the firelight showed a circle of great, broad faces and dilated eyes, staring with all the reverence every peasant has for that mysterious thing — a book.

"These books, twice as effective as oral work, were printed in secrecy at heavy expense. But many of us had libraries, jewels, costly gowns and furs to sell; and new recruits kept adding to our fund. We had no personal expenses.

"Often, betrayed by some spy, I left a village quickly, before completing my work. Then the hut group was left to meet under a peasant who could read aloud those wonderful fables. So they dreamed, until a few weeks later another leader in disguise came to them.

"In that year of 1874, over two thousand educated men and women traveled among the peasants. Weary work, you say. Yes, when the peasants were slow and dull, and the spirit of freedom seemed an illusion,

But when that spirit grew real, one felt far from weary. Then, too, we had occasional grippings of hands with comrades. We could always encourage each other, for all had found the peasants receptive to our doctrine. To own the land had been the dream of their fathers. Their eagerness rose; and stout words of cheer were sent from one group to another. An underground system was started, a correspondence cipher was invented, the movement spread through thirty-six great provinces of Russia and became steadily better organized. So the People's Party was established."

In September, Catherine and Stephanovitch were working near Tulchin, in Podolia. They had chosen this region because here the peasants had often banded themselves together against the Polish nobility.

In Tulchin they saw an old deserted palace in a great park. In the heart of the town they noticed a strange, gloomy building, surrounded by a high stone wall. Catherine wondered what it was. She was soon to learn.

They took up their quarters, as usual, with a peasant. He inspected their passports, and stowed them for safety in his great wooden chest. Beside it stood their packs. These were full of revolutionary literature, but they had no fear that any one would pry into them. It was an unwritten law that no peasant should ever meddle with another peasant's pack. Unfortunately, just the opposite rule prevailed as to letters. The arrival of a letter in a little town was a rare event, exciting general interest and awe. If one peasant received any mail, the other peasants expected to know all about it, as a matter of course.

Their host had taken the two travelers into his own hut until the little cabin beside it, which was partly filled with grain, could be cleared out and made ready for them. As his wife was ill, he had a servant girl. After a time Stephanovitch went to Kiev on business, leaving his pack in Catherine's care. She used to go every morning to the market to buy food. Coming home one day, with her modest purchase of two apples and a bit of pork, she passed the dilapidated palace, and was just thinking that some day the lofty throne of Russia might in like manner be given over to the worms, when she heard the rattling of a carriage coming rapidly along the road behind her. Turning, she saw that its occupant was a stout police officer.

"Halt!" he called to her roughly.

For a moment the world turned black before her eyes. Then she was herself again.

"Come here!" he cried sharply. "Where do you come from?"

"From the province of Orlov."

"Where is your passport?"

"At my lodging."

"Well, get in with the driver. We'll soon see the passport, if you have one."

The carriage started off, in a cloud of dust. Catherine was surprised to see that they drove straight to her lodging place, without asking where it was. Then she knew that there had been a discovery.

It was a hot day, and the windows of the hut had been taken out, to let in more air. The servant girl was standing at one side, near the stump of an old tree. She was deadly pale, and her face looked bewildered — almost idiotic. Catherine saw that she had been responsible for the misfortune. The simple girl had found that Catherine's pack contained papers and a map, and had told the wonderful news to her friends. It had passed from one to another till it reached the ears of the police.

"Passports!" growled the policeman.

The driver ran into the hut and brought out Catherine's host.

"Passports!" shouted the policeman again. The host ran in, and came out, waving Catherine's passport wildly in the air.

The officer began to question Catherine, and tried to take her by the chin, as superiors do to peasants. She resented the familiarity, and thus betrayed that she was no peasant. A wicked flash shot from his eyes.

"Where are her things?" he shouted, turning to the trembling host. The man thought his lodger was accused of theft. As he had seen nothing new in her wardrobe, he answered, "Your honor, she has no things."

"No things! What are those?"

He pointed to the heavy packs in the corner.

"Oh, those are her own things."

"Well, those are just what I want. Bring them here."

The packs were dragged into the middle of the room and opened. "Ha!" cried the police agent exultantly, as he pulled out a handful of revolutionary pamphlets. "So, you can read and write?" he said tauntingly to Catherine; but he had dropped the familiar "thou" and addressed her as "you." She made no answer. She had seated herself on the large wooden chest, and was eating her two apples with perfect coolness. She felt like an unconcerned spectator looking on at a play.

The officer was beside himself with excitement and joy. He seldom had to do with any case more important than tracing a runaway hog or a few stolen chickens. It was a great triumph to have caught a revolutionist. Meanwhile a crowd had gathered. Outside the windows, in the yard and in the room, men, women, and children stood looking and listening eagerly, full of curiosity and fear.

His eyes almost starting out of his head with excitement, the police officer began to read the manifesto of the revolutionists aloud to the crowd, with violent intonations and more violent gestures. Whenever a passage excited his particular wrath, he would swell his voice. Then he sent for the District Attorney, and the District Attorney read the incendiary document aloud all over again. The priest was summoned, and he too read it aloud. The officer sent for the judge and the chief of police. Meanwhile the peasants had been listening to the manifesto with very different feelings from those of the officials. As that simple but stirring proclamation of freedom, equality, and love was read, they supposed in their ignorance that it was the lost "original pages", the much-longed-for proclamation from the Czar. The good news spread, and the crowd grew larger and larger. Then suddenly the chief of police arrived, glanced at the wild, joyous faces around, and seized the document.

"What is this?" he asked Catherine roughly.

"Propaganda," she replied, "with which the District Attorney and the gendarme have been very viciously inciting the people."

"Search her," said the chief of police.

Some peasant women took Catherine into the little cabin and locked the door. But they refused to search her. They wept, and admired her calmness. She had nothing about her but two rubles, a blank envelope, and a few burnt matches.

She was taken under guard to the sinister looking building about which she had wondered, and was led down into the Black Hole.

"As I went down," she says, "two besotted wretches were stumbling up. I was pushed in, the heavy door slammed, and bolts rattled in total darkness. I took a step forward, and slipped, for the floor was soft with excrement. I stood still until, deadly sick, I sank down on a pile of straw and rags. A minute later I was stung sharply back to consciousness, and sprang up covered with vermin. I leaned against the walls and found them wet. So I stood up all night in the middle of the hole. And this was the beginning of Siberia."

Her first anxiety was to send a warning to Stephanovitch. Otherwise he would be arrested as soon as he came back. In Kiev there was a woman in the highest circles of the nobility who was a revolutionist. She had told her colleagues who were scattered over the country that in case of danger they might send important communications to her, and she would pass them on. With her burnt matches Catherine wrote in the blank envelope, "Aunt has fallen ill", and addressed it to the lady in Kiev.

When Catherine had been put in prison, twelve sentinels, armed to the teeth, had been stationed around the walls. Through the barred window she called to one of them, and gave him her last two rubles to send the message to its address. He took it to the chief of police. The local police authorities decided to send the message, at the same time notifying the police in Kiev, so that they might shadow everybody concerned, and track the conspirators to their lair. The telegram was sent, and a messenger boy brought it to the court lady. She read it and reread it, with a puzzled face. Then she handed it back, saying, "Why have you brought this message here? There must be some mistake. It is not for me. My aunt is staying with me at present." The boy took back the message, and the sleuth who had been a concealed witness returned to police headquarters perplexed. They did not know what to think; and, as the lady was of high rank and very rich, they did nothing further in the matter. She passed the message on to all the revolutionists of her acquaintance, and within twenty-four hours it reached Stephanovitch.

Catherine was held in prison in Petrograd for a long time, awaiting trial. She says:

"My cell was nine feet long, five feet wide, and seven feet high. It was clean, and a hole above gave plenty of air. My bed was an iron bracket with mattress and pillow of straw, rough gray blanket, coarse sheet and pillow case. I wore my own clothes. This cell I never left for over two years.

"In solitary confinement? No. I joined a social club.

"On that first evening I lay in the dark, telling myself that our struggle must go on in spite of this calamity, and yet fearful for it, as we fear for things we love. I lay motionless, and solitary confinement began to work on my mind, as the System had planned it should. Suddenly I sat up quickly. I could hear nothing; but as I started to lie down, my ear again approached the iron pipe supporting my cot. Tick, tick, tickity, tick, tick. I felt along the pipe, and found that it went through to the next cell. Again I heard: Tick, tick, tick, tickity, tick. I had once heard a code planned at a meeting in Moscow, but I could not recall it. At last I had an idea. There are thirty-five letters in the Russian alphabet. I rapped. Once! Then twice! Then three times! So on until for the last letter I rapped thirty-five. No response. Again, slowly and distinctly. My heart was beating now. Steps came slowly down the corridor. The guard approached and passed my door. His steps died away. Suddenly — Tick! — Tick, tick! — Tick, tick, tick! — and through to thirty-five. Then slowly we spelled out words, and by this clumsy code the swifter code was taught me. After that for three years the pipe was almost always talking. How fast we talked! The pipe sounded like this."

Her gray head bent over the table, her face was flushed, her eyes flashed back through forty years of danger and prison, and her strong, supple fingers rolled out the ticks at lightning speed.

"Our club had over a hundred members in solitary confinement; some in cells on either side of mine, some below and some above. Did we tell stories? Yes, and good ones! Young students — keen wits — high spirits!" She laughed merrily. "How some of those youngsters made love! A mere boy, two cells to my right, vowed he adored the young girl of nineteen, five cells to my left on the floor above, whom he had never set eyes on. I helped tick his gallant speeches and her responses continually along. They passed to the cell below hers, and were ticked up the heating pipe to her by a sad little woman who was grieving for her babies. Did they ever meet? Ah, Siberia is as large as the United States and France and England and Germany all together.

"Our club was not wholly a club of pleasure. Some of the members died of consumption; others killed themselves, and others went insane. Sometimes the pipe raved. It spoke many sad good-byes to wives and children. But the pipe was not often so, for a revolutionist must smile though the heart be torn. We older ones continually urged the young girls to be strong, for they told us how they were taken out and brutally treated to make them give evidence. A very few broke down, but there were many young girls who endured, unshaken, months of this brutality.

"From new prisoners we heard cheering news. The fire of our Idea had spread among workmen as well as peasants; in the factories many were arrested; some were imprisoned here, and joined our club for a time; but they were soon condemned into exile. Still the Idea spread. In 1877 came that tremendous demonstration on the Kazan Square in St. Petersburg. Hundreds were imprisoned; again many joined our club and were condemned, sent us last words of cheer along the pipe, and so were rushed off to Siberia.

"In 1878 we were tried. Out of the three hundred imprisoned more than one hundred had died or gone insane. We one hundred and ninety-three survivors were packed into a little hall. Over half had belonged to our club, and I had a strange shock as I now looked at these clubmates with whom I had talked every day. They were white, thin, and crippled, but still the same stout hearts. We nerved each other to refuse to be tried, for the trial we knew was to be a farce, with a special jury of only seven, of whom but one was a peasant, and with judges appointed by the Czar. They divided us into groups of ten or fifteen. The trials lasted half a year. When my turn came, I protested against the farce. I said to the judges: 'I have the honor to belong to the Russian socialistic and revolutionary party, and consequently do not recognize the authority of the Czar's courts over me.' For this I was at once taken out and my prison term was lengthened to five years as a hard labor convict in the mines. This is the punishment given to a murderer. I was the first woman to be sentenced to the mines as a political offender. My term served, I was to be an exile in Siberia for some years longer.

"Secretly, at night, to avoid a demonstration, ten of us were led out. Other tens followed on successive nights. In the street below were eleven 'telegas' — heavy hooded vehicles with three horses each. In one I was placed, with a stout gendarme squeezed in on each side, to remain there for two months. Just in front of my knees sat the driver. We went off at a gallop, and our 5000-mile journey began.

"The Great Siberian Road has been feelingly described by Mr. Kennan. A succession of bumps of all sizes. Our springless telegas jolted and bounced; my two big gendarmes lurched; our horses galloped continually, for they were changed every few hours. Often we bounced for a whole week without stopping over ten minutes day or night. We suffered that peculiar agony that comes from long lack of sleep. Our officer ordered the gendarmes never to leave us. At times we women held shawls between the gendarmes and our friends. Three wives who had come to share their husbands' exile were treated in the same way. We were all dressed in convict clothes. The men had also heavy chains on feet and wrists. Their heads were partly shaved. Our officer kept the money given him by our anxious friends at home, and gave us each the government allowance of four and one-half cents a day.

"For sleep, we were placed in the etapes (wayside prisons). Mr. Kennan has well described the cells — reeking, crawling, infected with scurvy, consumption, and typhoid. They had log walls roughly covered with plaster, often red with vermin killed by tormented sleepers. The air was invariably noisome from the open excrement tubs. The long bench on which we slept had no bedclothes. Through the walls we heard the endless jangling of fetters, the moaning of women, the cries of sick babies. On the walls were a mass of inscriptions, names of friends who had gone before us, news of death and insanity, and shrewd bits of advice for outwitting the gendarmes. Some were freshly cut, but one worm-eaten love poem looked a century old. For along this Great Siberian Road over a million men, women, and children have dragged, 250,000 since 1875,* people from every social class; murderers and degenerates side by side with tender girls who were exiled through the jealous wife of some petty town official.

* This was spoken in 1904. The numbers have increased enormously since then.

"You keep asking me for scenes and stories. But you see we were thinking of our Dream, and did not notice so much the life outside. Did any die? Yes, one by typhoid. Our officer rushed the sufferer on at full gallop, until his delirious cries from the jolting vehicle so roused our protests that he was left in the Irkutsk prison, where he died. Were there any children? Yes, one little wife had a baby ten months old, but the rest of us did all we could to help her, and the child survived the journey. Friends to say good-bye? Ah, let me think. Yes — as we passed through Krasnoyarsk a student's old mother had come from a distance to see him. Our officer refused to allow the boy to kiss her. She caught but a glimpse, the gendarmes jerked him back into the vehicle and they galloped on. As I came by I saw her white, haggard old face. Then she fell beside the road."

CHAPTER VII

On reaching the mines of Kara, she found that the prison year was only eight months, and that the forty months she had spent in prison would be deducted from her sentence. She found, also, that the political convicts were not required to take part in the actual hard labor of the mines. Their punishment, which to some of them seemed even worse, was that of enforced idleness. After staying ten months, she left Kara, as she then hoped, forever.

She was taken to Barguzin, a bleak little group of huts near the Arctic Circle. In an address given while in America, she told some incidents of the journey. She said:

"Picture to yourselves, on a cold day in autumn, with the ground frozen and the wind blowing hard enough to take your breath away, a long procession of hundreds of prisoners, traveling on foot across the steppes beyond Lake Baikal. They were a band of convicts who had served out their terms in the mines of Kara, and were on their way to the places where they were condemned to live in exile.

"I was one of those prisoners. I was on foot like the rest. I always walked ahead of the column, followed by several soldiers of our guard. The women who were ill and the children were crying and lamenting in the wretched carts that dragged them along at a foot's pace, jolting them and throwing them about. Every one was shivering with cold; nobody spoke; and the silence of the desert was broken only by the blasts of the wind.

"Then on the horizon we saw a black speck, which grew gradually larger and darker. After half an hour we could make out a crowd of men, hardly able to drag one foot after the other, staggering, thin, with livid faces, barefooted, and in rags. Among them there were no songs, no words, no sound but the rattling of their chains, which echoed like mournful bells in the cold air of the desert. The soldiers escorting this immense mass of people prodded on with the butts of their guns the weaker ones, who could hardly keep up with the crowd. They were runaway convicts, who had been caught and were being taken to the mines to serve out additional terms of hard labor.

"Our band halted, and I approached the unfortunate men. In Russia the ordinary (non-political) prisoners are always proud to have among them some persons who have been condemned for noble reasons. They look upon the political prisoners as superior beings, the more so as the officials with whom they are brought in contact are the last persons in the world to command any esteem. So I was surrounded by these convicts, these thieves and brigands, who made haste to offer me their services to carry letters to my friends at Kara, and to perform any other commissions with which I would entrust them. And it must be said that they kept their promises faithfully, regarding it as an honor to be of service to people like us.

"I asked them why they looked so wretched, and

why so many of them were ill. They answered,
'Because bread costs twelve cents a pound, and we are
given only six cents a day to buy food. There were
two hundred and fifty of us when we left the prison at
Irkutsk. Now there are only two hundred and ten
left. Forty have died on the way, of hunger and cold.'

"The soldiers, who had drawn near our group,
complained that they had not carts enough to take
up the dying. They said we should find six corpses
lying by the roadside, in the twenty versts between
there and the next halting-place. The gloomy faces
of the vagabond convicts showed that a similar death
awaited many of them on the march of hundreds of
versts that they would have to make before reaching
Kara.

"Most of these men, perhaps, had been made vaga-
bonds by the horrible conditions created by autocratic
officials, accustomed to look upon the common people
as chattels to be exploited for their profit. You can
imagine my feelings whenever we passed a dead body,
gaunt and almost naked, as we continued our funeral
march.

"A few days later, we arrived at another halting-
place, near Verkhni Udinsk. This time it was a
beautiful day, with the sun shining so brightly as to
rejoice one's heart. The great gate opened before us,
and we entered a large courtyard full of women all
dressed in white, with their faces painted and their
hair adorned to the best of their ability. For some
days the soldiers of our escort had been laughing and
saying that we should soon meet a band of women
condemned to imprisonment on Saghalien, to which
place the Russian government transports women con-

victs that are young enough to have children, in order
to increase the population of that desert island. But,
as it takes a great many months to get there, moving
from halting-place to halting-place, and as the convicts
in Russian prisons are regarded as having not only no
political rights but no human rights, the Siberian
government conceived the idea of transforming the
bands of women destined to Saghalien into bands of
prostitutes, to whom every officer, every functionary,
every soldier, and all their friends and acquaintances,
could have access at will.

"I knew nothing about it, and was greatly surprised
to see women prisoners, on a journey, adorned as if
for a festival. But at nightfall, when I heard cries,
sobs, shouts, the coarse voices of drunken men —
when I rushed to my cell window, and saw horrible
scenes, impossible to describe — then I understood
it all, and I thought I should go insane. When anyone
has survived such sights, how can he ever forget the
misery of his fellow creatures? How can he do otherwise than swear to devote his life to the deliverance
of his people? Next morning at sunrise, when, worn
out with sleeplessness and mental torture, I went out
to get a breath of air, I saw before me, going away
through the great gate, a herd of wretched women,
clad in filthy rags, their faces pale and drawn with
suffering. They were the unfortunate women prisoners, starting out for the next halting-place, there to
be subjected to fresh degradation."

Catherine reached Barguzin in February, with the
thermometer forty-five degrees below zero. Seeing
a few forlorn little children, she proposed to start a
school. The police agent showed her the police rules

sent out from Petrograd. They forbade an exiled
teacher to teach, an exiled doctor to cure the sick, or
any educated exile to exercise his profession in Siberia.
The government feared that if they were allowed to
minister to the people, they might spread their revolutionary ideas. In Siberia ex-statesmen were often
forced to hire themselves out to the Cossacks as common laborers at five cents a day.

In Barguzin there were three young students. They
were "administrative exiles" — that is, they had
been banished without trial, by "administrative order",
because they had fallen under suspicion. Catherine
and the students made up their minds to try to escape.
She says:

"We searched two years for a guide to lead us a
thousand miles to the Pacific. We found a bent old
peasant who had made the journey years before.
With him we set out one night, leading four pack
horses. We soon found the old man useless. We
had maps and a compass, but these did little good
in the Taiga, that region of forest crags and steep
ravines where we walked now toward heaven and now
toward the regions below. Often I watched my poor
stupid beast go rolling and snorting down a ravine,
hoping as he passed each tree that the next would
stop his fall. Then for hours we would use all our
arts and energies to drag and coax him up. It was
beautiful weather by day, but bitterly cold by night.
We had hard-tack, pressed tea, a little tobacco, and a
small supply of brandy, which was served out in my
thimble — one thimbleful for each. We walked and
climbed about six hundred miles; in a straight line
perhaps two hundred.

"Meanwhile the police had searched in vain. The Governor had telegraphed to Petrograd, and from there the order had come that we be found at any cost. The plan adopted was characteristic of the System. Fifty neighboring farmers were seized (in harvest time), and were exiled from their farms and families until they should bring us back. After weeks of search, they found us in the Apple Mountains. Their leader shouted across the ravine that unless we gave in they must keep on our trail, and escape was impossible. As we went back, around each of us rode ten armed men.

"The three students were sent in different directions up into the worst of the Arctic wilderness — Yakutsk.

"As punishment for my attempt to escape I was sentenced to four years' hard labor in Kara and to forty blows of the lash. A physician came into my cell to see if I were strong enough to live through the agony. I saw at once that, being afraid to flog a woman political prisoner, a thing for which there was no precedent, by this trick of declaring me too ill to be punished, they wished to establish the precedent of the sentence, in order that others might be flogged in the future. I insisted that I was strong enough, and that the court had no right to record such a sentence unless they flogged me at once. The sentence was not carried out."

On getting back to Kara, Catherine was overjoyed to find about twenty other women who were political convicts. At the time of her first imprisonment there she had been the only one. In spite of the prison hardships, this was one of the happiest seasons of her life, it was so great a delight to her to associate with

so many women of the noblest character, all of them
devoted to the cause of Russian freedom.

The women political convicts lived together in four
low cells. She says:

"Our clothing was a chemise of coarse cloth, a
skirt reaching to the ankles, no drawers, no stockings,
and a huge pair of coarse shoes. Each of us had also
a gray dressing-gown, with a yellow figure on the back,
marking her as a convict. We had plenty of clothes
of our own, but they were stowed away in one of the
storehouses of the prison, and we were not allowed
to have them.

"After a few weeks eight of the male political prisoners escaped, leaving dummies in their places. As
the guards never took more than a hasty look into
that noisome cell, they did not discover the trick for
weeks. Then mounted Cossacks rode out. The man-
hunt spread. Some of the fugitives struggled through
jungles, over mountains, and through swamps a thousand miles to Vladivostok, saw the longed-for American
vessels, and there on the docks were recaptured. All
were brought back to Kara.

"For this we were all punished. One morning the
Cossack guards entered our cells, seized us, tore off
our clothes, and dressed us in convict suits alive with
vermin. That scene cannot be described. One of
the women attempted suicide. We were thrown into
an old prison, where we were lodged in a long, low,
grimy hall, with little cells like horse stalls opening
off it on either side. Each of us had a stall six feet
by five. On winter nights the stall doors were left
open for warmth, but in summer each woman was locked
at night in her own black hole.

"There were no windows, only two small panes of glass, high up in the wall. At each end of the hall was a window, and a large stove where we cooked our food. The building was old, filthy, and dilapidated, with gaps in the walls, through which the snow and ice came into our cells every night. The roof leaked, and the icicles formed stalactites and stalagmites.

"At first we used to attack the icicles with knives, trying to clear our cells of them, but it was of no use; they always came back. In a Siberian winter the thermometer goes down to fifty degrees below zero, and at Kara the winter is eight months long. There are only two months when it does not freeze at night.

"The prison was literally swarming with vermin. They covered the walls, the floor, the beds, our clothes. For three months we did not use our bunks, but devoted ourselves to fighting the insects. We smeared the walls with tallow from our candles, and then set the tallow on fire. We used pails of scalding water. After months of incessant warfare, we succeeded in exterminating them.

"Our food was a little black bread and twelve pounds of meat a month, with which to make soup. The meat was blue and smelt badly. We had no vegetables.

"My fellow prisoners were mostly young women of the nobility, excellent and charming, but delicately bred, and not physically able to bear such hardships. They sickened one by one. Their bodies became blue with scurvy.

"In answer to our entreaties for vegetables, we were finally told that we might have potato plants — not the potatoes, but the tops which had been chopped up, slightly salted and packed in a silo as for cattle fodder. We tried these potato leaves in our soup for three or four days, but we could not eat them.

"We sent for the doctor. He came and inspected us, but told us he had orders from the government not to give us any medical care. My companions grew more and more ill. We made a small riot, battered on the hall door, and demanded the doctor with a loud noise. The ringleaders were bound hand and foot and shut into their cells.

"But the Russian government has not enough strength of character to stick steadily to any one course, even a course of cruelty. After refusing and refusing, if the prisoners persist long enough in keeping up a protest, being noisy and making themselves a nuisance, the jailors will often end by saying, 'Very well, the deuce take you, have the doctor, if you must.'

"The doctor was at last allowed to visit us; but my companions died one after another till half of them were gone."

Catherine herself did not even fall ill. She says she was too busy nursing the others. But her friends in America were impressed by her broad shoulders and deep chest, which showed that she had an uncommonly powerful physique. At the time of her visit to this country, out of all the women who had been her fellow prisoners at Kara, only one or two survived, completely broken down in health, while she was still active and vigorous. She says:

"For three years we never breathed the outside air. We struggled constantly against the ill treatment inflicted on us. After one outrage we lay like a row of dead women for nine days without touching food, until certain promises were finally exacted from the warden. This 'hunger strike' was used repeatedly. To thwart it we were often bound hand and foot while Cossacks tried to force food down our throats."

After serving out her term at Kara, Catherine was taken to Selenginsk, a little Buriat hamlet on the frontier of China. From Kara to Selenginsk was a journey of a thousand miles. They made it entirely on foot. They used to walk about thirty miles a day for two days, and rest every third day. There were two women in the party, and about a hundred men, most of them ordinary (*i.e.*, not political) convicts. They were guarded by a squad of soldiers.

It was at Selenginsk that George Kennan saw her. In his book, "Siberia and the Exile System", he describes her as follows (Volume 2, pages 121–122) :

"She was perhaps thirty-five years of age, with a strong, intelligent, but not handsome face, a frank, unreserved manner, and sympathies that seemed to be warm, impulsive, and generous. Her face bore traces of much suffering, and her thick, dark, wavy hair, which had been cut short in prison at the mines, was streaked here and there with gray; but neither hardship, nor exile, nor penal servitude had been able to break her brave, finely-tempered spirit, or to shake her convictions of honor and duty. She was, as I soon discovered, a woman of much cultivation. She spoke French, German, and English, was a fine musician, and impressed me as being in every way an attractive and interesting woman . . . She had been sent as a forced colonist to this wretched, God-forsaken Buriat settlement of Selenginsk, where she was under the direct supervision and control of the interesting chief of police who accompanied us to the Buddhist lamasery of Goose Lake. There was not another educated woman, so far as I know, within a hundred miles in any direction; she received from the government au allowance of a dollar and a quarter a week for her support; her correspondence was under police control; she was separated for life from her family and friends; and she had, it seemed to me, absolutely nothing to look forward to except a few years, more or less, of hardship and privation, and at last burial in a lonely graveyard beside the Selengá river, where no sympathetic eye might ever rest upon the unpainted wooden cross that would briefly chronicle her life and death. The unshaken courage with which this unfortunate woman contemplated her dreary future, and the faith that she manifested in the ultimate triumph of liberty in her native country, were as touching as they were heroic. Almost the last words that she said to me were: 'Mr. Kennan, we may die in exile, and our children may die in exile, and our children's children may die in exile, but something will come of it at last.' I have never seen or heard of Madame Breshkovskaya since that day; but I cannot recall her last words to me without feeling conscious that all my standards of courage, of fortitude, and of heroic self-sacrifice have been raised for all time, and raised by the hand of a woman."

Catherine gave Mr. Kennan a letter for her former fellow convicts at Kara. When she had been serving her term with them, she had often said to them, in joke: "America is a free country, and the Americans hate oppression. Some day some American will come here and help us to escape." Everybody understood that this was merely a fairy tale, but it amused the convicts.

When Mr. Kennan arrived at Kara, he found the political prisoners living outside the mines in little huts. A secret message was sent around to them that an American had arrived with a letter from Catherine Breshkovsky, and that he was waiting in a certain hut to read it to them. But nobody believed the news. Everybody said, "Oh, we all know about Catherine Breshkovsky and her American. That is just a joke." It was not until a second and a third urgent message had been sent that some one at last went, still incredulous, and peeped into the cabin, and came rushing back in amazement to announce that there really was an American there.

The eight years that Catherine spent at Selenginsk were the hardest part of the long term that she served in Siberia. Usually she had no one except a few natives to speak to, although from time to time one or two other political exiles were there for a few weeks. In winter, with the thermometer from twenty to fifty below zero, she used to put her chair on top of the brick stove, and sit with her head close to the thatch. In Selenginsk she caught the severe rheumatism that still affects her. She says:

"The government allowed me $6 a month. My hut rent was 50 cents, wood $1.50, food $4.00. My friends at home sent money too, but of course I sent this to my friends at Kara. At long intervals one of their many letters reached me — sometimes sewed in the lining of a Buriat cap. I grew almost frantic with loneliness, and to keep my sanity I would run out on the snow shouting passionate orations, or even playing the prima donna, and singing grand opera arias to the bleak landscape, which never applauded.

"My heart burned with a passionate desire to escape, to renew the struggle. I languished like a hawk in a cage. There was not a day when I did not think of escaping, and I was ready to run any risk; but the thing was impossible. Those eight empty years in Selenginsk have remained as a gray void in my memory.

"Only the thought of my comrades' suffering made me forget my own. I filled my time with work, so as to be able to send my earnings to the dark prisons, the snowbound wastes, the hungry, forgotten comrades. I read and studied, in order to know how mankind lived, and how far or near was the possibility of transforming it."

At last she became a "free exile", *i.e.*, she received a passport permitting her to travel all over Siberia. Her health had been much impaired, but she soon grew strong again. The last four years of her term in Siberia were spent in going from town to town, talking with the people, young and old, and preparing them for revolution. At Irkutsk, Tobolsk, Tiumen, wherever she sojourned, there grew up around her a circle of determined revolutionists. She made allies of some of the leading citizens of Siberia.

She still persisted in giving away to those more needy than herself the money sent her from home. Sometimes, when she had hundreds of rubles in her basket, she went around (to use her own words) "as hungry as a dog." She would walk the streets and make calls upon her friends, with the secret hope that someone might offer her a cup of tea or a bit of bread. She earned some money by sewing, but this also she sent to Kara. She became hardened to privation. Arriving in Boston once after a long railroad journey, she mentioned casually that she had had nothing to eat all day. When a friend expressed horror, she answered, "Oh, one day — what is that?"

As her term of exile drew toward a close, she knew by the increasing procession of political exiles from Russia that the work of the revolutionists was spreading. With hundreds of comrades, she planned for the future carrying on of the struggle. In September, 1896, her term expired, and she went home.

CHAPTER VIII

AFTER her return to Russia, Catherine spent three months in visiting relatives and old friends. To her surprise, she found that her surviving sister had aged much more rapidly than she had. She drew the conclusion that strong mental occupation and interest are more effective in preserving health, even under great hardships, than a life of comfort and luxury. She said of her sister's family: "They were worried about their coffee; they were worried about their garden; they were worried about everything. I had had no baggage for thirty years, and I was not worried about anything."

Barbara Tchaykovsky wrote in after years: "I remember how, when she stayed with us, the sight of her tiny handbag, containing all her worldly possessions, made me ashamed of attaching much importance to mere personal comfort, while men and women were being tortured."

Her son Nicholas had been brought up by kind but conservative relatives, who had told him that his mother was dead. Educated in the ideas of the aristocracy, he had no sympathy with her aims. She had one interview with him, and then parted with him, as she supposed, for life, or until the coming of the revolution; for she could not keep up any communication

with him without danger of bringing him under suspicion from the government.

Then she scoured Russia for the remnants of the
"Old Guard." She had not even the names and addresses of the old comrades who still survived. With
time and patience, she brought them together, and
promptly plunged anew into her old work of organizing the peasants. She found them greatly changed.
They were even more wretched than they had been
twenty years before; but they were also much more
intelligent, and more nearly ripe for revolution. She
says:

"When I began again to travel, I noticed at once a
vast difference. I no longer walked, but had money
for the railroads, and so covered ten times the ground.
For six years the railway compartment was my home.
I held meetings on river boats by night, in city tenement rooms, in peasant huts, and in the forests; but,
unlike the old times, the way had always been prepared
by some one before me. I was constantly protected."

For several years she traveled openly, under her own
name, although she did her organizing in secret. Then,
finding that she was suspected, she disguised herself
as a peasant, and thus kept on with her work for some
years more.

The government made every effort to catch her,
but without success. The peasants loved her, and
would no more have betrayed her than the Scotch would
have betrayed Prince Charlie. She had many hair-
breadth escapes. Once she was in a railroad station
when the police had guarded all the doors and were
watching every out-going train for her. In the waiting
room, she got into conversation with a party of nuns

and their abbess. The abbess was attracted by her and invited her to visit their convent. She left the station in their company, without suspicion, and spent several days in the convent, while the police scoured the city for her in vain.

Once the police surrounded a country house where she was visiting friends. It was the cook's day out. She put on the cook's clothes, and stood in the kitchen cooking the dinner while they searched the house.

Once she was staying in the south of Russia, disguised as a Frenchwoman. On some rumor, the police came along, examining passports in every house in the block. As they entered the front door, she slipped out at the rear, and into the back door of the next house, which they had just left.

At another time she was staying in Kiev with a girl of seventeen, an active revolutionary worker, who had been suspected and was under police surveillance. They slept together in her tiny tenement room. The spies watching the window observed that there was some one with her. The next night suddenly a gendarme knocked and said, "There is some one sleeping with you. Why have you not announced it to the police?" Fortunately, Catherine was out at the time. The girl was dreadfully frightened, but managed to reply, "Only my grandmother who has come to see me." The moment he had gone she slipped out into the rain and found Catherine at a secret meeting. She told what had happened, crying, "Oh, Granny, Granny! They are on your track, they are on your track!" "Do not be troubled," said Catherine. "If they had suspected that it was I, they would have broken the door down and come straight in. They only want to know who is staying with you." Her friends immediately dressed her up in silks and fashionable furs, and sent her to the railroad station in a carriage, in style, as a great lady.

During her visit to America a woman of wealth made her a present of a trunkful of handsome clothes. She was at a loss what to do with them, but finally accepted them, saying that they might be useful to her sometime as a disguise. This suggestion delighted the kind heart of the giver, who had been much disappointed at the prospect of her present being refused.

When hard pressed by the police, Catherine could change herself at will into an old peasant woman. She showed us how she once did this in Odessa. In a twinkling her shawl came over her head, her hands were clasped in her lap, her head nodded. A bent, decrepit old peasant woman looked from under the shawl with a vacant grin. When she wanted to evade the police in the streets, she would often kneel down before the sacred images in some outdoor shrine, and personate an old peasant woman praying with bowed head.

Catherine had begun as a Liberal, but long before this she had become an ardent Socialist. The aspect of the revolutionary movement in Russia had changed also. She said:

"Our old 'People's Party' had become the 'Party of the Will of the People', and had died when thousands of its leaders were sent to exile or prison. In 1887 the Social Democratic Party was formed, working mainly in the factories and mills. Here they found ready listeners, for the laborers, who had formed unions to mitigate their wretched condition, were often lashed to death. It was against the law to go on strike. Once when a labor leader had been arrested and a committee from the workers came to the prison to ask his release, they were shot down by the prison officials. Several times men were shot for parading on the First of May. Among the workers the new party gained strength until about 1900. Then all its Jewish members seceded and formed the 'Bund', which favored immediate revolution. Others too seceded."

About this time the party of the Socialist Revolutionists came into existence. Catherine Breshkovsky was one of its leading spirits, with Doctor Gregory Gershuni[1] and other fearless souls. They concerned themselves chiefly with the peasants, who make up 140,000,000 of the 170,000,000 inhabitants of Russia. Like the Social Democrats, they believed in the general principles of Socialism and worked to bring in the Socialist commonwealth. But they held that the first step must be to overthrow the autocracy. Freedom by revolution was their slogan.

In 1900, the government issued a general order to the police throughout the empire, that three revolutionary leaders were wanted — Catherine Breshkovsky, Gershuni, and Melnikov. By this time revolutionary circles existed all through Russia. Scores of secret printing offices, in Switzerland and in Russia itself, were working day and night, pouring out revolutionary literature, and the "underground mails" carried it from one end of the country to the other. The Socialist Revolutionist party was teaching the peasants the old lesson — that the land must be owned

[1] See Appendix.

by the people, and that the government of the Czar must be overthrown. In order not to take needless risks, the central committee of the party was scattered all through Russia. Its members seldom met, but constantly planned and directed the work, instructing the provincial committees, which in turn passed on the word to the small local committees, and so down to the thousands of little groups of peasants and laborers that met by night in country huts and city tenements. The leaders traveled constantly from group to group. As soon as one was arrested another took his place.

In 1901 the Fighting League was organized. It was made up wholly of Terrorists. Its object was to put to death officials who were guilty of particularly atrocious crimes, in the hope that their fate would be a warning to others. Catherine was in full sympathy with this movement.

Political assassination is rightly abhorred in America. But in Russia there was no possibility of obtaining justice by law, even for the most monstrous crimes. No subject had any legal rights as against the Czar: and the Czar's irresponsible power was delegated to a whole army of police and other subordinate officials, who oppressed the people at their pleasure. The country's noblest men and women were persecuted, imprisoned, and exiled; and the officials who treated them worst were thought to deserve best of the Czar.

In the Caucasus, a convention of women teachers met to discuss plans for an improved curriculum. A Colonel who disapproved of teachers holding meetings for any purpose ordered the assembly to disperse. Two or three of the more spirited teachers went to him to protest. He was so enraged by the remonstrance that he said to his men, "These women are yours", and turned the whole convention of teachers over to the soldiers to be outraged. He could not be brought to justice. In the eyes of the government, such deeds were a mark of zeal, and were looked upon as deserving promotion rather than punishment. The Colonel was assassinated. So was Von Plehve, who as Chief of Police had started outrages against the Jews in 1881, and later, as Minister of the Interior, had caused the Kishineff massacre. He had also revived the use of the knout to lash men and women. A number of other officials of the same type were condemned by the revolutionary secret tribunal and killed.

The Fighting League, however, had a comparatively small membership. It was a sort of guerrilla force auxiliary to the great revolutionary movement. Revolution by the whole people was the object for which Catherine and her friends were striving.

"In 1903," she writes in the "Neva" of Petrograd, "the Socialist Revolutionary party suffered great misfortunes. Wholesale arrests and searches robbed it of many of its leading workers, of its best printing offices, and stores of literature. It was necessary to replace all that. By this time the work of the party had grown strong abroad, thanks to our talented and zealous emigrants, who bent all their energies to the publication of party organs and popular books and pamphlets.

"In order to recall these young people to immediate activity at home, in Russia, I went abroad for the first time. In May, 1903, I boarded a steamer at Odessa and went, by way of Roumania, Hungary, and Vienna,

to Geneva, Switzerland, the centre of the party workers scattered in Paris, London, and Switzerland. At
this conference we were joined by the old fighters
of the '70's, Shishko, Volkhovsky, Lazareff, Tchaykovsky.

"The young people attended our meetings, and listened eagerly. Victor Tchernoff, the editor-in-chief
of our central organs (and Minister of Agriculture in
Kernsky's first cabinet), victoriously defended the position of the party. I urged the necessity of tackling
the real task, to propagate our ideas among the peasants
and workmen, to organize all the forces able and ready
to enter upon a battle with the old régime, ready to
sacrifice their lives for a free Russia. And thus a
stream of young people of both sexes began to flow
back to Russia, carrying with them our literature, and
the booklets 'In Battle Shalt Thou Obtain Thy Rights'
were distributed all through the fatherland. This task
of directing the forces of young Russia occupied two
whole years of my life."

In the meantime, in 1904, she visited the United
States, to enlist help for the cause.

CHAPTER IX

MADAME BRESHKOVSKY (I shall give her henceforward the name by which she was known in America)
was warmly received in the United States. She addressed great audiences in New York, Boston, Philadelphia, Chicago, and elsewhere. The meeting held
to welcome her in Faneuil Hall, Boston, was typical.
The following account is taken from the *Woman's
Journal* of December 17, 1904:

"Seldom has Faneuil Hall seen so great an audience
as gathered on the evening of Dec. 14 at the meeting
called by the society of 'Friends of Russian Freedom'
to welcome Madame Catherine Breshkovsky.

"Nearly 3000 persons thronged Faneuil Hall,
hundreds standing all through the evening. There
were many distinguished persons on the platform.
Hon. William Dudley Foulke, president of the Friends
of Russian Freedom, occupied the chair.

"Addresses were made by Professor F. C. de Sumi-
chrast and Professor Leo Wiener of Harvard, Mrs.
Julia Ward Howe, Abraham Cahan of New York, and
Henry B. Blackwell. In addition, Mr. John Romasz-
kiewicz made an address in Polish, Mr. Philip Davis
in Yiddish, and Dr. Shitlovsky of Berne in German.

"Madame Breshkovsky can speak English, but not
fluently enough to make a set address; so she generally

111

speaks in French. This evening, however, as there were many Russians present, she spoke in Russian, and Dr. Cahan acted as interpreter.

"When the 'Grand Old Lady' got up to speak, the great audience rose *en masse*. Handkerchiefs waved, hats were flung up into the air, words of affection in five languages were rained upon her from all parts of the hall, and the applause was deafening.

"Madame Breshkovsky had written out in advance what she meant to say. It was as follows:

MADAME BRESHKOVSKY'S SPEECH

"We are a long way from Russia, and it may seem strange to you to hear anyone speak with warmth of a country and of questions that are so far away, beyond the mountains and the sea. You who are sitting quietly in a beautiful, well-lighted hall in Boston, what have you to do with the gloomy prisons in Russia, and with the deadly struggle which has been going on for so many years between the vanguard of the Russian people and the autocratic Russian government? It is they over yonder who are waging the conflict, it is they who are suffering and dying to give posterity a better future. It is there that the martyrs are groaning, that the tears of their families are falling, and that the champions of freedom are being wounded and mutilated.

"You will be asked what their fate is to you? Many years ago, as I sat in prison surrounded by a gloomy silence, the wicket in my cell door opened, and my eyes fell on an envelope which brought me a greeting from afar, a good wish from a group of sympathizers in Switzerland. Then I was happy. My strength was revived by the consciousness that outside the prison walls there were friendly hearts that understood and sympathized, and longed to help me. The prison walls opened before me, and my mind soared fearlessly to meet new dangers and sufferings. Friends, all Russia is an immense prison to every Russian of progressive ideas. It is worth everything to the men and women who are working for freedom in Russia to know that free and civilized nations sympathize with them and wish them success.

"The party of progress in Russia is the more interested in having friends in all other countries, because it sees that the time of deliverance for the Russian people is coming nearer and nearer. All classes of the population are alike discontented with autocracy, all are longing to be freed from the yoke of despotism, and perhaps the happy day of our country's deliverance is not far away.

"But every political party that is in earnest, as ours is, wishes to secure in advance a friendly atmosphere, and to win auxiliaries that may help in case of need. Everybody knows that the struggle carried on by the progressive elements against Russian autocracy is not only difficult, but dangerous, and not only dangerous, but also very expensive. The autocracy has at its disposal armies of gendarmes, of police, and of spies; it spends millions to hunt down and annihilate all those in Russia who differ with its views. On the other side are only groups of people without money, and persecuted even to death. We have scarcely time to get together and organize when we are attacked, arrested, imprisoned, and exiled. In

Russia the government every year deprives the nation of the services of 10,000 men and women, the best, most capable, and most energetic in Russia, by imprisoning some, exiling others, and putting still others under police surveillance, which makes it impossible for them to work for their country.

"Nevertheless, what do we see? We see the progressive movement in Russia growing day by day, and all classes taking a widespread and intelligent part in it. The system of despotic monarchy has so disgusted all the people, and the miseries resulting from it have brought them so near the verge of ruin, that no one, except a few unprincipled men immediately around the throne, is willing to have the present régime continue. And that is why all the government's efforts to crush out everything that tends to emancipation come to nothing, and cannot check the victorious march of progressive ideas, which are permeating even the deep mass of the Russian peasantry. This is also why I appeal to you, friends, to help a cause which not only is worthy of every aid, but has a brilliant and not remote future.

"It is not weakness or lack of success that leads us to come to you; it is the enlargement of our work, and its success, almost beyond our expectations, that obliges us to appeal to the sympathy of free peoples, for their help in this hour of a decisive struggle, where the victory will bring happiness to the whole of our suffering country. We must take care not to leave ourselves without support, at a time when a decided gesture, a severe word addressed to our government by the free government of a free country, might turn the scale in the right direction — that of the freedom and happiness of our people. You know that every struggle is carried on by means of two kinds of forces, moral and material; and we ask you for help of both kinds.

"But, you may ask, where are the signs of this renaissance of the Russian people? What assurance have you that these people, mainly millions of peasants, dull, ignorant, and brutalized, can make a rational use of their freedom after they get it?

"The Russian government itself has answered the first question. By its present conduct, at once timid and hypocritical, it has proved both its own weakness and its fear of the progressive movement, which it hopes to turn aside by promises and postponements. By allowing the calling together of the zemstvos, the Russian government has frankly confessed that it has not strength or wit enough to deal with all the circumstances and events that in these days make up the life of the people. The shocks that absolutism is receiving on all sides have made it stagger so often that it has lost the habit of standing firm on its feet. This very war with Japan — this murder, this carnage, this suicide of the Russian people — was it not the act of a madman, who, seeing an abyss opening under his feet, tries to drag everything above down into it? Think of all the sorrows, atrocities, and losses resulting from this war — a war that nobody needed, and that is hated and despised by the people, and then say if a government worthy of respect, and convinced of its own righteousness and strength, could have rushed into it, and thus revealed to the world all its corruption, ignorance, and contempt for its people's happiness?

"We see Russia not only unhappy, rent by all possible evils, but also humiliated, disgraced, degraded, as she has never been since the terrible days of the Tartar domination. The best of her sons are being killed; the rest of her population is being completely ruined, and the country burdened with debt for centuries to come, the odious game of the present government thus enslaving future generations.

"After this, can you ask whether the Russian people could manage their own affairs better than they are managed by the Czar and his ministers? More than once the Russian people, as a whole, have shown themselves capable of deciding their own destiny and of making their own history, thanks to their common sense and courage. By searching the past, you will find that it was these same despised peasants who, with their own hands and on their own initiative, enlarged their country by territories such as Siberia, as all the northern part of European Russia, and all the lands that surround the Black and Caspian Seas. It was the peasants who saved the interests of their fatherland in 1613, when our great country was rent between aspirants to the Muscovite throne. They showed themselves dignified and wise at the time of their emancipation, forty years ago, waiting patiently for the justice of the Czar to give them a share of the 'holy soil', which is the Russian peasant's only wealth, his only means of subsistence. The people were much more intelligent than the Czar. It was impossible for him to understand, as they did, — they who work, and by their work feed the whole Russian empire, — that unless they were given land they would be left without their only means of getting a living, while those who did nothing would receive the land, which they would not know what to do with.

"Afterwards, when the different districts obtained the right to have their zemstvos, was it not the peasants who showed by their example how the money and other resources that come from the work of the people ought to be expended? To this day, the two peasant provinces of Viatka and Perm, where there are no nobles, have the best schools, the best roads, the largest number of doctors, of libraries and of technical schools of all kinds, and even a newspaper published by the zemstvos on purpose for the peasants, a thing found nowhere else in Europe.

"It is now forty years since the emancipation of the serfs, thirty years since we workers among the people first began to teach them. And now what a difference! The peasants have improved and developed till they are hardly recognizable. Experience has opened the eyes of our suffering country. She no longer believes in her Czar; she knows what he is worth; and, conscious of her own strength and her ability to act for her own welfare, she is asking for freedom. She is no longer willing to submit blindly to the will of a government that is ignorant and hostile to the nation's real interests. These same peasants, who formerly could not read, or understand the state of things, now read and understand perfectly the books and pamphlets that we distribute among them by hundreds of thousands, to show them the best way to get rid of the yoke which is crushing them, body and soul. And now that the happy time has come when the people read and listen to us, when they welcome our literature, our advice, and our presence, we find ourselves still confronted by Russia's evil genius, the autocratic government which persecutes everything true, which destroys everything great. But this time we are the stronger. The people are on our side, and we must serve them, at whatever cost. And therefore, feeling that the time of deliverance is near, we appeal to all the friends of freedom, saying, 'Please understand us, and please help us!'

"We say it with the more confidence because we know that the abolition of Russian despotism is a question which closely concerns other nations, both in Europe and in America. We know, as you also know, what the fate is of the Armenians, the Poles, the Finns, the Jews, under the rule of Russian absolutism, and you know whether their fate is a pleasant one. You know, too, that the Sultan, and all other monarchs inclined to despotism, derive their strength and safety from the power of the Czars, who always try to maintain the authority of crowned heads. In the name of justice and of the general good, I entreat you, friends, to help us as you can and as much as you can, so that we may see our immense and beautiful country, with its kind-hearted and gifted people, free and civilized as soon as possible."

"A great ovation followed the speech, and a collection was taken.

"The arrangements for the meeting had been made by Meyer Bloomfield. He was ably seconded by about a score of the best young men among the settlement workers, who acted as ushers. Mr. Foulke said that he had attended many political gatherings, but never one so enthusiastic.

"Letters wishing success to the meeting were received from Governor Bates of Massachusetts and from several labor organizations.

"At the close, Madame Breshkovsky received another ovation. Hundreds pressed up to the front of the platform, reached up their hands to clasp hers, and in some cases lifted up their children to greet her. Even those of us who had been familiar with Faneuil Hall meetings for many years had never seen such a sight."

Madame Breshkovsky addressed various other meetings in and around Boston, and spoke at Wellesley College.

She was welcomed by her own countrypeople with even greater enthusiasm. In Philadelphia, according to the *Philadelphia North American*, two thousand Russian men and women made her the object of "a demonstration almost unprecedented in America." At the close of her address in New Pennsylvania Hall, "a mighty cheer went up"; the people rose *en masse*, hats were waved, and the cheering lasted for five minutes. Then the audience surged toward the platform, took the aged martyr for liberty in their arms, and for nearly an hour carried her around the hall on their shoulders in triumph, shouting and singing "Du Biunshka" till they could shout and sing no more. Every one in the crowd tried to reach Madame Breshkovsky, and all who succeeded embraced her. Her clothing was nearly torn off, and the friends who had got up the meeting feared that the zeal of her admirers might cost her her life. These friends waited till she was borne near the platform, and then made a sudden rush and took her away from the crowd. Exhausted, but still enthusiastic, she sat

in a chair behind the wings, and begged to be allowed
to go back to her countrymen. Again and again the
crowd tried to storm the platform and reach her, and it
was with difficulty they were made to understand that
for her own sake the demonstration ought to cease.

In New York City she had had an enthusiastic
reception in Cooper Union, attended by thousands.
A New York branch of the Friends of Russian Freedom was organized, with the Reverend Minot J.
Savage as president, Professor Robert Erskine Ely as
secretary, and a long list of distinguished vice presi-
dents.

In January, 1905, she went on to Chicago, where
again she had a great reception. Later she returned
to Boston for a longer visit.

The impression that she made in private was even
deeper than that left by her public speeches. Kellogg Durland wrote in the *Boston Transcript:*

"To look upon the face of this silver-haired apostle
is like receiving a benediction. Her outward and
inward calm are superb. Her hands are beautiful in
their delicacy and refinement, despite the years in
Siberia. Her voice is low and sweet, her smile winning and childlike. Only her eyes betray the sufferings of the years. In repose her face is strong like
iron. The shadows of her eyes speak of deepest pathos.
We sat together in a little room in lower New York
one morning, Madame Breshkovsky, Abe. Cahan,
the Russian novelist and editor of the *Forward*, Katz,
I. K. Friedman, and myself. Madame Breshkovsky
was telling us her wonderful story. She spoke quietly,
yet the things she told of were so terrible they fairly
made our heartstrings quiver.

"Suddenly there came a sharp knock at the door, and a dark-eyed man of middle age stepped over the threshold. His black eyes glistened like jewels as he started toward Madame Breshkovsky. He spoke a few words in Russian, recalling an incident in both their lives, and with an exclamation of joy she stood up and threw her arms about him, kissing him first on one cheek, then on the other. They had last met as exiles in one of the prisons of Siberia."

Mrs. L. A. Coonley Ward wrote in the Chicago *Commons* of March, 1905:

"Not many days ago I stepped into a nursery. Four little children from two to nine years old sat watching a large, handsome, plainly-dressed woman with short gray hair combed back and waving over a massive head. Her brilliant eyes were full of merriment as she told the story of a wonderful doll, dramatically illustrating its accomplishments, even to its dancing. The little quartette had lost the sense of everything external except the charming story-teller and her fascinating tale. At its close she seated herself in a low chair in the center of the group, talking constantly, most entertainingly, while she cut and folded paper into bewitching shapes — cocks, boats, baskets, dolls, following in quick succession. In a few minutes the shy little three-year-old was on her lap, and the conquest of the children was complete.

"The story-teller was Madame Catherine Breshkovsky, the Russian exile.

"How has she come through her terrible experience with this child-heart fresh within her? Her companions in prison and exile are dead, or live with broken health. Many were made insane by hardships and loneliness. It was not her strong physique alone that saved her; it was this child-heart, companioned with a vivid imagination, a keen sense of humor, and a noble faith in the future.

"'How is it, dear Madame, that after all these cruel years you are without a touch of bitterness?'

"'Ah, it is because I believe in evolution. I am sure they act according to their light, as I act according to mine.'

"'You are sustained by a great hope?'

"'By great *hopes*,' she answered, while into her wonderful eyes there entered depths born of the world's ages of pain.

"Madame Breshkovsky is an altogether delightful companion. She is unselfish, interested in others, fond of books, music, and pictures, so that she becomes at once a part of the home life. She is impressive in her simplicity, hopeful, buoyant, sometimes even gay, a very human woman, and a winner of admiration and of love from every one who comes in contact with her rare, beautiful personality.

"Sitting in the twilight by the fire, with her shining eyes, her noble face, her melodious voice, she seems a splendid sibyl bringing to our modern materialism the simplicity, the poetry, the devotion of the mighty past, with its primitive virtues and its prophetic inspiration."

Madame Breshkovsky soon grew sufficiently accustomed to speaking English to make addresses in that language, with only mistakes enough to add piquancy to her talk.

CHAPTER X

MADAME BRESHKOVSKY found an especially sympathetic welcome in the social settlements. She stayed for some time at the Nurses' Settlement at 265 Henry Street, New York, at Denison House in Boston, and at Hull House in Chicago, and at each she left behind her a circle of strong friends. Miss Helena S. Dudley, who was then at the head of Denison House, said that no six years of her life had been worth so much to her as the six weeks that Madame Breshkovsky spent under her roof. Miss Lillian D. Wald, Jane Addams, Miss Ellen Starr, Professor Robert Erskine Ely, Arthur Bullard, and Kellogg Durland were among those who became warm and lasting friends.

She met Mrs. Julia Ward Howe, and the two noble old ladies took to each other at once. She called Mrs. Howe *"une vraie citoyenne."* Mrs. Howe invited Madame Breshkovsky to her home to lunch, and by way of welcome, sat down to the piano and struck up the Russian National Anthem. Madame Breshkovsky put her hands to her ears, with a cry. She explained to her astonished hostess that that tune was always played in honor of the Czar, and that the revolutionists held it in horror.

Emma Goldman did her utmost to help Madame

Breshkovsky, although their opinions were at opposite poles, Miss Goldman, as an anarchist, believing that there should be no government, while Madame Breshkovsky, as a Socialist, believed that the functions of government should be greatly extended, and should include the ownership and operation of the railroads, factories, and mines.

Madame Breshkovsky conceived a very tender friendship for me. Perhaps this good fortune befell me in part because of my long-standing interest in the Russian question. My parents and I had tried to help Boris Gorow when he lectured in this country on the iniquities of the Russian Government somewhere about 1884. I had been a member of the first society of American Friends of Russian Freedom, organized in 1891,[1] after Stepniak's visit to this country. The society never had a president; but it was formed chiefly through Mrs. Howe's efforts, and often met at her house. For some years it did active work, largely through the endeavors of its devoted secretary and treasurer, Edmund Noble and Francis J. Garrison. The society led the movement against the proposed extradition treaty with Russia, and obtained from Governor Russell of Massachusetts the appointment of a relief committee during the great Russian famine. A monthly journal, *Free Russia*, was published for several years, with Mr. Noble as editor, and L. Goldenberg as manager.[1] It was finally discontinued for lack of financial support, and the society's work was gradually taken over by sympathizers in New York.

Some years after this organization had gone out of existence, the reading of Tolstoy's "Resurrection"

[1] See Appendix.

impressed me afresh with the need that something should be done to better the terrible conditions described. The author speaks of a Russian official who wants to practise some piece of tyranny on the political prisoners, but refrains because he fears that the matter may get into the foreign newspapers. It is a maxim in war, "Always do the thing to which your adversary particularly objects." It occurred to me that it might be useful to spread news about the misdeeds of the Russian government through the American press. A new society of the American Friends of Russian Freedom was organized for this purpose, with the Hon. William Dudley Foulke of Indiana as president. George Kennan gave his services in translating the Russian news, and I manifolded it and sent it out. This society was merely a news bureau, and after a while it too came to an end. But it was still in nominal existence at the time of Madame Breshkovsky's visit to America, and was able to give her some help. A much better and stronger society of Friends of Russian Freedom, with headquarters in New York, was organized later.

But the most helpful of all the friends whom Madame Breshkovsky made in this country was Mrs. Isabel C. Barrows, the wife of the Hon. Samuel J. Barrows, secretary of the New York Prison Association and National Prison Commissioner. After Mr. Barrows's death, Madame Breshkovsky, then in exile at Kirensk in Siberia, wrote the following account of her first meeting with these good friends:

"It was toward the end of 1904. I was in New York, with no acquaintances, quite lost in that city which was wholly strange to me. I could hardly speak English, and had great difficulty in finding my way about that modern Babylon, that ant-hill of languages, nationalities, customs, and religions.

"We Russians are inherently timid, inclined to distrust our own abilities, our own knowledge; hence, when we find ourselves in a strange environment, we are filled with uncertainty, and our wish for a *point d'appui*, a person, a circle, a benevolent institution, increases because of the embarrassment felt by a person who is not sure of his ground. That was just my case when I arrived in New York. In spite of the large number of immigrants who came to meet me in the kindest and most affectionate way, I needed to make the acquaintance of the real Americans. I fancied that to impress a society accustomed to respect people in proportion to their wealth and outward accomplishments, it would take much greater gifts than mine; that it would be necessary to have a great reputation, and be able to carry one's self on the platform in a masterly manner and with full assurance.

"Alas! brought up in Russia, where every free word is forbidden, and having passed all my youth on my parents' estate, under a rather strict and serious régime, educated in the habit of keeping a close watch over myself, I was haunted by the thought of my own imperfections, the smallness of my knowledge, my total lack of talent. Although conscious of my inner power, and longing to act, and to spread my faith and my ideas, I felt bashful about appearing before an unknown public, and had no hope that I could do as well as I desired.

"So imagine my embarrassment when my friends, the immigrants, proposed to introduce me to an American family occupying an official position and enjoying a high reputation! Nevertheless, as I had my own mission, which was dear to me, and which I wished with all my soul to serve, I made an effort over myself.

"When I rang the bell at Mr. Barrows's office at 135 East 15th Street, great was my surprise to see two young women, modestly and simply dressed, writing and casting up accounts before long tables, evidently engaged in serious work, but not at all 'businesslike.' Their homelike dress, their quiet and tranquil air, without affectation or constraint, upset my ideas of the office of a man of business. It took me some time to realize that an American's office could be carried on like a family, where not only did the regular frequenters of the place feel as if they were at home, but where all comers were looked upon as possible friends.

"I did not yet feel sure, however, of being welcome in this inner sanctum, where a group of associates were working together for their common aim. Perhaps they would not like to be disturbed. But I had only to pass through a library and enter another little office to see that the two ladies who were writing there were not displeased by my coming. The elder, who was Mrs. Barrows herself, rose to meet me without the least sign of surprise or impatience. It was as if she had expected me, or as if she were so accustomed to meet all comers, at all hours, that no apparition could take her unprepared. Nor did the young lady show any surprise or curiosity upon seeing a person so awkward as I, arrayed more like an Indian than a European. All this convinced me of the high humanity of the master of the office, and I thanked God in my soul for having prepared for me a reception so simple and friendly. My relations with Mrs. Barrows, thanks to her benevolence and wisdom, were of invaluable assistance to me. It was she who translated my writings from French into English; it was she who taught me to pronounce the sounds in the English language that are hardest for a foreigner; it was she who guided me in regard to my later visits and acquaintances; and it was she who introduced me on the platform, at the first meeting in which I took part. In a word, before I had the honor of being presented to other distinguished Americans, interested in the cause that had brought me to the United States, it was from Isabel C. Barrows that I received as it were my baptism at my official entrance into American society. It was at the home of Mr. and Mrs. Barrows that I met their daughter Mabel, now Mrs. Mussey. It was there that I learned to know Arthur Bullard, whose friendship will be mine forever. It was there that I grew better acquainted with Alice Stone Blackwell, whose friendship, incomparable for its constancy and tenderness, has been a sweet sunbeam to me during the long days of an interminable exile.

"When I saw Mr. Barrows, I was struck at once by his tall, handsome figure, straight and graceful in spite of his age; his serious face, wearing the stamp of habitual benevolence, a benevolence inseparable from his exquisite nature. He made an extraordinary impression on me as one who would bring peace and love into the hearts of those who knew him well.

"I admired his beautiful face without ever daring to say how much good his gentle look did me. And my timidity lasted throughout the four months during which I had the pleasure of visiting the Barrows family. Sitting around a large table, spread with the frugal lunch prepared by the skilful hands of Mrs. Barrows herself in the next room, over a gas stove, we used to talk, each of the subject that interested him most; while Mr. Barrows, having finished before the rest, walked up and down the library, listening, stopping sometimes when any words attracted his special attention. It was only later that I learned that he valued what I said, and that the little he knew of me had made a deep impression on him. How much I regret now that I was not brave, simple, and frank enough to speak to a man the remembrance of whom has lived in my heart for seven years, whose image is still fresh in my mind, and whose portrait, in the little book 'A Moral Citadel', is a refreshment to me in the hours when I long to find myself in the company of the highest minds!"

Mrs. Barrows, through her large acquaintance, was able to furnish Madame Breshkovsky with many valuable introductions, and she helped to make her work widely known through articles in the press. She and I also acted as interpreters, on various occasions when she spoke in French.

Madame Breshkovsky not only gave her American friends a great deal of fresh and first-hand knowledge about conditions in Russia, and especially about the peasants, but she enkindled courage and idealism wherever she went. She made the same deep impression upon the educated and the ignorant, the rich and the poor.

She was convinced that revolution in Russia was actually at the door. "Our workers are already

400,000 strong," she said. "Day and night they work. In place of sleep, and warmth, and food, the dream of freedom!"

She resisted all persuasions to stay in this country and carry on her work from a place of safety. Kellogg Durland attended a small gathering of her friends in New York City, on the East Side, a few days before she went back. He described the scene in the *Boston Transcript* of March 29, 1905. After going up many flights of stairs, he found the small rooms crowded to the doors.

"'Baboushka is in the inner room alone. You may go in,' a messenger told me. As I pushed to the door, I saw Ernest Crosby, John Coryell, Katz, and a number of the New York radical ring, Tolstoyans, Socialists, anarchists, idealists, and dreamers of every shade. She talked to me of America and the Americans she had met; of her plans for the future, her bright hopes, and calm outlook upon her storm-swept country.

"'I see America a great plain,' she said, 'and all the people running about as little children — little children without a professor. You have nowhere a great leader. Everybody is bright and intelligent, but no big brain. In America there is too much specialism — too many people expert in one line, not enough who know many things. Your writers are too narrow. Write books that millions of people will read, but write about important things. If I lived in America, I would go from city to city and village to village, teaching and preaching. And I would write. The American people like poetry, but they also ask logic and consistency. When you write, be always logical, never contradict yourself, and be poetic in expression.

Then many people will read, and your influence will be great. That is what I say to all young men in America.

"'Yes, America has been very good to me. But I cannot stay longer. Some day I shall come back — perhaps in five years, when Russia is free.'

"The last days in America were full and memorable — the farewell meetings, the last articles to write, the final instructions to the bodies in this part of the world that are working for the cause in Russia. No one knew when she was to sail. The exact date was kept from all save her most intimate friends. There were but four at the steamer — Miss Blackwell, Mrs. Barrows, Professor Ely, and myself."

Two friends sailed with her. One had been for years a political exile, had escaped from Siberia, and reached America with health shattered for life. Physically a wreck, but still strong of heart, he was going back to renew the fight. The other was a young woman, the daughter of a well-known Russian family, who had spent two years in America, earning her own living and fitting herself to be a teacher among the Russian peasants. She was going back, with the full knowledge that three months was the average length of time that the propagandists were able to work before being caught and sent to prison or exile.

"Are you willing to sacrifice your freedom for twenty years, perhaps forever, for three months of activity?" she was asked.

"Certainly," she answered quietly. "It is only by many persons doing this that our poor people will ever learn, and be free. What else can we do? Many go to Siberia; why not I?"

As the three stood together on the deck, Madame Breshkovsky in the centre with her leonine head, and the other two on either hand, they seemed to Durland a type of the past, the present, and the future of the revolution.

Madame Breshkovsky took back with her about $10,000 for the cause, most of it contributed by the very poor Russians living in the large cities; and through her influence Arthur Bullard and a number of other young Americans went over to Russia and took part in the actual fighting.

CHAPTER XI

MADAME BRESHKOVSKY's expectation of a revolution in Russia was almost fulfilled in 1905. The great general strikes throughout the country, and the unanimous demand for a change in the old régime, terrified the Czar into granting a Douma and promising freedom of speech and of the press, with other urgently needed reforms. It is now a matter of history how all those promises were broken. The Czar had at first granted suffrage to the men of Russia on a fairly liberal basis. The first Douma chosen was too radical, and he narrowed the suffrage. The second Douma was still too radical, and he narrowed the suffrage again. Even after the electorate had been so changed as to make the Douma representative only of the rich, it was allowed no real power. Its decisions were constantly overridden by the Council of the Empire. The autocracy was preserved intact. Freedom of speech and of the press were soon taken away; the prisons were again crowded with the country's best men and women; and the procession of political exiles to Siberia continued, with ever increasing numbers. Naturally, the revolutionists resumed their work.

Through the treachery of Azeff, Madame Breshkovsky and that other veteran in the cause of Russian freedom, Doctor Nicholas Tchaykovsky, were arrested

133

in 1908. They were kept for a long time in the fortress of St. Peter and St. Paul, without trial. Doctor Tchaykovsky was finally released on bail, through the efforts of his friends, among whom Mr. and Mrs. Barrows and the editors of the *Outlook* were especially active. But Madame Breshkovsky was still held in the fortress, and word came secretly that she was failing and likely to die. Mr. and Mrs. Barrows were to sail for Europe in the spring of 1909, to meet the International Prison Commission in Paris. It was suggested that Mrs. Barrows should go on in advance, and try to get Madame Breshkovsky admitted to bail. Mr. Barrows said: "If you can help Baboushka, go. I would lay down my own life for her, and think it well spent."

Mrs. Barrows sailed in March. She had barely arrived in Petrograd when she received a cablegram announcing her husband's dangerous illness. She hurried home, but did not arrive in time to see him in life. A month later, she started again for Russia, provided with all sorts of letters from influential Americans to dignitaries on the other side.

Although she almost went on her knees to the Premier, Stolypin, she could not get leave to see Madame Breshkovsky. It was not until two years later that Baboushka even learned that this faithful friend had twice visited Petrograd in her behalf.

Mrs. Barrows found that a request for a prisoner's release on bail must be made by a blood relation. Madame Breshkovsky's son would have been the obvious person to make it. He had become a successful novelist; but he was still without any sympathy for revolutionary ideas. He was mortified that his mother should be in prison as a revolutionist, and he was not

willing to sign the application.   Mrs. Barrows thought
of appealing to an aged sister of Madame Breshkovsky's,
who was still living; but a Russian prince, a friend of
Tchaykovsky's, offered to use his influence with the
son.   He invited him to dinner, told him of the earnest
efforts that Mrs. Barrows was making, and said to him
in substance: "To-day your mother is old; and here
is another old lady who has twice crossed the ocean for
her sake; yet you, her own son, will not even lift a
hand to help her."   The son's feelings were touched;
perhaps he was a little ashamed.   At any rate, he
signed the request for bail; but it was refused.

He went to see his mother in prison.   She wrote him
the following letters while in the fortress.

She was allowed to write on no personal affairs save
her health; to discuss no politics; to make no reference
to the government; to speak of no recent publications,
etc., etc.

"January 22, 1909.

"My dear N: I was very much pleased to see you,
and I thank you for coming.   I wish that I could always
see you looking so well.   I appreciate the need of unity
between soul and body when one has singleness of
purpose, and I know very well what a tremendously
deep break is made in one's life even by a single crisis.
It may alter a man's life completely.   Preserve yourself, then, from every base and unwholesome thing.
Let pure motives only enter into all your actions.   Good
motives beautify the human being, and convey to the
face a beautiful expression.   I wish you success, my
dear child, in everything that leads to your perfection.
Kiss the others for me, and tell them my joy in seeing
you.

"I imagine myself sitting with you in your room while you are relating to me what you have seen, what you have heard, what you have in your mind to do. At first I listen to you patiently, and then I begin to argue. Do you know, I never could read or listen to descriptions of anything adverse to my soul, especially the horrid things which base people do to each other, even if the horrid things do not have fatal results. I have been reading Dickens for the first time, and I am obliged to skip whole pages. While reading I often say to myself, 'Oh, this happened a thousand years ago, and there is nothing of the kind now,' but still I cannot read the descriptions of horrors. I am afraid that in the books you write I shall have to skip some pages too, but I cannot help it. I will try to understand the plot without reading the horrors.

"Do you know what perfectly delighted me? 'Ivanhoe.' That is a novel of novels! If all historical novels were written in that way, they would be marvels. Still, I skipped nearly four chapters concerning the violence in the land. But it is a wonderful book. I think it would pay very well to publish a good translation, with illustrations. It is capital reading for youth, and delightful for grown-ups. Just imagine, I was always afraid of Walter Scott, because your grandmother inspired me with mistrust of him.

"Well, I wish you good health, my dear. Protect yourself from influenza, which attacked me as the autumn fell. I embrace you and bless you."

"March 2, 1909.

"My dear N: Soon it will be two months since I saw you, and still I have no books from you. Probably the time will soon come for your going away, and we shall not see each other any more. I constantly recall our interview, and always regret that I could not see you clearly, but I remember every word of our conversation. What you said of the Lake of Geneva often comes to my memory — that its beauty has been worn out by many commonplace pictures. But only think, my dear child, how everything that is beautiful in nature is 'tainted' in that way. Shall we blame the sky, the stars, the sea, the mountains, because they have been sung by so many poets and drawn by so many pencils, for so many ages? Shall we therefore cease to love them? Shall we think that it is not becoming for us to look on the Milo goddess with admiration, simply because there are so many photographs of her on every street corner? No, my friend, this is a prejudice, and it often prevents us from taking pleasure in things which deserve to be enjoyed. If it were true, there would be nothing left on the globe for a refined taste, because the crowd has looked upon all these things, on all sides and in all sorts of places. The sense of beauty lies in ourselves, and when it is strongly developed — that is, when we are capable of noticing and appreciating the very slightest feature of beauty — then everything that excites admiration in the crowd seems to us still more beautiful and more wonderful.

"It is another thing to prefer one kind of beauty to another. For instance, however picturesque and original Spaniards are, I never should prefer them to the French, because the creative spirit of the hidalgos and of the French people stands as one to a hundred in ability to create in the spheres of science and of art. And the Frenchman shares the fruits of his researches so willingly with others that his homeland attracts to itself the hearts and the affections of all other people. Believe me, my dear, Paris is so thickly populated with foreigners, not because life there is so gay, but chiefly because one can live there so freely and so usefully. Every one feels himself at home, and he has the right to everything that has been accumulated by ages of labor, of genius, of talent.

"I should like it very much if you would take Madame N. to the Lake of Geneva and go with her to the small village of C., near the Castle of Chillon, with the white mountains in the distance looking into the blue water at your feet — those white mountains whose summits melt into the transparent air. Oh, that mountain air, so full of health! When I saw this picture for the first time, I held my breath.

"Au revoir, my dear child. Come soon again. You can get permission for two or three interviews. I embrace you and kiss your hair."

"April 2.

"My dear Friend: I should very much like to know how you are. When I received your letter, I was surprised at your change of handwriting, but from the first word I understood what had happened. Such a healthy, vigorous man to look at to be ill in bed! One thing consoled me, that there is somebody who writes for you: it means that you are not quite alone.

"I was waiting to see you arrive, but you did not appear, and I lost hope. At last they said, 'Come,' and I went to meet you. As I was passing the clock I saw that it was a quarter before twelve, and I mentally reproached you for coming so late, and I walked briskly in order to look upon you sooner. But you looked ill. There is nothing more dangerous than to take cold with influenza. My dear, you ought not to trifle with your health. It is a great blessing, and its absence spoils life. Give my thanks to the one who writes for you, and be sure that I did not forget you those fifteen days while you lay ill.

"I intend in our next interview to speak less and listen more. You know that I know nothing about your life. I therefore ask you to prepare beforehand a concise, and as full as possible, story of your life, of your quarters, whether you live alone or with some one, what your surroundings are, how your time is spent, what you are writing now, what interests you very much, what your plans are. I am prepared to keep silent for the twenty minutes.

"Now I wish to tell you, as a lover of art, that it is quite worth while to see the picture gallery of Helsingfors. The Finns have skill, and their painting is original in execution as well as in subject. Folk-lore, the life of the people, and their traditions supply rich material for the artists. It is a country worthy of study.

"If you wish to amuse me, my dear, find me a book of travels describing different countries and epochs, with illustrations. It would be better if it were a work unknown to me, but anything that has appeared within ten or fifteen years will do, so long as it is well written and has plenty of pictures; but it must be without intrigues and cruelties.

"What Englishmen are writing now? What are they giving the public? You make me laugh with the question whether I 'follow the news'! My dear, I am entirely in the position of those fabulous creatures that have been stolen away and are kept living in such places that even the ravens and the wolves cannot peep in. Besides my four walls I see nothing, and hear nothing besides the ringing of church bells. My past was hedged in with all sorts of limitations, but such limitations as these I never experienced before. It is well that this happened towards my old age, when a large store of impressions and observations has been laid away in my memory. My whole past life appears before me as a tremendous school in which I pass from class to class. How many classes are still left, God only knows! Life is a great teacher for all who wish to learn, and he is fortunate who gets on to the proper road to learning, otherwise one may go through life without learning anything or thinking anything. The majority live in that way, and, alas! no one helps them. But he who knows how interesting and how blessed it is to know is bound to teach others. Ah, my dear, I begin to preach!

"I embrace you warmly. Give my greetings to all relatives and friends."

"April 27.

"My dear N: You told me that in about a fortnight you would come again. I should wait for you quite patiently if I were sure that you are well. The weather is wretched, and I know you ought not to expose yourself.

"Have you ever read what Lessing has written about the Laocoön? Having examined the history of this work of art, Lessing has devoted a great deal of time and study to it. The article is full of artistic taste and a deep understanding of the meaning of art. I read it not long ago, and it is deeply interesting in showing the relation between art and reality. It contains a good many sane thoughts, and every writer ought to read it carefully. It warns people about ascribing too much importance to the creative side of art, for, however correct it may be, it always remains an imperfect imitation of natural beauty. The world of our conceptions is very meager, especially if we place human productions above the spirit which produced them.

"Write me about N. I take an interest in every bit of domestic life — for instance, whom her chambermaid married, and is she content, and do they live together happily; and are they in the old house — the large one — or in the small one? etc. From the small things in life you can judge of the large ones. I think I owe my knowledge of life to that principle, or that peculiarity of my mind, that the minor things do not escape me. I notice them side by side with types of character and modes of life.

"You speak of M. and P. Their life is that of the provincial town. There is much good in it when it is enlightened by the spirit of knowledge and love. The smaller children may introduce both. My dear, try to appreciate all that is good and honest in people. Do not expect perfection from them, and do not try to fit everybody to one shape — even a healthful shape — so long as he is sincere. The human mind is growing and forming itself, and it is still shaking off the remnants of the old dust and dirt; and blessed are those who are already accustomed to hate that dirt in themselves and in others. It is the business of those who understand more to give their help to those who are climbing up out of the cerements of the past.

You have a good heart, I know it. Answer me soon, and receive my blessing, and my warm and loving kiss.

"Your Mother."

"April 29.

"My dear Kolinka : I have seen neither you nor the book. Although I am accustomed to wait patiently, still I wish to know as soon as possible what is going on with those who interest me. Your foster father and mother probably think I do not take any interest in small every-day affairs. It is not true. I know beforehand most of the events that happen in their lives. They are trifles, but these trifles make people joyful or sad.

"Tell your foster mamma that I wish she would describe to me her household and her friends. And will you ask one of your friends to buy me a crocheted shawl, soft and elastic, that I can wrap round my head, something costing about three rubles. I have still another request. I have received twelve rubles from my friend Isabel Barrows. This attention of my transatlantic friends is very dear to me, and I sincerely thank them for it, but I have no way to express these thanks myself. Therefore I ask you, dear, to help me to tell Mrs. Barrows and all her family and all the friends that I heartily greet them. So sure am I of their greatheartedness that I should not have been surprised if some of them had been here ! Blessed are those who cultivate in themselves a love for their neighbors, and who respect before everything the dignity of the human being.

"Yesterday I saw one blade of grass climbing from under a stone, on the sunny side. It presented a very sad contrast with the rest of the surroundings, the bare trees and granite walls. A small patch of sky also looked upon me."

"May 18, 1909.

"My Dear : After each interview I write you, for I feel that in the course of it almost nothing has been said. The shawl was received, but it is so good that I cannot find a proper place for it, and I have finally decided to keep it in the paper package, for I cannot make up my mind to put it on. It was too elegant for me, but I thank you for it. . . . My greetings and respects to all my old friends. I remember all, absolutely all, and love them, with all their children and grandchildren. For three days now I have seen the sun as I take my exercise walk, and I warm myself in his rays."

Influentially signed petitions from both England and America pleaded for leniency for the two aged revolutionists. When they were finally brought to trial, Doctor Tchaykovsky was acquitted. Madame Breshkovsky was again exiled to Siberia, this time for life.

Doctor Tchaykovsky wrote to Mrs. Barrows :

"We saw your old friend, shook her firm hands and kissed her cheeks. She is as firm and brave as ever, though her strong body begins to give way under the pressure of age and circumstances. She is not so erect as in former times. She was delighted to see Mrs. Tchaykovsky and my daughter, as well as the crowd of press correspondents, and kissed them all.[1] She

---

[1] On kissing the correspondent of the *London Daily News*, she said, "I am so glad to speak English again and to see an Englishman !" In answer to the press correspondents' expressions of sympathy, she said: "Do not let this trouble you. I have been through it all before."

wanted particularly to be remembered to Miss Alice Blackwell and yourself, and said, 'Tell them I love them — I love them all.' It was a matter of only two or three minutes between the verdict and the guards surrounding her.

"The verdict was a surprise. Her case was particularly hopeless, and she was ready to die in the course of the next two years if sentenced to imprisonment with hard labor. (She was sixty-eight, and the law permits hard labor only until the age of seventy.)

"The trial lasted two days, and both those days I sat with her on the same bench, guards with drawn swords on both sides of us.

"When my companion was asked what was her profession, she said, quietly but firmly, 'Propagandist of Socialist ideas.' In the course of the proceedings she made several remarks as to the facts, correcting the statements of the indictment and denying the lying assertions of the witnesses, but always admitting her participation in the work of the party, with an air of quiet dignity and epic greatness.

"Oh, how painful it was to see her gray head and erect form disappear among the crowd of guards in the corridors of the court! This, the noblest and bravest woman I ever saw, thrown into the realm of the down-trodden, deprived of all human rights, and subjected to the petty caprice of any minor official or jailer! I never saw her face so radiant and so proud as at the moment of listening to the verdict."

Madame Breshkovsky was exiled to Kirensk, a little town on an island in the Lena River several thousand miles from Petrograd.

Her friends were anxious to pay for more comfortable

transportation for her than was provided for the exiles by the government, but she refused. She wanted no special privileges. Neither would she accept the money that her friends sent her, except on condition that she might share it with the rest. She was held in prison till the large party to be deported to Siberia was ready. It consisted of one hundred and fifty political offenders, and a hundred ordinary criminals. The journey took from spring until nearly autumn. First they went from Petrograd by train to Irkutsk. In the prison there she was ill for a fortnight with scurvy. One person only was allowed to see her and give her some of the money that had been raised for her, but nothing else was allowed to pass from his hands to hers, not even a lemon for the scurvy. Then the prisoners walked for two days, about twenty-five miles a day, to Alexandrovsk. Thence they started in carts for Kachug. The train was made up of eighty peasant carts, each holding three prisoners, besides the driver. The only extra comfort that Madame Breshkovsky would accept was additional hay in the bottom of the cart, and probably that was for the benefit of the sick woman who was traveling with her, and who died on the way. She herself stood the journey well. Another political exile saw her when the convoy stopped at Manzurka, and wrote in a letter dated September 24, 1916:

"When Granny passed here on August 14th she asked with evident sorrow about Joseph. 'Oh, what is going on in the prisons! It is impossible either to remember or to speak of it.' Her face darkened, although a moment before she had been quite lively and bright. This thought of her unfortunate comrades pains her like a terrible sore at her heart. This was the only moment that she was gloomy while we saw her. All the rest of the time she was so exceedingly bright and kind that it was hard to believe she is nearly seventy years old and had just got out of prison after two and a half years of solitary confinement. A full figure with rosy face (I paid special attention — there were no wrinkles), sparkling eyes, and gray hair showing from under her hood and hanging upon her forehead. The train stopped beyond our village to change horses. It was quite a camp, of two hundred and fifty human beings surrounded by a chain of escort.

"Among this crowd in gray coats under a gray sky and in the rain, her imposing figure struck every one immediately. It seemed to me that since 1905, when I had seen her last, she had grown younger. She was in good spirits. A crowd of young people accompanied her. This brightened and encouraged her, and colored the impression that she produced upon us. And this was after five days of an awfully hard journey, all the time under a pouring rain, in a shaky cart, with the nights passed in barracks or around camp fires. Many persons would have been quite prostrated, but our Granny looked as if she were at a students' party.

"We were admitted inside the chain of the convoy, so that we were able to see her, as it were, amid her home surroundings. She was the centre of the party and the object of general attention, not only to her comrades, the political prisoners, but also to the ordinary criminals and to the soldiers of the convoy.

"It is a curious fact that when we were traveling under escort to our destination in April, the convoy repeatedly asked us, 'When is Granny coming up? Lord grant us to see her!' The prison in Irkutsk also was expecting her. The whole of imprisoned and exiled Siberia was waiting to see this 'miracle woman.'

"Unfortunately the train stopped at Manzurka only a little while. There was hardly time to speak to her, so many wanted to see her and pay her their respects. She was joking almost all the time — kissed us all — was very glad to see our Volodia, now a grown-up youth — kissed him. We had hardly time to exchange greetings and remember common friends, yourselves amongst others, when the guards approached her and said, 'Please, Baboushka, get up on your cart,' and accompanied her to the telega. Pointing to another comrade, who was traveling in the same cart with her, she said, 'This is my friend. He has taken care of me all the way.' There was a third passenger in the cart, a feeble woman, so exhausted that she could hardly sit up, and lay down at once upon the hay. 'A Dissenter,' said Granny in an undertone. 'And this is our dear kind Starosta,' pointing to a tall, bright student, the deputy of the party.

"She was wearing a sort of dressing-gown of superior shape and cloth, and a peculiar hood."

From Kachug she made the journey partly by boat, partly by cart, and finally reached Kirensk on August 27, 1910.

CHAPTER XII

On August 29 she wrote to her old friend, George Lazareff, a political exile at Baugy sur Clarens in Switzerland, who for many years had watched over her welfare with great affection, and supplied her with money:

"Dear Brother: The day before yesterday I arrived at my destination. I shall not dwell on the details of my journey, but shall mention my needs, since winter is approaching.

"Neither the money nor my belongings which I left behind at the forwarding prison at St. Petersburg have been received as yet. While I remember the beautiful warm blanket that you brought to show me at the moment of my departure, I want you to let me have in addition two broad warm flannel skirts and two pairs of warm stockings, as well as a warm head shawl and a light waterproof, and also some yards of cotton sheeting, out of which I shall make all the clothing I want.

"Living is very dear here; lodgings especially are growing expensive owing to overcrowding, and they increase in price with every new party of exiles. I have engaged for myself half of a log house divided into three small rooms, bedroom, kitchen, and reception room! with a separate entrance, for five rubles a month (about two dollars and a half), which includes firewood, water, and cleaning.

"I have become used to eating little food, and can now live on very little, but I cannot eat rough food. My monstrous swelling is going down. It appears to be severe inflammation of the kidneys, and I was ordered baths, for which I hope to arrange with the assistance of kind friends. Had it not been for the care of comrades, I should have fared very badly on the journey.

"Au revoir. I am waiting for money and books, novelties, serious ones. I embrace sister M. and all relations."

The first letter from Madame Breshkovsky received in America was dated September 29–October 13, 1910 (the Russian calendar is a fortnight behind that of the rest of the world. The date is given according to both calendars).

"Dearest and best friend Alice Stone Blackwell!

"My good and lovely friend Helena Dudley!

"Five years and a half ago, when you asked me to remain with you in America, I answered that in five years, when everything was restored and put in order in Russia, I would come back. In my mind, restored and put in order meant Russia renewed and quietly working for her further progress. Certainly, when I said that, I did not expect that my wishes would be exactly fulfilled. I know that great historical cataclysms do not take place without 'flux and reflux' of success and mischiefs, without many and many new efforts and battles before the end is attained. But, dearest friends, I did not foresee that the recommencement of my relations with you would follow from the place where I now am. Your old acquaintance is once more in Siberia, farther than ever from your charming homes. But what is distance if our imagination can transport us wherever we choose, and represent to us all the scenes and images that we remember and love? So I feel, and instead of fixing my attention on all sorts of disagreeable conditions environing my everyday life, I prefer to visit all the places and people that made me contented and happy. In doing so I feel myself always among the best company in the world.

"I am not quite without good company in reality. There are a few people who have access to me, and who take care of my small needs. Two exiled families anticipate my material wants. A young exile takes me to walk around the little island whereon is situated the so-called town of Kirensk, surrounded by two rivers, the immense and cold Lena and the less majestic Kyrenga. The boy helps me to heat my stove and to make my few purchases. The two years and eight months in the fortress of St. Peter and St. Paul having impaired my health, the young man is of great use to me, for my gait is not yet sure enough, and it will take some time before my strength and activity come back enough to let me exercise my feet without help. The winter is severe. The cold mounts to over 56 Reaumur [1] and perhaps during two or three months I shall not be able to go out. Nevertheless I hope to regain my health, and to live to see you again. Why not? My own experience has proved to me how greatly circumstances change. Happen what may,

---

[1] The name of the thermometer used in Russia instead of Fahrenheit. They speak of it as going up to zero instead of down. Zero is the freezing point.

I shall always believe in the coming of progress, mental as well as moral, and in the capacity of my country and my dear people to go forward.

"During my imprisonment I wrote a great deal, setting forth my opinions on various questions of social life; concerning the education of children and young people; on the destiny and vocation of women; some psychological questions; on the arts and on culture in general. In a word, I explained at length my thoughts and the result of my experience gathered during my whole life. There was no allusion to politics, nothing that could arouse prejudice on the part of the government, and yet all these writings of mine, more than six hundred sheets, have been taken from me, and my request to have my own work given back to me has had no result. I am sorry, for in it there are counsels and opinions worthy of being listened to, especially by the young people, who among us are always eager to learn the opinion of their elders.

"I am not sure that you will receive this letter. It is quite possible that I may be deprived of the joy of corresponding with you. A watch is kept upon all my doings and my every step, day and night, and my position in exile differs little from that in prison. The guards are permitted even to wake me in the night to see if I am safe. There is always one of the spies watching me from a distance. But all this cannot transform me into a miserable creature, for I find everywhere some good souls that wish to be useful to me.

"Tell dear Mrs. Barrows I sympathize with all my heart with her sorrow in the loss of such a noble man as her husband. Her daughter, her son-in-law, and the estimable young ladies I saw working with her are before me. I remember every one with whom I was acquainted in America, especially the women who gained in my soul the best nooks. The young men of the settlement in New York will never be forgotten, as well as Mr. Ely."

To Miss Blackwell. December 29, 1910–January 11, 1911.

"The new year has come, and I wish that you, my dearest daughter, may be as well as when I saw you. You see your Catherine is strong, although she is twice as old as you. Your two letters and the card from George Kennan gave me great pleasure, and made me so proud of myself I cannot express it. To have the confidence of such people as you both, as my dear Helena, it is a great comfort — a great comfort. Only see how happy I am — persecuted, banished, and yet beloved! All these days, for instance, I have had so many visitors, poor comrades from all the corners of the large territory where we abide, that during the whole week I could not select a moment to write, to read, to be alone. My means are very small, but if one desires to be useful, it can be done in some way or other. The comrades are especially in need of books and papers, and of different tools for various kinds of manufacturing. There are shoemakers, carpenters, locksmiths, etc. The places where they live are so small and so far from all good markets and shops that nothing worth while is to be found there. The want of money is a second reason, and the prohibition against leaving the place of residence assigned to them is the third. All these difficulties have to be overcome, and being older and more ex-

perienced, I can sometimes help the poor boys to arrange their little affairs. Many of them are without
clothes, especially those who have come straight from
prison. They are not allowed to take their clothes
with them. All their belongings are left at the prison,
and have to be forwarded to the owners at their place
of destination; but the prison officials are allowed to
steal all they wish, and only about a quarter of the
goods are restored to the owners. One may plead
and write as often as possible, without receiving any
answer, and remain naked and hungry. How many
deaths take place as the result of want, of despair,
and of alcohol! for there are natures that cannot support such a way of life — the solitude, the daily privations, the lack of hope. You understand my situation, — that of an old mother who wants to aid every
one of them. I help, I scold, I sustain, I hear confessions (like a priest), I give advice and warning;
but this is only a drop in the ocean of misery. With
all this, I feel myself strong and ready, always ready —
perhaps because of this.

"Write more about yourself, Helena, and the boys and
girls whom I saw through you and with you. Is the
New York settlement as interesting as ever? There
were a dozen good young people. Some of them have
visited Russia; I read and heard of it, but had not
the opportunity to meet them. Very sorry. Give
them all my best wishes. You may read all the letters
enclosed in yours, my dear Alice. No secret that
you would not know. My life is very open now. I
am under close surveillance. I cannot take ten steps
without a spy at my heels; but up to this time my
correspondence is safe. It is only in the prisons now

that letters have to be inspected. But they never hesitate to break their own rules. Your friend and second mother, Catherine."

To George Kennan. December 29, 1910–January 11, 1911.

"Thank you, old friend, for your readiness to fill my life with your attentive goodness. I would like the *Woman's Journal*,[1] and one of your best papers, and a review for which some of my American friends write. For books, I would like your works about Japan, and some others concerning some new questions that are occupying the attention of the world. Now that I am out of prison, the classics do not attract me, and my imagination keeps traveling over the whole world, around all the earth, — even farther. How long it will last, who knows! Often and often I see in the papers how many of my old friends have passed away forever, but I myself feel as if I were fifty and not sixty-seven. So glad, so happy to hear of you, to see your writing!

"Yes, our dear old friend, I remember your visit as well as if it were but yesterday. The first time I read your book about Siberia [1895], I laughed much over your saying that I should finish my days in Selenginsk and be buried there. Many and many times afterwards I looked back to those words, and was so eager to see you, our dear friend, the celebrated author of your beautiful book. Even the young people, so apt to forget or ignore history, are well informed about the writing and the author himself. And now, notwithstanding all the horrors we have survived in

[1] A woman suffrage paper edited by Miss Blackwell.

Russia, your book is translated and read everywhere, and those who knew you personally never speak of you without the best feeling of gratitude. I am sure you are as young and energetic as you were."

To Miss Blackwell. January 25, 1911–February 7, 1911.

"The many pictures you sent me made a great sensation around me, for, after looking at them for some days in my cabin, I began to distribute them among the children, many of whom visit my poor dwelling, curious to see the 'grandmother' known about all the town as a persecuted person. Only two pictures I kept for myself: 'Hello, mamma!' and a view of a villa; both pleased me much. Six letters from you, two cards from K., and one letter from Miss Starr. It is lucky, very lucky, for I am now quite alone, without my young boy who used to serve me and to nurse me. Michael Borash has been arrested, imprisoned, and sent away to another district, and is not permitted to quit his abode. What had he done? Nothing except to visit the old woman every day and do her housework. It is the second case of a man being banished for his acquaintance with your old Kitty, who thinks herself to be a witch, swallowing every one that approaches her.

"No news, no theatre, no festivals. I avoid all sorts of routs, for the government is lying in wait for any pretext to wrong somebody or to do me harm. A week ago one of our comrades was buried, and there were some of us present at the cemetery. Now the police are making capital out of this token of sympathy, though not a word was spoken, not a song sung.

The name of every one present has been written down, and two young men were arrested before the funeral, as if to prevent any disturbance. . . . Nobody is sure of living in the same place even for half a year. Such insecurity deprives men of all energy and activity. How many have settled down to follow some trade and begun to work and to earn their bread, and suddenly, without any tangible cause, they have been arrested and sent away to a place where there is no work, nor means to obtain it! Such persecutions drive men to despair.

"But you, dearest, can write as often as you will, without fearing to be arrested, imprisoned, and exiled!

"It is cold — 40° and 45° frost. My cabin does not suffer too much, but out of doors it is too severe for my health. Yet I am going directly to take a bath, for my feet suffer without hot water. Half a mile to go there, another half mile to come back. Up to this time my bodily strength has not entirely forsaken me.

" January 26–February 8.

"Yesterday, when going to take my bath, I was accosted by the postilion, with a packet in his hand, searching for the address. He guessed it was for me, and handed it over. It was a beautiful book, 'The Tragedy of Pelée', by George Kennan. My thanks to the author. How is his health? His little photograph would be welcome in my cabin. I am very sorry my boy is not with me so that we might read the book together. The frost is intense. I remain in my log house quite alone with my books, newspapers, and letters. Many of them are full of good words, and make me contented with my destiny."

With a picture postcard:

"Everything is covered with deep snow now. In three months the spring will do her work, and this picture shows what poetry is the share of this north country, and what are the walks that this climate affords. Some hundred years hence, when people are more sensible, Siberia will be unrecognizable; but now, O God! how wild it is, how desert and rough! It is good fortune for us that the peasantry and the islanders are good-hearted people and do not molest any one."

To Miss Ellen Starr of Hull House, Chicago. January 10–25, 1911.

"Certainly I was wrong when I said you would lose the vivacity of your feeling toward me, my beloved friend, my dear Ellen Starr! The American women are not so expansive in words and manners as we Russian women, but the stronger they are in their faithfulness, the deeper is the foundation of their attachment, once formed. That I knew always; nevertheless it was difficult to be persuaded that persons who are so constantly occupied, working so hard for a great many people, as you, as our kind Helena Dudley, could have time to think about a far-off friend, buried in Russian prisons and Siberian forests. The better for me, always so eager for love and friendship from those whom I love myself. Alice Blackwell was an exception to me. I saw during my personal acquaintance with her that she was apt to embrace the whole world with her beautiful heart, her strong soul; to press it to her bosom, and never be tired of working for it. But she did too much for her human strength, and now she must rest a while.

"Now I see there is no distance, no time for us; and, sitting so far one from another, we speak, we relate, as if we were together. For instance: I should like to know about the 'clever' lady that used to sit at the post in the first room of your settlement. About Mr. —— the *commerciant* that used to learn Italian with you. About the author of the book, 'The Soul of Black People' (if I am not mistaken). He pleased me especially. And very much I should like to know about Dr. Yarros, with whom my sympathies were growing every day. She and her friend (a teacher) were so hospitable, so eager to be useful. I do not ask about Miss Addams, being sure she will always remain in Chicago as the head of Hull House, surrounded with her old and new friends. But the life of many others is apt to change often, being more dependent on various circumstances.

"As to my young man, who continues to be my devoted nurse, he is so much pleased with the flattering words with which you and Alice gratify him, that it seems to him almost impossible that he should be so highly appreciated. He is very modest. Each of the letters from America I have perused with him once more for his sincere satisfaction. He is a Social Democrat,[1] but the difference of creeds (of programs) here in exile, as well as in the prisons, is very often annihilated by the necessity of sympathy and friendship. The use of personal capacities, and often the want of

[1] The Social Democrats spread their propaganda mainly among the industrial workers in the cities and towns. They held that peasants who owned any land, even though they were wretchedly poor, must be classed as capitalists. The Socialist Revolutionary party worked chiefly among the peasants, and emphasized the importance of enlisting the peasants in the common struggle against oppression.

what one would desire, make people less fanatical, less dogmatic.

"I have many young friends in these districts, near and far. All are working hard for their living; all are so glad when they receive any token of love or encouragement. That makes me responsible, for I consider the young people (of whom there are six hundred in the district of Kirensk) as my own children, my grandsons. And, just as it happens with a large family, there are good children and those who are less satisfactory. Some of them would be better if they were at home, where it is not so frightfully hard to overcome all the difficulties of life. But the heart of a mother is indulgent. Certainly I choose the better, but the wicked shall live too.

"Thank you, dearest, for your desire to aid me. I have not received or heard of the money you sent. And yet it would do well here, where the need is so great that many boys have their feet frozen for want of suitable boots. How often my heart overflows with sorrow, seeing and hearing about such misery! I do my utmost to spend as little as possible; and yet I cannot keep my expenses under ten dollars a month, for my own wants. Even rye bread is twice as dear as in Russia. My health does not permit me to eat meat and many other things. Milk, tea, white bread, and some eggs, or a little macaroni, is all my provision. And yet I feel myself quite at ease, and strong enough for my age and all the odds. I never feel any discomfort in my little log house, having lived such a long time like a beggar, without my own shelter, my own bed, my own table to write a letter, never writing letters when I was living 'illegally.' And now I am as rich as a queen, and want nothing for myself.

"Oh, dearest Ellen! forgive me my English. But I heard so many times in Chicago and everywhere else such words as: 'Your bad English is better to us than your good French,' that I consent to be laughed at, and to have my writing mended by your amiable hand.

"Thus far I receive all the letters sent to my address. No letters can be read without a special order to the gendarmes. They know that I never permit myself to write anything compromising; nevertheless their curiosity is without end, and the habit of persecution is so old and strong that they are never tired of doing it.

"Now during the Christmas festivals, when many young people here took pleasure in disguising themselves and going through the town in masks, my keepers were afraid I should escape in that manner, and they ran about like lunatics, searching and looking after every one, intruding themselves into every house suspected to be the place of my visit. And I was sitting in my cabin, reading or talking with one of my friends. Every path I take is watched by a gloomy figure shrouded in black furs from head to foot, and standing immovable near the house I visit, waiting for me to return. Without permission I cannot set foot on the frozen river, for it would be regarded as an attempt to escape. All night they keep looking into the windows of my den (so low and blind it is), and I do not hang any curtains, to keep them from entering the interior of my dwelling. A thousand thanks for your desire to soften my fortune."

To Miss Blackwell. February 4–21, 1911.

"What a disaster, what desolation! I never suspected such bad things of you, my dear friends, Alice and Helena! You are both ill and overpowered with your everlasting efforts to do the best, the most; to be always working, and tired over and over. It was your mode of life all the time I saw you.

"Pray, both of you, conserve that health which is so necessary to many and many of your friends. You ought to feel that people have acquired the habit of addressing themselves to Alice Blackwell, to Helena Dudley, in all their needs and sorrows, as to their legalized officers, always ready to act and to aid. What a disappointment to them not to find these two invaluable ladies at home! Think of me, too. You do, I know.

"My best time to work at my table is the morning, but there are many who want me and take up my mornings, when my strength is fresh, my body strong. The days are very short, and shorter in my hut, with its small and badly arranged windows.

"I confess I am tired to-day, especially because I could not be as useful to some persons as I wished. But my uneasiness will last only till early morning.

"Your father has passed away. Oh, my daughter, how many good people we have lost! In every newspaper I read an obituary concerning one of the best. And all these people are younger than I. How glad I am you have understood my religion and accepted it! Glad for you, for me, for the world. — Now, my mind is full of belief and hope, and this makes me quiet and sure of the future. Here I have to do with many and many unhappy boys, who (some of them) are not so strong in their faith. I speak, I write, I exhort. That takes much time, and leaves not enough to read books. Do not send French translations, but only some English books. I prefer the originals. Some newspaper talking about our affairs would be very interesting.

"December 4–21.

"The whole day interviewed and interrupted. Not tired, but disturbed. And yet I try to be patient with everybody, for I know how much happier I am than others.

"Many of the exiles are ill and lie in the hospital, where the food and all the treatment is horribly bad, dirty, and poor. The doctor, as well as all the officers of the government, is unworthy of the name. He receives very large pay, and will do nothing for the welfare of his patients. We have to prepare the necessary food and clothes to see them in any degree satisfied. For shame! How bad everything in our country is now!"

She encloses two picture postcards, showing views of Kirensk. On them she writes:

"This beautiful river Lena has very few shores to be built on; big hills and stone mountains accompany its current from the beginning to the town of Yakutsk. Then it is very wide and flows between flat and boggy lowland, covered with a short and poor wood, sometimes with grass, where the Yakuts pasture their cows and horses. Farther north there is nothing but the moss that satisfies the humble and useful deer, which are the livelihood of the Yakuts and other tribes of the far north.

"This beautiful islet with its town, viewed from the

next mountain. The diameter of the place is little more than a mile. It has nearly two thousand inhabitants of mixed population. Most of them are descended from the convicts (ordinary malefactors) sent here for many and many years. Some come of their own will. Two or three big firms, having millions at their disposition. Telegraph, post office, boards of treasure, many police of various grades, an enormous whisky factory (a government monopoly), two clubs, three churches, and many shops of every size. You will see the site of my dwelling near the dark park belonging to the little old monastery, with two or three monks. Before the town you see the river Lena, and behind the river Kyrenga; both are equally large in this place. All provisions are transported here from the west, and are twice as dear as in Russia. The culture is very low."

To Miss Helena Dudley. February 17–March 2, 1911.

"You are all too kind to me. This makes me forget my position as an outcast, destined to a solitary existence, and always apprehensive of a mischief that is awaiting me or my nearest comrades.

"The book sent by George Kennan gives me the best moments of my evening, so vividly and so engagingly are described all the scenes of the tremendous event seen by our excellent author. With much interest would I read the work of Mr. Walling, 'Russia's Message', as well as the book prepared now by Arthur Bullard. If it will not be ready for a long time, let him send his writings about Russia, printed in several magazines. It is a great satisfaction to read the writings of people whom you knew and loved. It is like a conversation. When I peruse the 'Tragedy of Pelée' I am in the society of our old friend. I see him, I hear him, I examine his every act and intention. The characters he describes are of a high interest to me, for I am fond of brave and honest men. The other day I received a box from him containing a nice shawl, white as snow. The post office officials exclaimed: 'Even in America they take an interest in your destiny!' It is true, I feel myself watched by my friends from all sides of the universe. And this my good fortune is felt not only by your grandmother, but by all around her. This last fact gives all these signs of benevolence a very large meaning and many good effects. Every grandmother has a lot of grandsons about her, and they are dear to her heart. Ask it, my dearest Helena, of Mrs. Barrows.

"Yes, I have my family in the United States of America, and I look upon all your homes as my own. How beautiful it is! It makes me stronger and cheers me up, and even if death should take me away before I see you, my best feelings, my soul will remain with you.

"Fortunately for me, this Siberian winter is so warm and soft that the inhabitants say they do not remember one like it for many years.

"Your grandmother and your Catherine.

"As for clothing and other matters of domestic use, I have only the necessary, and do not want more. All the surplus is divided among the necessitous people of the colony; but money is the most needful thing to apply to the demands of the situation.

"February 22. All these days I have been uneasy with the wicked influenza, and did not go out, — could do nothing except read papers and be tired to death with the visits of many boys, who, feeling the approach of spring, are walking from place to place in search of some work and change of life; of that gloomy and dim and miserable life that makes them endure all sorts of privations and offences from rough Nature, as well as from the government, always ready to spoil every attempt to improve their mode of existence. Sometimes I wonder, abashed and terrified by the actions of the government towards the political exiles. They are persecuted merely for efforts to gain their bread, and it is not astonishing if some of them have recourse to violence, deprived as they are of all possibility of settling down like other people. The beasts of the forest are incomparably better organized and more satisfied with its institutions."

To Arthur Bullard. About March 2–16, 1911.

"I have all the best Russian newspapers and magazines, and my friends are doing all they can to render my abode as comfortable as possible. Yet I accept every donation with gratitude, for around me I have an innumerable quantity of people who are in want of everything. There are about a thousand young men in our district of Kirensk, nine tenths of them without any resources. I have the possibility of knowing about their needs, and I do what I can.

"My greetings to your three friends. I remember them quite well. Oh, how cheerful it would be to make visits to the houses with wives and babies! God bless them.

"My health is improving. I am stronger than when in the fortress."

To Mrs. Barrows and Miss Blackwell.
"April 1–15, 1911.

"My sister Isabel, my daughter Alice: North America is my second patrie. I have often said: 'The United States is the country I would choose to inhabit, after my own great and poor country.' You both, Helena, and the rest of the women I knew in America, made my presence in your country so full of good impressions that nothing can efface them. I must add my gratitude to some young men who took part in the idea that fills my mind and my heart. I have friends, good and devoted friends, in Russia. They have known me for sixty-seven years, and it is quite natural to see them accustomed to appreciate one another. But with you I passed only a few months, and only enjoyed, only enjoyed. Yet you believed in my sincerity, my earnest wish to be good and faithful. For you are sincere and faithful yourselves."

To June Barrows Mussey [1] (Mrs. Barrows's grandson).

"When you grow up, your grandmother Catherine Breshkovsky will tell you some stories from her own life, and you will learn from her experience how wholesome it is to care to endure all the roughnesses that we encounter marching through the vicissitudes of the circumstances accompanying the sinuous ground of the way we are thrown on. She feels herself happy and strong because she is always faithful to her religion, which bids us love our brotherhood, mankind, as dearly as we love ourselves."

[1] Written on a picture postcard representing an old Yakut telling stories to his grandson.

To Miss Dudley.[1] (Undated.)

"I cannot and shall not forsake my poor boys, even for the happiness of spending my last days amidst such friends as you. I am sure that you will understand me, and love me no less. I am a mother of a large family, who are accustomed to see me devoted to their interests and to have me share their fate, bad as it is. Now, represent to yourself a mother forsaking her children, and going to those that are rich and happy without her! Not only my boys here, but all the young people all over the country would be grieved, and their faith in their grandmother would be broken. For myself, I confess, such a life (for a long time) as you desire for me would be difficult for me, who am accustomed to an existence very scarce and modest. You cannot imagine what a want of the least comfort we support, having always in view the mendicity of the budget of our people for every day's needs. And think of the feelings of a mother who should leave her children scourged by their foes, and go herself to enjoy a company where she finds only friendship, love, and worship! What would you say of it?

"Yesterday there were two good boys with me, and I asked them, laughingly, if they approved of such a course. The faces of both became sad and severe, and one of them said: 'I do not conceive it.' As I understand it, that was not merely my own opinion and feeling, but the voice of every sane and uncorrupted soul. If till now I am anything in the eyes of my countrymen and yours, it is for my sincerity, and

[1] Miss Dudley had proposed that an effort be made to get leave for Mme. Breshkovsky to come to America.

the simplicity of my existence. I am even afraid that
I should not suit quite well such a rich country as yours,
with its habit of having great talents of every sort at
its service. I have no talents, you saw that yourself.
But my simple nature suits my people's simple heart,
and we understand and love each other. We are slow
in our doings, we are devoid of the ambition that
stimulates the doings of others, but we are faithful
to our Ideal, which is brotherhood."

To Miss Blackwell. March 30–April 13, 1911.

"Two letters from you, one from Isabel and one from
Helena — all this is so much luck, so much delight,
that I am quite unable to fulfill your request to describe
my health in every particular. You can judge for
yourself when I say that I inhabit my cabin quite
alone, moving about very slowly, but being able to
do all I wish except to split the wood, to clean my
walks, to bring water, and to scrub the floor. I do
not wash my clothes either. All the rest I do myself,
for it is very little. I never dine, and do not cook.
Tea, milk, white bread, and some eggs are my every-
day eating. I could have excellent supplies, very good
provisions, although very dear, but I don't wish them.
First, my health requires an abstemious diet, second,
I do not want to spend the money on myself, having
around me hundreds of hungry young men, frozen
and exhausted. Certainly there are some gaps in my
every-day régime, but we Russian people, we political
exiles, we cannot imagine our life otherwise than as
full of privation. Therefore anyone who is as well
situated (comparatively) as I am has no reason to
complain. I receive for myself a lot of money that

would make me rich and comfortable. I enjoy a large correspondence, thanks to the desire of my friends to know about me. This liberality, as I perceive, has alarmed the government, and the story of my deportation to another place was invented to interrupt the exchange of news between me and my friends. And it was stopped for some time. But there were other people who wrote the truth, and now all is going as before, to my great joy.

"Certainly it would be better for me to have a young, devoted comrade at my side, who would be free enough and willing to serve me. Yet, as that cannot be, there is an old cobbler (a political exile too), a good drunkard, but an honest and devoted man, very reasonable when sober. This Platon comes to see me every two days, drinks tea with me, and speaks abundantly on the deeds of which he was once a witness or an actor. He loves and reveres the memory of many of our comrades who were exiled twenty-five and thirty years ago, now dead, or old and crushed by illness and all sorts of disaster. Now that he knows he is to visit me once in so often to fulfill his duty, he refrains from drinking, is always polite, and does his best to please and to be useful.

"April 1, or your 13 April.

"I wish to be polite too, and to answer as well as I know how your question as to my health. My chronic troubles are: (1) neuralgia through all my organism, the feet, the hands and the back, including the head; (2) rheumatism in the feet and the shoulders; (3) kidney trouble, which made me very ill during my last imprisonment, and was not cured at all, for the doctor (intentionally or unintentionally) took no notice of it, and cured me only of the hemorrhoidal attacks which were the result of want of motion. Now this last disease is nearly gone, but as for the first three, they will remain, I think, till the end. When I am cautious and prudent, these three foes of mine behave themselves supportably enough; when imprudent, or forgetting to provide for urgent needs, then I feel badly, but not so much so as to be unable to move and to eat. Besides these maladies, fever during the winter once or twice a month visited my old body, and made me feeble, unable to do the least work. The intense frosts are over and I feel better."

To Mrs. Isabel C. Barrows. March 28–April 10, 1911.

"Dear, dearest and a thousand times dearest friend and sister, Isabel C. Barrows! From this my letter you will see what a martyrdom it is to have to do with a certain class of people. Your dear letter, sent to me through the hands of a bureaucrat, has reached me only to-day! You wrote it November 17, 1910, and I received it April 10, 1911. It was traveling from one board to another, from one administrator to many others, till a policeman brought it to my little blockhouse, where I read it with tears in my eyes, learning only to-day how much you were doing for your old friend and how good, how exceedingly good your excellent husband was to me. God be blessed that your letter has reached me at last. It is such a great comfort, such a delight, you cannot imagine it. I only supposed all that you tell me, but never knew the details of your coming to Russia, and the great interest that your countrymen took in my fate. I

am quite ashamed of such sacrifices as you undertook
for my sake. My soul is filled with pride and glad-
ness at the same time. What is exile and all persecutions compared with the joy of having such devoted
friends!

"March 29–April 11.

"Oh, yes, the boys keep coming to see me and to
tell me their needs; rarely have I time to finish my
letter without interruption. Now I am so anxious
to know if this letter will reach you. Never to be
sure of the lot of one's correspondence, of to-morrow,
— to be a thing in the hands of others, — it is a disagreeable position; especially when we wish so eagerly
to get our feelings transported there where our best
friends are. It would be a wound to my soul if you
thought me ungrateful. And what do you mean by
saying you are too old to hope we shall meet again?
I do not think so. On the contrary! In some years
we shall meet and spend many good hours together.
Why not? Only sixty-seven years old I am, and you
are much younger. My health, if not strong, can yet
endure for some time the uneasiness of the life that
awaits me for some years longer. I hope to see your
(our) grandson, the little June Barrows Mussey, who
is dear to me as your and your husband's descendant,
which makes me sure we shall have in this young
man a brave, an honest, a beautiful boy, always
ready to serve the interests of humanity. Kiss his
hands and little feet for me."

To Miss Blackwell. May 8–21.

"The letters from Miss Julia C. Drury and Mr.
Lewis Herreshoff, Bristol, R. I., written April 13,

1911, reached me only yesterday. I am not only touched, but transported into quite another world of thought and feeling.

"While I perceive all the exaggerations concerning my qualities and capacities, I understand nevertheless that the friendship and sympathy which you all, my friends in America, show me, are not in vain, that there is a solid foundation on which these feelings are built. The better for me!

"You will comprehend me when you remember that for half a century my whole being has been full (from top to toes) of one straining: to improve the moral, mental, and economic life of my people. It is too old a habit, and one cannot break the bond that unites him with the existence of his folk. And what an example it would be to my youngest comrades! God forbid!

"Seventeen letters from you, two from Isabel, two from Ellen Starr, three from my Helena Dudley, one from Arthur Bullard, my boy, from Mrs. Kennan one. And so many Easter cards that all the children of Kirensk and my boys too had a present from you.

"Every one of my friends asks what comfort would best suit my life in Siberia. I answer: A suit of winter clothing, from head to foot.

"I shall never be able to provide it myself, for all the money I have I destine for others, who are suffering more than I. My friends have often asked me to buy winter clothing here in Kirensk, but I never did and never shall do it. It must be light and warm. Boots, pantaloons, overcoat, and a cap; gloves, too. That for my health: and for my soul's welfare, some money to aid the needy, to buy them tools and materials for work.

"Your devoted and a little excited and enerved
Catherine."

To Ellen Starr.   (Undated.)

"Twice I have read your letter and the verses of
Sophie Jewett. It is the first time I have seen them.
I read also those in the New York Times,[1] and I am
ashamed. Ashamed, yes, for I do not believe myself
a heroine or a saint. It is natural to be reasonable
and loving when you have inherited these qualities
from your parents. But why should we speak about
me, when there are so many questions that interest
me much more? For instance: There are some
writings of mine that would be read with no little
use by young people who desire to form, to improve
their characters. My sayings and reasoning are very
simple, and therefore very clear and practical. I
have never retouched them, and don't feel able to do
it, but if somebody else would go over them and trans-
late some of the best places, I should be glad. Alice
ought to be of the council, and you, being stronger in
health, ought to help her. As soon as I get my writings from the hands of the police, I will copy some
sheets and send them to you.

"I agree with you that the presence of honest and
inspired minds is a great blessing for mankind, and
we ought to teach our children to honor above all the
nobleness of the soul, for there is not a greater treasure
on earth. And yet we should teach them, too, that
this ought to become a fact of every day, and, speaking
truly, every human being must try and can succeed
in attaining the highest grade of mental dignity. It

[1] See Appendix.

is our right and it is our duty. Otherwise why should we be better than the rest?

"When I see one of the noble hearts of my boys, I become as poetical and sentimental as you, dear friend, and I admire the earnestness and strength of their feelings. But when I hear people praise my own qualities, it makes me feel confused and abashed. Too long have I carried on my work, and have had time to be accustomed to see it as an everyday task. Nevertheless I confess that your letters and the good words I have heard from my American friends gave me great joy."

To Miss Dudley. May 20.

"Overpowered! Overpowered! Overpowered! Nine letters, besides postcards and innumerable magazines, books and papers! All at once, for our mail was cut off for a whole month because the great river Lena and our less great river Kyrenga were carrying the ice to the north. The spring is cold, but I feel well, and I am happy because of the tokens of love my American friends send me in such numbers.

"I will not repeat all my words of gratitude. You must know once for the rest of my life that I am a creature full of gratitude, and prize every token of friendship and goodness. One thing makes me wonder a little: it is the admiration for my character and my patience in enduring my fate. First, I will say that there are many and many people among us who have shown not less but more courage and grandeur of soul during their whole lives, — so many people who have died like very heroes. Secondly, we Russians are a people of religion; we have one in our soul, through all the nation, and the worship of the beloved Idea is our national trait. This capacity of appreciating the worshiped Idea above all the rest of the material world makes us strong and willing to sacrifice ourselves for its sake. This conviction makes me bashful and confused when hearing or reading beautiful words about myself. I would think it is so easy and so comfortable to serve a cause chosen by ourselves! Certainly one is tired sometimes, and sometimes irritated against all the silliness of mankind, yet it does not continue, having no time to mourn, obliged as we are to think how to do better.

"I hope some day to get my manuscript written in the fortress. I hear that it has already come, and the chief of police is reading it, out of curiosity or fear. You see with what might it is endowed! The administration of the fortress consented to give it out to me. The Police Department in St. Petersburg consented too, and yet the chief of police in Kirensk is allowed to decide whether my writings ought to be given over to me. And he has kept them for many weeks, and will keep them for months perhaps. I never speak with him, and have no wish to meet him anywhere. This winter some comedies and dramas were given here many times, and some vocal and instrumental concerts (thanks to the unofficial participation of some boys); but I never go to see or hear them, disgusted to be in the same room with the policemen, who are always there in force, never paying for their places.

"I have to answer 32 letters this week. Lady Mackintosh's letter made me glad; very."

To Arthur Bullard.   (Undated.)

"Bullard, my boy! Already in Panama! You grind yourself into pieces and will be old at forty. I would have you always young and active, but without excitement, or, better, without too much strain. It is so delightful to know our friends are in good health, and strong in body and soul, and it makes us so sad when we hear that one of them is declining in strength. Pray, do not exhaust your nerves; preserve your capability of work for the future too. It cheers me up to know that here and there are boys and girls who keep in their hearts an unexhausted desire to aid the world to do better. Such minds and characters are the flowers that embellish our earth. Only think how gloomy and cold it would be without the best! I once asked you: 'What would become of your country if every year 10,000 of your best people were exiled from it?' You answered, 'If only fifty men, the best of us, should go away every year, our country would remain like a desert.'

"My friend! You must work, you must love and feel heartily, you must make efforts to improve yourself and others, and yet you must learn to be more abstract, to consider the world and its phenomena with more coolness — all the phenomena, not excluding those that concern us personally. You have long known, I am sure, that a person who cares much for his own welfare, and is much affected by all that happens in the sphere of his own life, is much more enerved and tired with the world than a person whose mind is dwelling on the questions that concern mankind as a whole. I don't mean that one can live like a machine, never hurt by the acridity of the atmosphere

created by our silliness and ignorance, by the mischiefs that come over and over in a very wonderful
miscellaneous form and quantity; but one can get
the habit of struggling through all his existence and
never being disappointed, never exhausted. More
philosophy, more contemplation, more perception
reaching into the future. — You know well yourself
how to do, and it is only my longing for your welfare
that makes me speak about questions so thoroughly
studied by every one interested in the existence of his
own psychology. I wish to know you safe and conserved.

"Now I have to answer twenty letters more. The
day is warm. My window is open. The little meadow
before my blockhouse is full of hens and cocks . . .
so peaceful . . . and so much grief around!"

CHAPTER XIII

To Miss Blackwell.   May 27–June 9, 1911.

"You ask me what I think about woman suffrage. In Russia the question of the equality of rights of both sexes has been decided affirmatively, not only by the intelligent people but by the workmen and peasantry too.   Like many other progressive ideas, that of the equality of rights is delayed only by the same force that holds back all the best beginnings in the country.   We have no need to preach the equality of the sexes, or that of the races inhabiting our country, for the idea as a principle is accepted by the majority of our people.   This idea is included as a part of the whole faith we confess.   But as we have on the other hand a body of black-meaning rascals, there is, in Russia also, a group of women writing and speaking on the necessity of conferring on women all the political rights which men enjoy.   (Up to this time I have never seen the papers and magazines of the Russian suffragists.   Now I shall ask to have some sent me.) Here, the women and the men alike are deprived of every right, and alike they understand that before all other rights one ought to struggle for the right to breathe.

"In a country like yours, it is indispensable to further the question of equality by all means, for, firstly, the means are very large and open, and, secondly, every line of progress advances more swiftly when there is a strong group of active and intelligent

heads and arms to promote it. I welcome with all
my heart the intensity of the efforts shown so clearly
and so gracefully in your estimable and beloved
Woman's Journal. When yesterday I read the issue
of May 6, 1911, I felt myself in such an admirable
society, so witty, so elegant and so devoted, that it
seemed to me a beautiful festival made for the sake
of equality, humanity and brotherhood.

"Certainly, I do not think that the decision of the
question of women's fate consists only in the suffrage.
Their destiny is so great, so big, so broad, and so endless, that it cannot be defined by one casual, though
historic, episode of their existence. Therefore, when
in the fortress I wrote on women's destiny, I took
the question in a larger sense, and considered their
whole significance as one half of the human race — a
half that holds in its hands the future of mankind.
The development of body and soul depends on women's
capacities, their experience, their love, their accomplishments, moral and intellectual. As man has found his
destiny in nourishing and keeping safe his race, so
woman must take for herself the duty of improving
the race and making it worthy of the name of *homo
sapiens.* All that is love, tenderness, grace, beauty,
courage, abnegation for the sake of large ideals, for
the welfare of the future inhabitants of the world, —
all these feelings and capacities are the result of our
organism, are innate in us, and prepare our natures
to be not only wives and mothers, but teachers, doctors
of medicine, professors, ministers, statisticians, hygien-
ists, psychologists, Socialists, and all that is necessary
to be known by persons whose duty it is to educate
and elevate the human race. Certainly, women have

all political rights as well as men, without which they never will have their actions as free as they should be. Every human being has a right to be all the best he can be, therefore nothing ought to embarrass his efforts, his strivings. That must be understood by every one. But the question of duty is much more complex, for Nature herself has made some differences between the sexes, and these differences, in their turn, have created different instincts, sympathies, feelings, likings, as well as different dispositions of mental capacities. I never wish to discuss which half of mankind is better, or more genial. For my part, I am sure that both halves are wonderfully, beautifully made! And yet I prefer to remain a woman, for I relish very much the most delicate sides of the human soul.

"So, dearest daughter, agreeing that the happiness of our race consists in *everlasting struggle against the wicked habits of the past and in everlasting straining to elevate ourselves to the highest degree of perfection*, I have found out that of the two halves of mankind it is the women that can better, and ought to, as more inclined to it, work (more successfully in every sense) in this field of human action.

"And it makes me very and very sorry, seeing that many women, well educated and intelligent enough, instead of doing this beautiful work, instead of carving out men's souls and giving to the world more and more accomplished examples, are eager to become, if not policemen, yet something like agents of the administration, officers of various institutions that concern only the exterior side of the life of our country. They are not trying earnestly enough to prove and to improve their own talents, their own creative force,

They are not doing for the welfare of mankind all they can do as women, as mothers, and governesses, as sisters and companions, as leaders of the morality of our world, as philosophers of the great love that unites all souls together and establishes such a brotherhood among us that no exterior forms or political constructions, no new principles or teachings can deprive us of it. Our very souls ought to be cultivated in such a direction as to choose and to prefer the higher, largest and clearest ideas. This poor earthball of ours ought to be our home instead of our world, and we ought to be all one family, not at all so large as not to be known to everybody. The more you think about the affairs of the earth and its population, the more you remark how limited are the bands of the life of the place we dwell on. In comparatively few centuries, every man will know every nook of our globe, and will be acquainted with every tinge and color of our skin, while industry is making so great a progress as to permit us to fulfill all the desires of our curiosity. And if we remain only indifferent spectators of all we see, we shall very soon be tired of our character of idle spectators. Quite another thing when our heart and our mind are interested in what they are contemplating. In this case we not only look, not only satisfy our curiosity; we feel strongly, and all our capacities are working with the desire to improve the status quo when it is bad, or to learn to assume the witnessed, when it is worthy of it.

"I am sure there are men who possess a very delicate and beautiful soul, a fine mind, that picks out of the world all the best it can encounter. Yet I am sure such minds, belonging to the masculine sex, are rather an exception; while the construction of our feminine mind has been cultivated during so many thousands of centuries in a pacific direction, preferring the sphere of sense and meditation. . . . Yes, I am sure it is time for the women to step out as educators, as creators of new relations between one another. There must be principles, but there ought to be practice, too. Who will set the example? Only those that can observe the functions of our body and mind from the very infancy of its growth can inculcate successfully new habits and new inclinations in the coming generation.

"For the winter I shall take another cabin, more comfortable; this one being too old and demolished. Cold, rain, wind, all comes through."

To Miss Blackwell. July 1, 1911.

"You wish to have news from me oftener, and I am so slow with my answer. Perhaps I am getting old, though I cannot believe it. When, feeling myself uneasy, I am tired, not so alert and brave as I am accustomed to be, it seems to me it is a stranger woman, and I consider her as a queer and drollish being, looking at her with disgust. It is not I. Not only in my imagination, but in my innermost sensation. And you can be at ease about the disposition of my mind. Even when feeble in body, I shall remain always strong in soul. I cannot be otherwise: the mind has worked too long in the same direction, and the habit is formed."

To Miss Dudley. June 20–July 2, 1911.

"I have many cards coming from various parts of the world; Japan, Australia, Honolulu, Canada, Cali-

fornia, Florida, and other places in your great republic.
It is very pleasant to have every mail bringing some
new magazine, some new view of far off lands and
countries.   Nevertheless, being a Slavonic woman,
— therefore slow and fanciful, — I am not able to
respond to all these tokens of benevolence, and feel
myself always guilty toward the good people who send
me so many delicacies.   And so, if it has been said
in one of the magazines that I am delighted to receive
news and pictures, it must be said, too, how thankful
I feel."

To Miss Blackwell.   July 11–22, 1911.

"You have spoiled me so that the two weeks without your letters seemed two months to me.   During
this time I have had letters from many American
women unknown to me, but very amicable, full of
sympathy toward the old exiled 'Baboushka.'   The
book I got from Mr. Lewis Herreshoff ('The Seven
Ages of Washington') made me cheerful, for I like
much to read about great characters; but all this
cannot make up for the lack of news from my daughter.
You are my own; so I felt even in America.

"Now I want to say some words about the *Woman's
Journal*.   It is a special publication for the study
and propagation of one serious idea, which ought to
be realized as soon as possible.   And you are quite
right when all that does not concern this idea, directly
or indirectly, is excluded from the paper.   In this
way your journal has acquired a vigorous and warlike
character, and makes a strong impression.   I was
glad to see that your parents were commemorated.
You and I are happy in having had such excellent

parents. I thank my fate every day for this good fortune.

"I find that all your magazines printed for a special purpose are much better than those which are destined to entertain their readers. *Life and Labor*, the *National Geographic Magazine* for instance, even those for young people and children are very well edited. The *Outlook* is welcome, too. As for the magazines you pick up in the railroad train and send to me, they make a beautiful store of books that furnish reading for the scholars and beautiful pictures for the children. To-day I must congratulate two young girls (nine and four years old) because it is their birthday, and I shall give them some of the pictures, bright with colors, made to attract the attention of the public to some new ware or invention. How glad will be the young damsels getting such unseen tableaux!

"Long ago I formed the habit of looking upon people like growing children, and these last as little animals, growing with every day nearer and nearer to the human being; and, surveying the course of their development, I learned to understand the psychology of our mind, our soul; also to distinguish the inclinations of the two sexes, and to find out how many exceptions there are on both sides, which form a lot of miscellaneous examples of our race. Many, many types there are; the combinations being so manifold, so fanciful. Very interesting.

"I strain my energy and my English trying to answer every address sent to me with cards, postals, magazines, and yet I am sure that many remain without answers, and it torments my mind.

"Somebody said Miss Addams is a living proof that

a woman can do very much without voting. One
can answer: She would do much more when the
votes of her sisters were with her. The book Miss
Addams wrote, Miss Starr must send me.

"Soon I shall have two albums full of American
postal cards, and it will be a commonwealth object,
everyone will enjoy it.

"Next month I shall change my cabin for another
one, not so old and dilapidated. It is on the same
street, and not far from the neighbors who are so
good about helping me in my little wants, but the
courtyard is not so large, and will not be my own
domain, for there is a house on the same yard, peopled
with a widow and her two daughters. The owner of
the house dwells there too. Perhaps they will be
good to me. I hope so. My health is always better.
I take care of it, and pray you, as well as my sister
Isabel and our dearest and best Helena, to take example and follow my system. Spare your forces as
long as possible, for a life devoted *long* to the chosen
cause is the best example we can give to our posterity."

To Mrs. Barrows.   July 12–15.

"I am sure the parents of June will not spoil the
boy with too much cajoling and nursing. I wish he
might have a sister. I love the girls; there are excellent ones."

To Miss Dudley.   5 A.M., July 21, 1911.

"You see, I shall begin very early, in order to remain alone and be able to write. During the day my
cabin is never empty. The boys keep coming and

going out to see the grandmother, to tell their affairs, to take counsel, to ask, to pray, to be consoled, to get books, papers, some clothes, money, and oftener to spend some hours with a soul they know to be devoted to their mental and material interest. I was uneasy last month, and so much visitation made me fatigued; yet, knowing the boys have not a nook where they feel themselves as well off as with me, I only once cheated them for coming too late in the evening, for at ten I go to bed. Oh, poor children, they put up with everything from their grandmother, and are delighted to be loved and cherished by her. Working very hard they earn a very poor subsistence only, for every path, every effort on their part is checked and confronted with the hatred of those who have the might to do all the evil. They are arrested and transported from place to place on every occasion of the ill humor of an official. Not one knows what will become of him to-morrow. I am not willing to speak about it, otherwise it would be impossible to find colors and expressions to depict all that we are subjected to.

"I do not complain. For my part, I am too well accustomed to all these spectacles, and support my fate bravely enough; but seeing the best youth of the country mutilated, deformed, exterminated, one cannot remain indifferent.

"A very few days have been warm; in two months we shall see snow again, and for seven and eight months. There are many beautiful flowers in the woods and vales here, but I never leave the town, and can see them only when brought. I am happy in the devotion of my boys and the love of my friends in America."

To Mrs. Barrows.   May 30–June 12, 1911.

"Lincoln's statue and seven other cards ornament my window before me, and the mignonette [1] will make the delight of many houses. 'The Order of Peace and Good Will' (by Charles F. Dole) is a beautiful copy.   Pity I am reading it alone."

To Miss Blackwell.   August 24–September 6, 1911.

"Why do I write to you in English and not French? Because I feel myself nearer to you, to Isabel and Helena. I like very much this rich and original organ of expression.

"You were jealous about my mentioning the 'boys' only. The reason is that in the district of Kirensk there are a thousand boys and only eight or ten girls, scattered all over it. Here in the town I have had only one. The exiled and condemned women, who are not in the hard labor prisons, are settled part of them in the west of Siberia and part in the southern districts of Irkutsk. Only those who were not tried, but exiled by administrative order, are settled in the region of Yakutsk, 1500 miles to the north.

"Aug. 25–Sept. 7.

"Yesterday this letter was interrupted by the visit of a squadron of gendarmes and police. They came to make a search in my lodging, and turned over all my correspondence and all the papers and magazines. They remained an hour and a half. There was nothing to be sequestered, and as the gendarmes could

---

[1] Mrs. Barrows had sent Madame Breshkovsky a package of mignonette seed.

not go away without taking something, they took the photographs showing me with some of my comrades.

"Again the police of Kirensk are troubled about my safety; again the chief himself is tripping around my cabin every night now, in fear that I may be transported to some secret place and vanish away. It is very disagreeable, for the neighbors' hounds keep on barking for hours after these nightly visits, and I cannot sleep. It was the same all last winter, and now it is beginning again. I laugh very much about these fusses, and yet I am fidgeting about the fate of those who come to visit me, the boys who cannot avoid the connection with me, having nobody else to nurse them.

"Your songs, Alice, I sing them when alone, inventing tunes of my own.

"Now I am not alone in reading English. In my vicinity (400 miles from me) there is an exiled professor who reads English with much delight, and the *Independent* is appointed for him. After having looked it over, I send it to Kachug, a village on the shore of the Lena, where our professor lives. Another boy comes to read with me, and I let him read your letters.

"We have in Russia a great many devoted girls, full of abnegation; but their sincere earnestness makes them timid; they think too little of themselves. And see, how beautiful is the character and how multiple the capacities of our Aunt Isabel, and yet she never minds it, never cries out, when in her place a man would be a celebrity known all the world over. And remark that her mental activity does not prevent her from exercising her womanly feelings and being tender towards all with whom she sympathizes. The female organism, as well as the habit of observing and analyzing, makes us women more inclined to sympathize with the feelings of others. The mode of life in every country has made the men more bureaucratic, more formalists, and more hardhearted. Undoubtedly a reasonable education will by and by modify this difference between the sexes; and also the female sex will become stronger in mind and body.

"I remember always how beautiful and how heavenly sweet and splendid was our best woman, Lucy Stone, the ornament of the human race.

"My health is still improving. The rheumatism and neuralgia are insignificant during the summer; and my splendid lodging, which awaits me, will render me safe during the winter too, with the aid of your flannels.

"I have a dinner every day now, and feel strong and lofty, as if I were a princess, young and rich and proud. The calf which is pasturing in my courtyard has become a friend of mine, and I prance before him like another calf."

To Lillian D. Wald.　August 29–September 11, 1911.

"Beloved and esteemed friend, Miss Wald:

"How rich you have made me, sending me such a beautiful choice of magazines, which now (and with every day more) begin to be a source of delight to many people at a great distance! Yesterday, for instance, there was with me a mother on her return from Yakutsk, where she had visited her exiled son of twenty-two years old, who in learning English feels an absolute want of English literature. There are other boys who share this study, and all will be quite comfortable when they receive from me the interesting *Rest Evening* and the *Atlantic*.

"Yesterday, too, the *Independent* and the *Public* were sent to the professor of whom I wrote to my Alice. He is a fine man, highly educated. He does not wish to forget the foreign languages, and reads eagerly the English literature that is so scarce in Siberia, especially among the moors and woods where we are settled.

"The rest of the magazines are with me, but they do not serve me alone. Among the newcomers (who do not cease to arrive) some can do well enough to be able to profit by the rich stock in my room. And, making mistakes myself at every phrase, I teach them how to pronounce, remembering some principles that I got from Aunt Barrows, when in New York. What an excellent teacher, what an incomparable adviser, what a wise corrector she is!

"And myself, when tormented by the mischiefs surrounding us, I have recourse to the magazines, so richly illustrated, and spend hour after hour in reading, commenting, fancying about far-off people and countries. They give much material to think of, to laugh over. The pictures in some periodicals, and their covers, so splendidly painted, have been presents and surprises to a number of children (even boys of mine), whose bare log walls are ornamented with what makes the chamber much more cheerful.

"I wished to make an album out of the quantity of postcards I get from America,[1] but seeing how

---

[1] I was in the habit of enclosing in my weekly letter to her a bunch of picture postcards. A. S. B.

much pleasure it gives to every one to have some with him, some pretty things, I resolved to treat my poor guests by giving two, three, or four cards to every one. Some have sisters and brothers at home, and use the cards when writing to them. Others choose some subject to keep it on their wall, before their table. Many of them are living five or six in one room, little and dirty. These keep their cards in their pockets. When they are working hard, their better clothes are left at home, and the cards within. So much for the printed matter and pictures; but I have myself a superior gift from your country, the letters showing so much interest in a far-off old woman, buried in a little wild spot, where she is destined to live henceforward — I will not say, destined to die.

"This correspondence enlarges to a high degree the world of my acquaintances, of my sympathies, and the traveling of my fancies. It engages me to feel myself as if living amidst a large society full of faces that are smiling and greeting me with the cordiality of true friends.

"The little freedom left to me is restricted more and more. As the days begin to be short, I shall have very few hours to move about. All the evenings will be spent in my room, for I have been told that the spies following me everywhere are not to remain in the street during my visits, as they have till now, but are to penetrate into the courts of the people whom I visit. And as nobody is pleased to have spies looking into the windows, I prefer to remain alone in my own cabin. And when alone I try to call up all that is dear and agreeable. The mail vivifies my imagination, which transports me into a less rude, less rough environment. In October there will be no mail. The stock of magazines and some stuff for making shirts and trousers for the boys will fill my leisure.

"August 31–September 13.

"I am sure you have printed some articles on your visit to China and Siberia. If so, I should read them with interest. Four intelligent women, such as you were, must have caught a lot of impressions during such a long journey, which afforded half a world to be examined. China and Russia were for a long time terra incognita to the rest of mankind. Nevertheless there was a superstition against them, especially concerning the Russian people, who were known, even in 1905 (the year I was with you), as a conglomerate of hordes of Kirghis and Tartars. Nobody was willing to believe me, when I represented my folk as intelligent enough to desire improvement. Although in these last seven years a vast progress has been made in the historical beliefs and the political vigilance of these millions of minds, yet our inherited slowness follows us.

"My greetings to all the inhabitants of your settlement, and God bless them!"

To Mrs. Barrows. September 26–October 13, 1911.

"Once more and once more I have gone over the list of Jaeger goods,[1] and I get more and more affrighted at the cost that will be paid for my sake. Too many things, too much dress! I have not the habit.

[1] Mrs. Barrows had arranged to have a complete suit of Jaeger flannels sent to her.

September 30–October 13.

"When you described to me your summer walks, so richly ornamented with splendid scenery, and when I look at the cards and pictures coming to me from America, Switzerland, England, France, from the Caucasus or Central Asia (Tashkend), I am delighted, and I wonder how people feel if they live in such beautiful places. It is impossible to admire every time, for you will have no time to do anything else; but it is impossible to remain indifferent, either, when facing such a gallery of supreme pictures.

"When I have before me a splendid view, I feel myself thrown into a beatitude akin to consternation, as if I were before a piece of witchcraft that turned a commonplace into a miracle. It only shows that our own country is lacking in scenery. Russia, except for some of its conquered territories, is a flat and monotonous land, where the eye searches for a new point, a relief, a more vivid color, a picturesque group of trees. Perhaps this equality of lines and tints, this ever-gray nature, has made us Russian people rather dull, with a tinge of melancholy, our fancy always dwelling on a better world.

"I believe that when they are free, our people will transform the country into a garden. The soil is rich and easy to cultivate, and beautiful forests, fields, and farms will cover the plains, while in the mountains, like those of the Urals and Siberia, there are plenty of materials proper for use. But now nothing prospers. The forests are destroyed, the rivers nearly impracticable on account of the sands, the soil badly tilled, and the buildings so ugly and uncomfortable that one might think they had been made so on purpose. No education, no good examples.

"We see that the wild people are so faithful to their customs that, even when they are neighbors of more civilized races, they do not want to make any changes. But when they begin to accept some changes, and begin to acknowledge science, then it is not hard to introduce innovations. The ice is broken, the waves can flow freely and rapidly.

"Especially is dirt abominable to one who had the good fortune to grow up in a clean and orderly home. Too much dirt is painful to a person who is above all delicacies. And when I think how good it will be in the future, I represent to myself all over the country a cleanness and neatness that will make it possible to sit, to walk, to eat in every place in the land. It is not nature itself, but the dirt and disorder which people themselves make, that is so disgusting. Therefore I do not like the life of the big towns, where there is so much dirt and so many bad smells. You will laugh at the topic of my letter. Yet it is not wondrous, for before my eyes are hedges, palings, dilapidated cabins and barns and stalls, all these black with time and rain, and covered with a cloudy, heavy gray roof that seems never to be sunny. And yet we are pleased with rain and wet, fearing the approach of a fiercer enemy, which will imprison us for half a year.

"We have now some young women, winning their bread by sewing linen and clothes. An American fashion magazine serves them very well."

Sometimes she cheered her friends by writing gay bits of *vers libre* on postcards:

"Helena dearest, don't be sorry,
Soon, very soon, thanks to your goodness,

I have my bath in my own room.
And soon again instead of linen
I shall be wrapped in Jaeger's wool.
The samovar will wait on table,
The Chinese tea will smell the best;
And your old friend, renewed, reyounged,
Absorbs the sugar, milk and bread.
She could have many, many others
Of delicacies of the world,
But the old stomach is so trained
That can't endure no sorts of dainties.
But for the space, and light, and air —
I have them for the rest of life.
    Dearest friend!
I will be merciful and never more
Write in verses.   Forgive me."

To Miss Blackwell.   October 4–17.

"You see me dancing,
    You see me prancing!
    The Jaegers are coming,
    I have the notice!

In some days there will be in my new dwelling a shop
of clothes and beautiful things!   And now, my daughter, you must be at ease.   Your old Catherine will be
soon like a cocoon, from head to foot accoutered with
wool.   No frost of Siberia can hurt her more."

To Miss Blackwell.   (Undated)

"I have read 'The Ballad of the Brave Man' over
and over, and wondered why you could not write all you
know about your mother, that blessed and holy woman,
in similar ballads?   Every act and circumstance of
her life could be chanted as a psalm.   It might be done
in two parts: (1) a short and compact chronology of

the events of her life; (2) a thick book composed of many ballads, describing her acts, her experiences, her sufferings and success, with all the love and admiration you keep in your heart for this woman, who remains till now a unique example of energy and cleverness, devotion and love.

"Be not afraid to profane a great cause or a great character by setting it forth in a simple style, full of plainness, and feelings of tender love. Everything great is sympathetic with what is natural and comes from the depths of our souls.

"I often ask myself how I would write the biography of a great spirit, and I always feel that not the details of the material side of the hero would prosper, but that only the mental, the spiritual world which was his own, could flourish under my pen. One must write as for himself, with earnestness and freedom of feeling, as the bird sings its song. When we read the old ballads, the sayings, legends, psalms and descriptions of the lives of saintly people, we are more touched and impressed than when we read very serious accounts of the world and the acts of any famous character. The personification of Lucy Stone is a spiritual one now, since the present day public can only imagine her being and her face, the more beautiful and attractive for not being set forth in a rude and rough account, which suffers always through being dry, notwithstanding the endeavor of the writer to make it living and gracious.

"In recent years we have had in our magazines many memoirs, biographical sketches and descriptions of the most remarkable Russians who have served the cause of their people. And the best are those that

show us the soul, the tastes, moral and spiritual, of
the person described, his behavior among his friends
and in his family; in a word, all that made up his
inner world, the complex of the soul, that remains in
the reader's memory like a celestial light."

To Doctor Tchaykovsky.   November 10, 1911.

"I wanted to write you a cheerful and jolly letter,
as both these states of mind are not foreign to me.
On the contrary, it is a long time since I have laughed
as much as since my return to the world from solitary
confinement; and here I often laugh at every trifle,
and look lovingly at the few youngsters who like to
take care of me, and whom I like to see about me.
But just on account of these youngsters I am suffering
a good deal of discomfort at present, not to say sorrow.

"From the very beginning it was known that every
one calling on me was entered in the 'book of life.'
In time it came to the notice of the police supervisor
that some called on me seldom, others more frequently;
that some did not stay long, others remained to chop
wood, sweep out the rooms, go for provisions, or else
to work at some foreign language, or sit and wait until
the time came to close the chimney with its heavy
flue-plates; or else to take the old lady out for an air-
ing, or to the bath-house and back.   Particularly there
was a young man living within a mile and a half of the
town, beyond the Lena, supporting himself by odd
jobs, with a little help from his relatives.   He came
every day after dinner for two or three hours; he was
very kind to me, and very attentive to all my household needs.   He got into trouble once because he had
given me a ride in his boat (it was only in the beginning

of September), and now he is being constantly reminded that he has no right to remain in the city after 8 P.M. I have already told you that only those few exiles who have obtained special permission live in Kirensk itself, or those who are under special surveillance, like 'poor' me; the rest have to live on the other side of the rivers, and go a long way to their work. But as there is a dock on the other side as well, many work there in Glotow's steamboat shops, and in the town there are Gromov's work-shops.

"Well, about a month ago, another young man came, an assistant surgeon. He got employment as a carpenter at the city wharf, quickly made a success of his trade, and was already in hopes that by the end of winter he would master all the secrets of carpentry and house-painting, and in the spring would open a shop of his own. Being inclined to do favors for close friends, he called on me daily after his work and gave me massage; in the afternoon he would call to take his scanty portion of dinner, so as not to have to go a mile and a half to attend to me. It appears that this sort of laborious life was considered a crime: the district police captain has taken away his passport (a yearly one for travelling over the district of Kirensk, which he had just obtained), then arrested him, imprisoned him, and on Saturday he is sending him away escorted by gendarmes to the Mukhtuiskaya district, 700 versts down the Lena nearer to Yakutsk, a starving settlement where there is no work, deserted by its own population, and filled with convict settlers who think it less dangerous to escape from there and be caught again than to remain there without work and without bread.

"Then again, yesterday and to-day they are summoning other persons also to the police for examination, a short list of seven or eight names, alleged to be people particularly intimate with me. On another list all those who visit my hut are recorded, and what will be done with them I cannot imagine, unless they station an armed guard to drive away all those who step upon my grass-plots. Aside from the fact that I like people generally, that a feeling of gratitude is deeply implanted in me, that distressed young lives are particularly affecting to me, so that I am simply ashamed to be the cause of anybody's misfortune or trouble, I see that complete loneliness threatens me within a short time, either in the form of a hut prison here in Kirensk, or somewhere in Bulun, on the Arctic Ocean, where they send exiles for complete isolation. What they are afraid of I cannot understand; I only know that I would rather stay in Bulun with white bears than to see how, on account of me, they are persecuting other people and depriving them of bread and of the most necessary freedom. They are even going to send away the sick, so that they may not pass by me on their way to the hospital.

"All their tricks are the fruits of an idle imagination, and the attractive prospect of honors and promotion. But how can others be expected to endure all these pleasant jokes? I personally have been used to these conditions during all my long life; nothing surprises me nor will surprise me. But young hearts cannot feel themselves as well, and every unexpected, unreasonable blow baffles them, and leads to an enormous loss of energy. It is a good thing, however, that people are not angry with me, whence come all these evil machinations, spreading out net after net — plague take them!

"Send me not only magazines, but books. There is a common library here, but through the preponderance of foolish voters it has passed into the hands of careless people, so that now it will be either ruined entirely or reorganized in a more or less remote future. Since this mess was made before my time, I do not intend to be responsible for it, the more so as I should be compelled to deal with various antagonistic interests. Therefore I prefer to receive the books myself, and to give them to whomever it seems best, keeping order and system. Do not think that I am greedy for myself personally; I do not read so very much, only what is necessary; but young brains need food.

"Now the boasting begins: To-day at last came the package with my prison belongings (coat, dresses, etc.). Taking into account things sent by you and gifts received on the road here, it appears that I have half a dozen 'costumes,' one finer than the other — such wealth as I have never before accumulated since I was born. I have hung them around the walls, and I look at them and think: 'What shall I do with all these things, even if I should order a wardrobe!' And as for handkerchiefs, gloves, little rags that have been sent — so many have accumulated that I can't imagine where to put them all. To my relief, your gingham will go for shirts for the boys (I intend to cut as many as four out of 15 arshin).

"The new handkerchiefs I have given away to neighbors who have been kind to me, and everything that is old I have kept for myself, except the beautiful blanket, which I hide under my pillow in the day time, and at night spread over my ordinary every-day one, which has seen many things in its time. Even my old cloak is about ready to go into retirement. I have acquired two wadded coats and a few warm skirts; in a word, enough to get married on (such a bride!), and the people are still dissatisfied, and are always grumbling: 'A fur coat, grandma, a fur coat, by all means a fur coat.' I will show them a fur coat! Soon I shall have a bear skin for my feet. So far, nothing but a calf skin from Yakutsk lies under my table as a beautiful rug, and warms my feet, which are clothed in felt shoes and rubbers. The hut would be good in every respect but that there is a draft from the floor and the cold comes in. But we shall overcome that, with the bear's help.

"Heigh-ho! my life is nothing but a genuine carnival.

"Abundance of earthly gifts, and the sincere love of kind friends more than the wickedness of the enemies; so that the cup of joy outweighs that of bitterness. Just now, for instance, I have returned from my walk carrying in my hands a package of pies; one made of fish, another of carrots; — got them without paying a penny, and they took such pleasure in wrapping them up in a newspaper! And if my clothes have to be washed, kind women are found (from our own circle) who will take them and wash them. But I myself like to freeze my washing out on the line in front of my window.

"Oh, what a great surprise my hut would be to Boris and Marusya! Merely the heating of my little stove and baking potatoes in it would fill up many hours with the most pleasant occupation. The tin of which my samovar is made even reflects the moonlight

during the night, and its bright shining is the cause of
no little admiration. And the small, queer cupboard,
turned on one side, — that is my pantry; and my
small windows, consisting of a lot of little pieces of
glass; and finally a hole in the wall opposite the stove,
through which sometimes the bright sunbeams fall
on the chips of wood scattered upon the stove. This
hole is open, and many eyes have looked through it,
how many that are not known, nobody has any idea.
But neither I nor anybody else objects, since, owing
to these ventilators, the air in the house is fine, and no
one ever has a headache."

George Lazareff to Miss Blackwell. (Undated)

"I was so glad that Baboushka had found in the
assistant-surgeon Rogestwensky a very useful and
devoted man, who came every day to bandage her
swollen legs. But the local authorities found he was
too earnest and too frequent in his visits to her. Suddenly he was seized and sent to the remotest and
worst hole of the district. She was in despair.

"'What for?' she cried. 'Miserable executioners!
Send me to the devil, if you like, but why do you torture my poor, innocent, and generous friends and comrades, all those who approach me?'

"Everybody who came to see her the guards
stopped, and asked them who they were and what they
came for. It made so much trouble, not only for her
but for her landlord, that nobody liked to let a room to
her. It was for this reason that she lived so long in
a miserable half-rotten hut, which she liked because
it was solitary, so that the guards did not bother the
hut-owner — the hut standing apart, with the windows

looking on the snowy desert. For her health's sake I insisted that she should find a more comfortable lodging. After long consideration, she decided at last to do it. She gave me two weighty objections. The first was that the more comfortable lodging might spoil her character and definitely corrupt her spirit. She would live in a comfortable house of three neatly furnished rooms, — salons, as she called them; meanwhile some of the other exiles, after a hard and long day's work (if they were lucky enough to have work) could hardly find a hole in the warm stall of some native to spend the night. If she could take some of her poor comrades into her lodging to live with her, how happy she would be! Of course there is no legal objection to it, but her experience with her comrade, Assistant-surgeon Rogestwensky, to whom she wished to give a permanent lodging in her former miserable hut, had taught her that such generosity on her part would cost her co-dweller very dear: he would be removed altogether from Kirensk. Meanwhile she badly needs the assistance of her comrade exiles, who love and adore her as their mother, as the model of human devotion and self-sacrifice.

"In her last letter she writes me that she has changed her lodging at last, and is now settled in her three neatly furnished 'salons.' And she finds her expectation is fulfilled; she feels herself gradually becoming corrupted. The criminal thought is knocking at her mind, how nice it would be to make a bath-room out of one of her pretty 'salons' and to furnish it with a comfortable bath-tub, where she could warm her sick legs! One of her comrades, being an expert, is ready to realize this ideal, and is going to install a home-made tin bath. I hope she is now so corrupted that in the next letter she will tell me of the realization of this great enterprise. She cherishes the idea that her comrades will find an opportunity to wash their poor bodies free of charge from time to time, and to enjoy themselves in the most American style. You see, with money in hand it is possible even in the Russian hells to get some comfort.

"You know how strictly she is watched. They fear her escape from Siberia. Money sent to her all at once in considerable quantity would excite suspicion. The same sum of money divided into parts, and sent regularly and periodically, would seem of no importance to the local authorities. There are many common convicts who have rich relatives and receive much money from them. We could easily send to Baboushka $100. a month, if we had it, but only on condition that it was sent regularly.

"There is no person in the world who can prevent her from doing what she considers her duty. Above all things, she bothers herself in visiting sick native people, in giving them good advice as to how to feed the children, and so on. Very often she carries them her milk, part of her own daily food. In answer to my reproaches for her unreasonable philanthropy, she mocked at me, saying that I was greatly mistaken in my appreciation of her conduct. She was a very sly old woman: by giving a trifle to these poor little wretches around her, in return she got more from them for herself. They are so stupid, she says, as to bring her all the sweets they can get in that arid region; butter, different kinds of berries, eggs, little cakes, and so on. They are stupid, because she is only one, and cannot give them much, but they are hundreds, and little by little, bit by bit, they bring her a great deal. And they help her with so much zeal and love (in return for her pretended attention), that she cannot help accepting the gifts. 'So, in the long run, I am the gainer,' she concluded. 'Light gains make heavy purses.' In a word, she is a really incorrigible old woman. However, by force of her indomitable energy and good-natured character she is spreading everywhere an atmosphere of consolation among the suffering people.

"In my opinion, the agitation in America at present in behalf of Baboushka, old, ill, and almost dying, will have a good effect in the mitigation of her lot. They might let her live in some warmer town of Siberia."

"November 1–13, 1911.

"All my beloved friends!

"Like a queen in a palace, like a princess in an armchair, like a scholar before a large table, surrounded by magazines, papers, letters, and a lot of beautiful post-cards is sitting your old Catherine, proud and happy, strong and well. All October she was mute, enjoying her new dwelling, where she is as comfortable as one can imagine. A large room, divided into four chambers, represents a house that would suit a person of much greater pretensions. It would take a great deal of inspiration to depict all the benefits of my new apartment. This letter will announce only: (1) Having space enough to walk from one corner of my house to another (passing through three chambers and a line of 30 feet) — I remain at home all the time,

having no desire to take cold and to get the influenza.
The same cause forced me to order a bath, which will
stand in one of my chambers and will be heated by a
little engine, attached to one of its ends, so that the
traveling of half a mile to take a bath (as last winter)
is excluded from my pastime.

"There is only one brick stove in the centre of the
four rooms. It is large, and without the aid of the
old cobbler it would be difficult to get it ready. This
old friend of mine returned to his offices near my person with the return of cold weather. Every morning
he is there to bring wood, to get water, to clean and to
brush all my apartments. Many chairs, many tables,
one commode, and a kitchen with a fireplate (an iron
disc on which all can be cooked) . . . all that depends
on his activity and zeal. We have a samovar now, and
drink tea together, but as for cooking, we don't occupy
ourselves with such trifles. My various friends bring
me very often every sort of food.

"(2) I wish to tell you what I received during October from America, that great and benevolent country
that fills my existence with surprises, caresses and en-
dowments of all kinds. Many letters were received,
and many cards. The magazines reached me safely,
and were much read by myself and by many other
exiles, who, learning that I have a lot of them, ask for
them from various parts of Siberia. I send them,
being proud and content. The two excellent books
from Chicago, with a letter from my Starr, gave me
real joy, for I longed for news of her. All my visitors
are surprised to see such a quantity of printed and
written riches. I only smile and enjoy it in my heart.
But all the Russian material, except the letters, is

immediately distributed among the visitors, who come from several near-by places, and take it to be read by all the comrades in the vicinity. They keep robbing me to the very last, and when I see anything very interesting, I hastily stick it under my pillow, and when alone I hurry to read it, before I am robbed of it. But my English literature is with me. Never one little scrap of English printed paper has been lost or destroyed by my hand. One of my tables is covered with heaps of books, and magazines, and the *Evening Post*, before being sent to Yakutsk and other parts of East Siberia. *Life and Labor* [1] is my favorite, and the *National Geographic Magazine* enjoys the favor of everyone for its splendid pictures. One young man is going to photograph them and make them fit to be shown in the magic lantern.

"You are all working too hard : meetings, readings, visitings, writing and establishing new and new settlements and different places of help and education — it is too much for the same persons, already tired and exhausted by a work of twenty or thirty years. Now you must only survey the work of young people, and bring them up to be able to take your places, and to continue what you began.

"There is a change concerning my custody : now there are four spies going around my house and looking into my windows. Two accompany me when I go out. This escort is so disgusting that I have no wish to walk out of doors. What they are afraid of, I don't know ! I see only that they think me able to vanish like a cloud before their eyes."

[1] The organ of the National Woman's Trade Union League, edited by Alice Henry.

To Mrs. Barrows.   November 8–21, 1911.

"Do you know where the crabs are wintering? [1] I see you do, while examining my new wardrobe, brought to me from the post office yesterday afternoon.   It was a glorious apparition, which enchanted all the boys that were occupied with the matter; for the package was big and heavy.   The goods were so well wrapped that everything is as fresh as if just out of the shop.   Even the paper and the cardboard are safe enough to be used by our bookbinders.   Everyone touched the stuff, and everyone was sincerely glad to know that grandmother will be clad as warmly as one could desire.   I am sure the whole winter there will be examination and appreciation.   It is the first time in my life that I have had such beautiful things for myself.   This very letter I am writing enveloped in the delicious overcoat, fearing no frosts, weather or storm.   The old cobbler, Platon, my faithful servant when sober, laughed and cheered, examining the big shoes I received, and did not dare to touch with his rough hands the exquisite Jaeger's linen displayed on my table.   'Oh,' said he, 'did your friends in America get the photograph of your old cabin?   They would be as much astonished to live in it as we should be to wear such beautiful linen!'

"Everything of best material and skilfully made.   Even the duties were paid.   So I got a quantity of foreign goods without paying a kopek for them.   All this, thanks to persons who not only know where the crabs are wintering, but who can arrange the matter

[1] A Russian proverb concerning people who know where to find the best things.

so finely that the receiver has no trouble; he has only
to take and to use.

"Yours for ever."

To Miss Blackwell.   November 20–December 3, 1911.

"Certainly the women of the United States are
remarkable for their energy and cleverness! The
campaign carried on in California by the suffragists
is a whole *épopée* in the life of your people.   It is a
beautiful example for countries where the political
institutions allow people to act with an endeavor so
largely developed.

"The portraits of Miss Addams and Miss Blackwell were such a charming surprise to me, such welcome guests among many others, many beautiful
women!   In my room, large and convenient, I received
them all heartily, and, sitting alone during the long
evening, in a corner near the stove, I held a long conversation with both girls on a series of interesting topics
which occupy my mind.

"November 29.   For instance, since I got the leaflets
about the work done by Denison House, I thought
very often of the great difficulty of fulfilling as well
as one wishes all the enterprises we take upon us in
doing so many things at once.   So much hard work
and such large outlays do not show to the world the
results of a sane and clever education of children,
which question is the most serious among those that
concern our race.   And I am sure that this question
can be solved only outside of the life of the big towns.

"The children that have grown up far from contact
with country life, from all that composes so-called
'nature,' are only half of a human being in its com-

pleteness. The children of the well-to-do have the possibility of traveling and seeing many sides of country life. And yet they are not (on the whole) so richly endowed as the children of farmers. As for the poor children, they grow up in the large cities like little apes, never thinking about the beautiful and marvellous scenery of the great world. All our great men (in science, literature and social life) are natives of the provinces; all the best scholars, the most active workers in every kind of social activity are people who grew up outside of the capital cities and large towns. There are exceptions, as always, but they are so few that I could not cite an example. In a country as free as yours, why not make experiments, why not establish some institutions (settlements) for poor children and orphans in some wholesome country district, where all this large family would constitute one farming association? The little ones would learn how to work, the biggest would study and work at the same time; several handicrafts might flourish, too. The arts would be an every-day luxury. Such an institution would be a splendid proof of the possibility of producing a race of men able to be useful in every place and in every state of life.

"I do not say that the settlements you have now are not necessary. I only wish that your women might show the world what is the best mode of education while we are living under the conditions of this century.

"December 4–17, 1911.

"I have a telegram that I am to receive a pelisse and a watch. Never was I so rich.

"Pray tell Helena I embrace her from my soul.

Her kindness, her delicacy in connection with every one is remarkable. I love people in general, but good people are my delight, and I don't need to see them, to know them personally, in order to love them sincerely and strongly.

"It is wonderful to me how much your women can do, and have time to enjoy parties and visiting. Full of energy.

"I never heard of Isabel's son before, and was sure she had only one daughter. I am very glad she has a son; it is a great comfort to have such a near friend and companion."

To Miss Dudley.   December 15–25, 1911.

"Our dear Euphemia and you will send me some cards. Very glad! They give such great amusement to my young friends. They are fond of symbolic pictures. The Slavonic mind is very poetical; and all that recalls the beauty and greatness of the world is eagerly sought.

"But the goodness of my American friends grows greater and greater, and I am afraid I shall be spoiled. Yesterday the mail brought me a little bag in which I found violet soap, ribbon dental cream, violet talcum powder, cold cream, and a bottle for hot water. This reminded me of Lucy Smith's present, which I found once on my table when I occupied her room. I would be so happy to embrace this very angel of a girl, and take her on my lap, and kiss her over and over."

"December 16.

"Where will you go, what new work is to torment you farther? Dear friend, it is enough of sacrifice;

you must live as long as possible, and not wear out your health. It is a desolate situation to know one's best friends on the verge of peril, and to be sure they never will take care of their safety! I very often fear to hear that your health, that of Aunt Isabel, that of our Alice, is declining. Many persons in your country are dear to me. But you three were especially good to me, and so kindly good that I became familiar with you, as if we had understood and loved each other from the beginning of the world. I am never sure I shall not hear something bad concerning your health. Don't think I am in the same condition as you are. I do not strain. I have been working all my life like a Southern ox (such as our peasants labor with) that goes his pace, no faster, no slower, never tired, but never much at once. Consequently my strength is better conserved. The work of all three of you is, on the contrary, a work of race-horses, with the great difference that race-horses are well nourished, very well looked after, and tenderly nursed, while you three run without rest, and without that necessary comfort of soul which can be gained only by a leisure which occurs often and gives us time to collect our thoughts, feelings, impressions, and conclusions. I could not be myself without such conditions."

CHAPTER XIV

George Lazareff to Miss Blackwell. December 20, 1911.

"There are two classes of exiles in Siberia. Those who have been banished by administrative order, without trial, are sent for terms of not more than five years to the remotest part of the empire, as dangerous persons, and are temporarily deprived of all their civil rights. They are given a money allowance by the government, the amount varying with their rank and with their place of exile, which they may not leave. They are under constant surveillance.

"The second class of exiles have been tried and banished for life, and are permanently deprived of their civil rights. They receive no money from the government, but after they have stayed for six months in an appointed place, they are entitled by law to receive a passport authorizing them to live where they please in their district, and to travel about and look for work.

"Baboushka belongs to the second class, but she is illegally deprived of all its privileges, and has to bear the worst features of the treatment of both classes. She gets no money from the government, yet she is not allowed to choose her place of residence, nor to travel about, nor even to go freely through the streets of the miserable little town of Kirensk; and she is watched continually by police spies."

213

Picture card [1] to Miss Blackwell. December 30, 1911–January 12, 1912.

"This is the greatest festival of the Yakuts; the young horses will be killed, roasted, and eaten.

"A beautiful fur coat and a clock with a bell have been received. I remember Miss Wald said something about it. My thanks to her. The Christmas was a merry one. Nobody was hungry nor cold, — I mean my company.

"La Follette's autobiography is beautiful, — a splendid man. 'The Eleventh Hour' [2] that I got to-day is dear to my heart. Julia Ward Howe was a wonder."

To Mrs. Barrows. January 5–18, 1912.

"The *Survey* was received, and your article on the prisons read first of all. If you knew all the truth about our places of confinement, what horrible scenes would engross your descriptions of what occurs there, where many, many thousands of our best youths are dying!

"January 11–24.

"Already your letter with the news about the death of our Durland has come to me, and this letter of mine is not finished. Why? Never alone! never alone! I do not complain, for I feel and understand that the constant visitation of our people is the only good that can be done. From 9 A.M. to 9 P.M. I must give all my attention to the needs of others, after which pastime I am tired, and able only to read papers or articles. Thanks to the money I have received from

---

[1] The picture on the card shows a crowd of Siberian natives standing around some shaggy horses.

[2] By Mrs. Howe's daughter, describing her last years.

my American friends, I eat well, I have had many comfortable novelties. And with my Jaeger clothes, my pelisse, and a young lady who takes me every day at noon, I go out to walk and breathe the pure, fresh air.

"Durland was a good heart. What a pity! When I see one of my boys failing, I suffer much. I scold them often and hard. I never knew you had a son before you wrote it me this autumn. How glad I am he is a good boy! Mabel is a noble soul. I remember her, and her husband too, though I saw him only once. Every corner of your residence in New York I remember as well as if I had seen it yesterday."

Doctor Tchaykovsky to Miss Blackwell. January 20, 1912

"Baboushka writes:

"'I should be quite contented had I by my side always a dear female face and a kind heart. For an old woman like myself, often ailing, there is nothing more soothing than a caressing female hand. To help in the bath, in the bed, to hand food or drink, to sew or to cut — she could do all, my darling; but I have no such darling, and there is no chance to get one here. It is true, it would be very lonely for her to stay here with an old woman like me, always exacting correctness, economy, foresight, and other virtues. If I could have her at least temporarily, just to stay with me, so that I could feel by my side one who is quite near to me; some one who could take care of me, instead of my always taking care of others. It is true there are many here who remember me, who try to serve me or to bring me something nice, but all this is done occasionally, in a hap-hazard way, and it

often happens that I have either too much of everything, or nothing at all. There is no constant eye
watching how I behave myself. One often needs to
get something, to send somewhere, to run to the post,
to the shop, to an outdoor cupboard, etc. Of course
one could do all that one's self. But I am not what I
used to be. In short, I am too old.'

"And again on December 12–25 she writes: 'What
I said before about a female friend, of course refers
to one who would not be worried by staying with an
old woman, who would be prepared to stay here, say
a year, or at least half a year; would forgive me my
grumbling, and exacting correctness and economy (but
not greediness or meanness, of course) in everything.
Where one could find such a treasure, I don't know.
On the other hand, it would be as useful for her to pass
through a school of care and attention to her neighbors, for it would not be of myself alone that she would
have to take care here, but of many others.

"'I received yesterday twenty rubles, and at once
bought butter and sugar — the greatest expenses
here. It is remarkable how particular our boys are.
Those who have work or a position will not touch food
in my hut, but only those who are unemployed."

To her friends at Wellesley College. February 10,
1912.

"Wellesley College gave me one of the greatest
pleasures I ever experienced. When I was there, I
found one of the most beautiful institutions I ever
saw. The establishment itself is perfect, furnished
with all the improvements of the last word of pedagogy.
But what charmed me most of all was the body of

teachers and pupils. When, after the few words I spoke, I sat with my cup of tea in the salon, where a hundred dear young faces looked at me with friendship, with sympathy, I felt so cheerful and familiar with all that surrounded me, I had at once so many words to say, so many thoughts to express, so many feelings to discharge, that it was very hard for me to leave the dear society when it was announced that the horses were at the door.

"If words came as readily as ideas and feelings, I could say ten hundred kindly things.

"'I would be true, for there are those who trust me;
I would be pure, for there are those who care;
I would be strong, for there is much to suffer;
I would be brave, for there is much to dare.'

"'I would be a friend to all . . . I would look up — and laugh — and love — and lift.'

"'As long as we do not surrender the ideal of our life, all is right.'

"'Is thy burden hard and heavy? Do thy steps drag wearily? Help to bear thy brother's burden . . .'

"'Be noble! and the nobleness which lies
In other men, sleeping but never dead,
Will rise in majesty to meet thine own.'

"'When courage fails and faith burns low,
And men are timid grown,
Hold fast thy loyalty, and know
That truth still moveth on.'

"'Kind hearts are the gardens,
Kind thoughts are the roots,
Kind words are the blossoms,
Kind deeds are the fruits.'"

"These words are in 'The Calendar of Friendship,' received from a dear friend. I quote these golden words not only for their beauty, but also I have experienced them all my life as an irrevocable truth.

"After my visit to Wellesley I received many tokens of friendship from its inhabitants.

"I pray you both, elder and young ladies, pardon me for my long silence. I recognize my fault and feel ashamed. Oh! my ignorance of your beautiful language makes me miserable very often. For I desire to speak with you, to correspond with the American women whom I esteem and admire now more than ever. Their energy in all they undertake is wonderful, and is an example to the women of all the world.

"Accept my greetings, lovely ladies, and pardon

"Your friend

"Catherine Breshkovsky."

To Miss Dudley. February, 1912. (Written on the back of a picture postcard representing Jesus before Pilate)

"Pilate, after having heard what Jesus said to him, asked with a smile of doubt, 'And what is truth?' So many and many people, wishing to preserve their independence of action in things that flatter their tastes and the weak sides of their characters, make the same suggestion, in the hope of withdrawing themselves from any responsibility towards the requests of humanity. And yet the truth is born with us, and lies in the souls of all sane people, and teaches us to love our fellow sisters and brothers, and to do to them the best we desire for ourselves. And we see that only those who fulfill this law of our nature are sincerely esteemed, and happy even in their distresses."

To Miss Blackwell.   February 24–March 8, 1912.

"Women's enfranchisement, after the Chinese revolution, is in my opinion the greatest event of our century, as regards political reform. For I am sure the enfranchisement of women must be followed by a store of new reforms for the welfare of humanity.

"Yes, this century from its very beginning has been full of miraculous events. One can live with plenty of sensations without even taking part in all these beautiful evolutions, otherwise than by surveying and digesting the events which cover the earth at this moment. I feel as if I were in the very middle of all the perturbations which threaten to overthrow all the old prejudices and evils. I think it is thanks to this faculty of pursuing in my imagination the course of life in general that I conserve that verve of character which is familiar to me. And now, besides the possibility of following the course of progress, I have the good fortune to have many relays of young people around me, which makes me mother of an infinite family, whose members are in a state of everlasting circulation. This state of things keeps my mind awake. I stay like a watchman on my post, overseeing on every side. And when we add to all this my personal material welfare, and the possibility of furnishing what is most necessary to those who are in need, one can understand why I do not feel cast down or mournful. Not one of our exiles is so richly off as I. And George Kennan is quite right in saying that he found me in Selenginsk lacking all the comforts I enjoy now. And my luxury of to-day comes from America. For my Russian friends would not be able to send me so much money and such beautiful things.

"This month is a cruel one: cold and wind day and night. The winter is so long and unrelenting (frost and snow the whole eight months) that we forget the feeling of better weather, and the summer, the two months of warmth, seems to us a far-off dream.

"Professor Ely and his wife! I see them both at a party, or a musical evening, when the young miss, his bride then, stood on a tabaret and spoke nice things, and we stood around her. I recollect, too, how angry Mr. Ely was with me, when, confused, I could not speak on my life in Siberia and at Kara. Everything about the Americans I remember as clearly as if it were yesterday. First, I was eager to see, to hear, to understand the characters, customs, all the ways of life; secondly, I was so pleased to find a friendly reception, so pleased! To this day I am always surprised to be welcomed, beloved, cherished. Therefore every token of friendship and love is to me like a new happiness in my life. I have always wished and strained to deserve my own respect, and that of honest people, but I look upon this as a duty common to every rational being.

"I am afraid Lucy Smith is gone. What a sacred heart it was! A very saint. I am afraid about Helena, too. She is always tormenting herself with the thought that she does too little, giving all her life for others, and yet imagining herself not worthy enough. I do not think so about myself. I look at it in this way: Everyone must endeavour to be useful, but nobody is obliged to do more than he can.

"Oh, your old Kitty is very seldom tired of life, and she needs but a sparkle of light to feel herself as young and strong as ever."

To Miss Blackwell. March 14–27, 1912.

"If this were not such a cruel climate, which uses up so much strength and expense for food and clothing, we would make many improvements in our life, for there are many skilful, strong and clever people among us; but without money, tools or provision, it will take many years of persevering efforts to obtain any amelioration. All you earn during the short summer, you eat up during the long winter, when the country presents an immense bare wilderness. No plants except the big trees, no birds, no movement from place to place, except the mail post, speeding on six or seven sledges, with two horses to each. The caravan runs very fast, or fast enough, considering the state of our roads, always very bad. The little bells ring far and loud, and all the inhabitants, especially our boys, run towards the post office, where they receive the same answer: 'Not ready, — to-morrow.' It is absurd to see how slow the employees of all Russian offices are. And they are accustomed to treat the public like intruders, that have no right to ask.

"The last two months my health has been much better. The clothes you sent me have much to do with this, for I am never cold now. You have much to do, too, with my present position. I am sure my enemies will not show themselves too cruel towards me. Some time ago, one of my friends wrote me that she was trying to have me removed to a place further south. I forbade her to do it, and got for answer: 'Your prohibition came too late. I had already asked for your transfer to a less cold place, and received the reply : "Let her thank God that she is in Kirensk and not farther north."' Yes, and I think I should be farther north but for the tokens of friendship I get from your country.

"In some days it will be Easter. I am already preparing pastry and meat for my poor guests and myself. Now that my excellent Platon is too often 'unwell', I have taken a young girl into the house; she dwells with me and serves me. Fifteen years old, she could not read or write, so I am teaching her. Then she sews clothes for herself, and makes flowers to ornament her parents' home. She is a Siberian native, of Slavonic race. But the Russian peasants that have inhabited Siberia for centuries are very different from those of Russia. Here they become rough, lacking in benevolence and gratitude, and always suspicious. It is the result of a severe struggle with wild surroundings, and of the fact that, ever since Siberia came under the Russian government, the officials sent to rule it have been those who could not be tolerated even in Russia. Those who are too bad to be endured there are sent to Siberia, and reign here without any restraint. In consequence the natives look on everyone coming from Russia as a scoundrel and a brigand; for Siberia is the place where all the convicts are settled. No wonder the 'Tchaldans' (the nickname for Siberian people of the Slavonic race) have a strong prejudice against anyone who comes from Russia, and it takes time before the best of them are trusted. Now, the number of good and honest people who constitute the majority among our exiles have made a favorable impression on the population, and the inhabitants are not able to distinguish a true 'political' from a false one. Hundreds of such are here, too, for the government throws in one heap with people struggling for the right, many unworthy people who have had no share in any honest activity. So our enemies are spoiling the reputation of the whole mass of 'politicals.' We have many troubles on this account, many afflictions, and many judgments, which have sometimes ended with the exclusion of the guilty person from the society of the rest. One cannot be severe enough in such a position as ours. If anyone wishes to preserve his human dignity and his calling of a struggler for the right, he must be an example to the rest of the population in all his concerns; in his exterior as in his interior life. And here, where no other means exist to prevent degeneration but self-control, and the public opinion of our comrades, here we must be stronger in our principles than elsewhere.

"What a beautiful life Isabel's has been! I have translated your account of it, and it will be printed in a journal for young people. I often watch her in different phases of her present life. I see her running with our June; her face is radiant, like a saint who sees heaven. The child is a symbol of the best future of mankind, especially a child that has for its forefathers such people as Isabel and her distinguished husband. Another time I see her speaking at a Congressional reunion, and she is beautiful, with her strong speech and her severe expression. And then I see her among her friends, animating the whole group, giving interesting news and comments, inspiring those around her with a benevolent feeling towards all the world. Now that I know she has a companion in her son, I imagine her walking with him in the forest, with searching eyes and aroused mind, trying to penetrate into the secrets of nature. She is far from any trouble, amidst the beautiful and silent creation, and her soul is wandering in God's region. . . . It would be so well, so well for the youth of every country to have a full description of her life, which has been an uninterrupted course of reasonable labor and noble actions — a soul full of love and energy. Her God must be satisfied with such a daughter. Such a woman is to be chosen as a model, for she has not only preached all her life, but also acted. She has never been tired, or never permitted herself to be so, and all she could give away she has given. A rare and idealistical example."

To Mrs. Barrows. March 31–April 13, 1912.

"It is long since I have seen such a collection of brave, witty, and sympathetic men as in 'The Moral Citadel.' It rejoiced me the more since, except for a dozen excellent characters, I had not the opportunity to make so close an acquaintance with American men as I had with the women. I saw that the men were so occupied with their business, always so serious, and I dared not approach them. Certainly such men as Professor Ely and the young students in New York I felt to be good friends; and I looked upon Mr. Barrows with veneration, mingled with fear of being a burden. Now that I know his life of devotion and love for all humanity, his beautiful face, yes, his whole tall slender figure are so near to me, so wholly near, that I often address him, and approach him like a beloved relative who is glad, too, to find out his old sister.

"What wonderfully good examples of the human species we have on our earth! How can one be distressed or become disenchanted after having known such people as I have known in my country, in yours?

"The *Woman's Journal* is a clever and warlike piece of work. They repeat very often the same arguments, but it is well in this case, for one must '*battre le fer quand il est chaud.*' Once a week you must cry aloud, not to be forgotten the other six days.

"The *Survey* is a friend whose presence with us can last very long, for it treats of subjects with which we shall have to do for a long time, gradually ameliorating the innumerable defects of our social life. Every worker in social questions would do well to read the *Survey*, for every one of them would find there some investigations useful in his own specialty. If not new, the *Survey* is never old.

"Easter was spent well. I got a beautiful gramophone, with excellent songs and musical parties. For three days we have had music from 9 A.M. till 9 P.M. One relay of young men came for three or four hours, then another, and I was afraid it would continue the whole week, so I sent the instrument for a while to my friends, a very good family of our people.

"I have some pupils in French, German and English. But my time is spent for the most part in preaching, and hearing the confessions of hundreds. Every one has his own secret or sorrows to tell me, and to get an answer.

"As for my health, it is good while I sit at home. The body may be very well wrapped up and not feel cold, but it is enough for me to breathe a cold air to begin to sneeze, and to have miserable bronchitis. It is very abominable, but with milder weather my health will be restored.

"I have received this printed card: 'The Holy Spirit of the Spring is working silently.' The thing is done with much taste. I shall write on it and send it to the lawyer who defended my cause so heartily. But we have no mail this month. We have friends so far off, on the border of the Ice Sea, that they can receive mail only once a year. We are fortunate."

Picture postcard [1] to June Barrows Mussey. April 2–15, 1912.

"My beloved grandson! These three creatures are little pawns. Now they are plucking prunes, and eating them with great pleasure. But they work very hard every day, and have no time to do much wrong, like the kings and queens, who remain always lazy, for all is done for them by the laboring pawns. Many of the little pawns have excellent capacities; they learn well, and work for the welfare of the whole people. So will you, too."

"June 2–15, 1913.

"I would cross the ocean like these ducks, to see our Nonna, to kiss her hands, and to know how strong she is now. Tell her that Catherine is well, walking every day, and looking after her vegetables that she has planted in a large bed."

[1] The picture shows three peasant children picking fruit.

To Miss Dudley.   April 3–16, 1912.

"Your letter gave me great joy. Dearest girl! I
see you are taking a right course, and you will find a
profound relish (yes, a relish) in approaching 'the other
half' of humanity, so unknown, so disapproved. If
you find there many sides of life which are too heavy
and sometimes too disagreeable, yet you must feel
that only in approaching this sea of laboring human
beings, investigating their mode of life and their
psychology, can one act reasonably and rightly. For
'the other half' is the basis on which the whole organization of our society is built. If the foundation is
wrongly laid, it will crack, and all the structure above
will be thrown down.   And if a citizen wishes to be of
use to his country he must begin with the basis. All
the rest is only palliatives, and, if we have nothing
against philanthropy, yet we cannot admit that such
work can solve the social problem. For my part, I
esteem and love tenderly the people who work sincerely as philanthropists, but I am always sorry to see
such mighty forces choose a line of work that does not
bring the great benefit which results from work amidst
'the other half.' When working there, a person of
mind and heart will see and understand at once the
state of things, of social relations and needs. Without books, without being taught, you see clearly where
the talent is buried. You will see at once that the
world is now divided into two parts, and that we have
to make these two parts like one body. We see, too,
that one part is willing to do so, and that the other
does not wish it. . . . Oh! much to do! But, when
once the people have found out the place that makes us

suffer, time only will be needed to restore the wrong. And you see how fast this teaching is now spreading. There are quite plain, uninstructed minds of peasants and workmen that need to be informed only once not to forget it during their whole life, and to explain it quite distinctly to every one who will hear it. For it is life itself that is teaching, learning, and suggesting; there nothing is invented; there is no place for fancy or poesy, — a naked truth.

"I cannot tell you how glad I am. For I am sure your nearest friends will follow you, and devote more attention to the labor question. It is very good, if only you will not speed like young horses, and lavish your forces so that you will be dead in one year. Only see how long Julia Ward Howe lived, and many other old ladies of whom I have read with delight in the American papers. How beautiful it is to see and hear an old woman of eighty or ninety addressing words of love and reason to the young generation! I have experienced myself that the words of an aged person carry much more weight with young people than those of their mates. They believe in the teaching much more when they see that old people preserve a young faith in the religion they have chosen. Therefore I urge all your company to spare their strength and health. There are not so many worthy people that they should be treated with neglect. I read much about what happened in Lawrence, not only in your papers, but in the Russian papers too. Our best papers never fail to mention all that concerns the cause of 'the other half' throughout the world."

To Mrs. Barrows.   (Undated.)

"There are some very good women here (exiles too) that take care of me. Morning, noon, and night, they come to make all right, and to prepare my food. One wished to remain with me to nurse me, but she was arrested and turned out of the cabin. I knew it would be so, for any one must have a special permission to live in the town, and this girl had none. And even if she had had one, it would have been the same, for every one who approaches me closely is contaminated. Now instead of four spies I have six at my doors and windows. And yet I am happy in spite of all these villainies, for I do not think about them. I think how good people are to me, receiving tokens of love and friendship. I think this very fact makes my enemies very angry, and they permit my frequent and large relations with the world only perforce. Oh, they make searches and hope to find something prejudicial near me. But I have nothing to conceal, and my feelings, my philosophy, are open to every one. Never mind! Very soon I shall be well, prancing and dancing. Then Alice and Helena will receive long letters full of jokes and foolishness.

"I am annoyed to be careful about my health. I want to feel joyful and strong. It is my habit, otherwise I am angry with myself. And it seems to me it is another person, an old foolish person. I do not recognize myself. I miss my soul, my very self. Very disagreeable! Such a bad state makes me careful about my health. I am afraid of becoming an invalid. And I eat an excellent soup, and fine white bread and boiled milk. Dry fruits give a beautiful compote.

In a word [I am] like a chess queen sitting on a throne.

"With all this I pray God to give me reason and patience to remain as careful forever, to remain strong for the rest of my life. Perhaps God will hear my woes, and send me more character and attention. I detest being an invalid. For I think my age is not at all so great as to throw me out of life. And life is growing more and more interesting. I wish to witness it. Do you wish so too, dear sister, for there are many young people who learn from us to be honorable and brave, and we want to see them acting.

"Do not address yourself to those that have no heart, no reason in their tops. It will never do. Your interference makes them more prudent and less rough, I know — but for your own tranquillity."

To Miss Blackwell.   June 6–14, 1912.

"One thing causes me sorrow. It is the thought that the name of Lucy Stone, so often mentioned in her *Journal*, is known to few persons, and that the young generation pronounce that venerable name only by heart, without understanding how great and holy it is. Who could better relate her life, who could tell so clearly and sincerely how great and tender was this beautiful soul, how attractive this face that I remember so well in the portrait in your room? Now that you have a wide and long experience, that you can compare the immense difference between the two degrees of difficulty of the work done by your mother and those of to-day, you can show the world a wonderful picture of energy, perseverance, and self-denial exercised by a woman that won her cause by her own strength, fighting her way and rights like a knight of unrivalled honor and courage. You have no right to leave the world without giving it the biography of your noble and beautiful mother. You have no right to rob posterity of such a treasure. Humanity is not yet too rich in beautiful examples not to show them to us as largely as possible. We need to have before us such images as can inspire us, teach us.

"June 11–24.

"It has been good weather these days. I have been often out of doors, and felt as if I were intoxicated.

"Once you asked me what I thought of theatrical representations which are given only to satisfy our lowest tastes, our frivolities. I am against them, and never would recommend them to children and young people, understanding that grown people will go to such spectacles only to get some idea of them. Young people should be maintained only by high and beautiful pictures of our life. Children have, without our intervening, too many wicked and dishonorable examples before them. I am sure the only reason there is so much bad literature, so many bad performances of all kinds, bad music, and bad morals is because the people are not well enough acquainted with that which is healthy, high, and beautiful. Most people, even now, would prefer what is good, what is thoroughly good. Oh, yes, humanity has already developed the senses which can catch the more delicate traits of progress.

"I send Mr. Herreshoff a big face of mine. It is very like me, and reminds one of the ancient statues made of stone and worn out with time.

"The skirmish and all the wrongs that are committed during the election time wring my heart. I cannot read the description of it without suffering for a free country. Oh, if we had what you have already! But it is our own fault.

"We have had some warm days. I am sure there will be more, and there will be time enough to get strong and beautiful (!) before winter comes. Just now my cheeks are red and brown, my feet alert and gracious, my mind full of hope. A magnificence of different sorts of flowers are brought to me as splendid bouquets by our boys, who are climbing the mountains and searching the forests and valleys. A very rich flora, but for a very short time flourishing and ornamenting the rude and monotonous nature of the country. I cannot leave the town, and cannot breathe the air of the fragrant vegetation of the forests. But we have so many flies in our town, and other atrocious insects in all the houses, that it must be taken as a compensation for the want of living beings, inhabitants of the immense spaces surrounding us.

"Oh, if you were as well and strong as I am, notwithstanding all the defects and deprivations of my liberty!

"Miss Addams is always in action, and many other women, the pride of your country. Certainly, when once we get our rights, we shall prove our fitness. It was proved long ago. But, for my part, I think never was given such an excellent answer on the suffrage question as was given by Clara Barton, that majestic and wonderful woman."

To Arthur Bullard.   July 4–17, 1912.

"Le monde se reveille."

"Yes, politics in America, as everywhere, is more hopeful now.   I am very eager to be aware how great is the progress in your country, being sure that its example will have a world wide significance.   The thousands of immigrants that invade your country will promulgate the reforms made there in their own native lands, for many of them are only temporary toilers in the United States.   Therefore all the news concerning the state of political questions in the United States (the election of the president included) is a matter of great interest to me.

"The book about Panama is a rich piece of literature for people who have a poor idea of what the physical and social life of the place is.

"As for the 'ineffectual reformer', as you call him, it is exceptionally interesting.   I am waiting for it.   Perhaps I guess the character that may be the model of the man you describe.   I remember a figure among the people of your set, very long, somewhat dull and melancholic, walking like a person of a world apart. Such figures are familiar to me, and I have learned to perceive through the outward loneliness and melancholy of their faces, an emptiness of mind and feelings. Pardon me if I am wrong in regard to your hero; but I never saw courage and abnegation combined with a lack of enthusiasm and faith.   I think that a true exposition of the before mentioned character in his efforts to be useful to mankind will be of great profit to your readers; showing how little or nothing a man can do who is not sure enough of what he is doing.

I hope our fatherland will move too; it cannot rest behind. Being pushed from East and West, it must go forward."

To a Friend. July, 1912.

" You are not married yet, and you gaze like a philosopher on the happiness of your friends, without bitterness, enjoying their family life as if it were your own. Well! you are young; you will choose a nice, working suffragist, who will embellish your life without giving you much trouble about getting a great deal of money.

"To-day I saw two of my boys going to visit their brides. They have to go more than a thousand miles, half of which they will travel on foot, and eating only bread and tea. The boys and the two girls have recently finished their terms in the hard labor prisons, and yet they are young, fresh, and full of hope. They are enthusiastic enough, and will reach their ends."

To Mrs. Barrows. August 6–19, 1912.

"*Life and Labor* suits me as well as the best Russian magazines, for it is simple and noble.

"I have a terrible photograph of myself, very like indeed. I will send it to your son, but he mustn't be afraid."

Picture postcards to June Barrows Mussey. August 17, 1912.

"You see in this picture a horde of ancient Cossacks, when they formed a nation of their own, and were really brave and independent. Free as they were, they elected every year a new chief, a colonel, who ruled all their affairs. When the ceremony of election took place, the ex-chief would transmit to the newly chosen 'Ataman' all the relics, or jewels, which were regarded as the treasure belonging to the whole army, and a sign of honor for the person that kept them. So, my dear grandson, I will transmit to you the keeping of my best sentiments and thoughts."

October 26–November 9, 1912.

"You see that this boy takes his toy for a living bear. He is a little afraid of him, yet courageous enough to encounter him in a fight. So often in our life we are mistaken, taking quite childish things, trifles, for serious or dangerous circumstances, and we waste our time and forces about nonsense. Do not cry unless you are badly hurt, and never be a coward."

CHAPTER XV

George Lazareff to Mrs. Barrows.   November 8, 1912.

"After the peaceful strike at the Lena gold mines, more than eight hundred men, women and children were shot, killed and wounded, and all the political exiles, many of whom were working there, were expelled from the place.   This trouble happened in the district of Kirensk.

"The police made two searches at Madame Breshkovsky's.   They took away all her papers, postcards, and photographs, but later returned them.   She is practically imprisoned in Kirensk.   Meanwhile she is doing incessantly a great work in her immense district in organizing help for the starving exiles, and through them medical and other assistance for the local population.   The whole population love her, and this again excites fresh suspicion on the part of the police.   I send her regularly forty rubles a month" (a little more than twenty dollars).

With three picture postcards sent to Miss Dudley.

"1. This is a typical Russian student.   She comes from a far-off province, lives on eight or ten dollars per month, and is studying day and night, till she grows as lean as a dying woman.   She wears these clothes autumn and winter, till she catches some illness, very often fatal. She wishes to be useful to her people, and to know everything in the world. Too eager for knowledge, and therefore not seldom missing its main object. The painter of this picture is a connoisseur of Russian types, especially among our youth.

"I have here this year many young women. Some came with their husbands, others came here as political convicts, and very often I wonder to see how excellent they are. So modest, so zealous, clever and good. Working very hard, for all of them have to earn their bread, except myself, provided as I am with every comfort imaginable."

"2. This girl is musing on what will be the destination of her knowledge. Her heart is not glowing, but her reason is strong, and she fears to spend her forces cheaply. She is not a Puritan like the first, yet she appreciates herself highly enough to wish to be a first-rate woman. We have had many of this kind, and nearly all have been sentenced to many years of hard labor. Proud and strong characters. All the pictures I send to America are bought here in this little town. One merchant makes a large profit by selling these cards, for all our boys are very fond of good pictures, and they give up their last kopek merely to have some sympathetic face, or landscape, or symbol."

"3. Never tired and always ready to sing and to dance are the young girls of the Russian peasantry. Working in the fields sixteen hours a day, they return home, as well as the married women, with songs which are heard miles away. And while the mothers prepare the supper and take care of the little ones, the girls are out of doors, out of the village, running 'horovod.' A large ring of girls, and often young boys, hand in hand, keep slowly moving and singing one song after another till the summer sun rises again, and all this squad disperses to begin work anew. Sometimes there is a violin, and more lively dances animate the numerous groups, where youthful peasants, poor and rich, feel themselves equal and free. There are beautiful examples of womanly beauty. And I imagine what a magnificent society we shall have when all these young wild beings get a serious and wholesome education."

To Miss Dudley. October 6–19, 1912.

"What an extra fine present, what a beautiful album of Wellesley College! And Ellen Fitz Pendleton, what a majestic figure! The life of Wellesley College students pictured there is like the paradise of Mohammed: joy, beauty, and festivity. Sorry there are not photos of their cabinets full of books, and desks, tables at which the nice blond heads I saw during my short visit at the college are working.

"How fond I am of the articles George Kennan is giving to the *Outlook!* All he says about Japan I agree with to the last word. For I have had the same experiences with other peoples, whose psychology is strange to the whole body of our nation. How well it is that science is making a successful advance toward giving different countries a knowledge of each other! It is so dull to have only strangers around us in every place on earth, when we are brothers, all coming from one source The soul is the same, the habits are different.

"Alice sent me Mrs. Pethick Lawrence and Miss Christabel Pankhurst; very agreeable pictures, but I should pity them now, after all the sufferings they have experienced these last years. They do not laugh, and their cheeks are meagre and pale. I would not follow them, yet I cannot blame them, for they are sincere and distressed. I mean that, with the energy of Englishwomen, and the large possibility of carrying on their propaganda, the women could work their way out without militancy run to the extreme.

"As to the war in the Balkans, I wish it would end the sordid question, the so-called 'Eastern question.'"

On a picture postcard:

"This is just the cell in the fortress of St. Peter and St. Paul. Everything is stone, asphalt, and iron; it is very dark in the cells on the first floor, for the wall which surrounds the buildings is high enough to keep out the light of the sun, and you never see the sky and stars. An old creature, like me, can support all the privations of air, light, motion, etc. But the young suffer seriously, and the silence and the mysterious running of all the ways of life there exert a distressing influence on the spirit and imagination. It is like a tomb. No human sounds, but very many sounds coming from outside, and from underground, the origin of which you cannot explain. Nobody answers your questions except the chief, very seldom seen, and you can torture yourself with visions and horrible pictures till you go mad. Many, many young lives have perished in this awful place, the best souls and best characters."

To Lewis Herreshoff. October 10–23, 1912.

"All those around me are too young to be a match for me, or, if I speak to the aborigines, too foreign to me.

"I am not able to write more than I do, having on my hands a lot of cares concerning the health (mental and physical) of more than fifteen hundred youths. I cannot do the tenth part of what I want to do for my unfortunate family, but my thoughts are with them, and my heart is always busy with all sorts of sentiments. Hope, love, care, pity, are mixed with sadness, impatience, anger.

"When alone or in my bed, I imagine to myself some unexpected chance that brings me large means of guaranteeing the welfare of my young family for some time. And I distribute and I keep the goods for the future, and so I fall asleep. Otherwise it would be impossible for me to keep up my humor and presence of mind, for every day's need and every day's misfortune would crush my heart.

"My imagination has been very vivid from my childhood. I cannot read stories or accounts that tell about perversity, crimes, or cruelty. I am sure none of us could support the sight of tortures, for instance, yet nearly every one can read the description. I cannot, without being hurt mentally; I become furious, for I represent to myself all the horror of the fact. Often I think it is only thanks to my imagination, always inclined to picture high or beautiful events, that I have preserved the strength I possess until now. Even all sorts of deprivations, moral or physical, are disgusting to such a point that I cannot read of them.

"One of our best writers, Dostoïevsky, translated into English, French, Italian, etc., is dreadful to me. I never read him. He is a psychologist and a scientist in all mental diseases. My body and my soul were always healthy; I see a great mischief in every species of psychopathy.

"The letter of your niece on the election of Roosevelt and Taft reached me. In the American press, as well as in the Russian press, I follow the race of the election, and I fear that no one of the candidates is fit to arrange matters better than they are now. Yet all goes with you much better than with us, to the shame of our people."

To Miss Blackwell.   October 20–November 2, 1912.

"It has been a quite peculiar pleasure to me to read 'A Man's World,' by Albert Edwards. Why so? It is well written, and includes a lot of interesting questions and facts; but that is not all. The book captivates me for its very near approach to the style of our best autobiographers. It is even difficult for me to conceive, when reading it, that it is by a foreigner: just like our own method of setting forth the things which are dear to us, and those which concern our ideas and feelings. No effects, no self-admiration, no desire to move the reader by any sentimental pictures or descriptions — plain and true. And yet you feel all the time how intelligent and profoundly meaning the author is, how awakened is his spirit. The constant sadness and melancholy of his heart is not underlined by himself, but the reader himself sees this rather stern figure, that keeps in his mind a world of thoughts and observations. Having missed the happiness of the outer world, he has acquired, by a long way of study and philosophical watchfulness, an inward world of knowledge of the secrets of life. And, as our acquaintance with human psychology makes us masters of life with all its vicissitudes, we feel that the author of this book stands strongly on his mental feet, and is capable of discerning distinctly the wrong from the truth.

"You must notice how bad my writing is growing. It is because I am always tired. My head is full of the needs of those around me; and when you add all the mischiefs coming from our enemies, it becomes a heavy load. Sometimes I feel ashamed before the young people, having no words, no voice to express myself.

"I have sent three cards to Helena Dudley, our growing friend, whose majestic figure I imagine on the platform at Lawrence. How glad I am, how beautiful it is, without any flattery!

"How different is 'A Man's World' from 'Fifty Years of Prison Service,' an autobiography by Zebulon R. Brockway! This man assures us that every functionary was the most venerable officer, yet he finishes his account of nearly every one by adding that the officer was killed by some convict for his cruelty. It is a narration of a very uniform performance of service of a pedant, and no signs of the psychological growth of a human soul."

Mrs. Barrows wrote to her, protesting against this judgment on Mr. Brockway. I insert her reply here, although out of chronological order.

February 5–18, 1913.

"You were right in saying that I had read only the first part of the book, 'Fifty Years of Prison Service,' when I wrote my letter. Now that I have read it to its last page, I am entirely of your opinion, that the author, venerable Mr. Brockway, was an imposing figure in the tenacity and the devotion of his character, which never failed him. And it is above all the last chapter, 'The Ideal of a Prison System,' which proves the sagacity and sincerity of this remarkable man.

"I must tell you that it is just the difference in character between our two peoples, the Americans and the Russians, which keeps us from mutually understanding each other at first. For instance, ignorant and grotesque as are our people, and consequently our criminals, they are particularly susceptible to the smallest kindness, to the least indulgence, even on the part of their persecutors. The expression, 'He is our father,' is always used in good faith in regard to the officials who pay the least attention to the needs of their subordinates, and never in my life have I heard of prisoners permitting themselves to ill-treat warders who were at all good to them, or who were even just to them. Our people acknowledge the law, and are always ready to obey it, and it is only a clear injustice, an intolerable persecution that makes them impatient and rebellious. Everything that is just, everything that is benevolent toward them, they appreciate and respect. But, as the whole world knows, these poor people are ill treated to the limit, in their everyday life; they are still more so in the Russian prisons, where every monster of a jailor has a right to tyrannize over the prisoners as much as he chooses. The most hideous of these scoundrels sometimes get the fate that they deserve; they fall by the hand of a rebel, who, in most cases, is avenging the outrages endured by all his comrades, and not his own personal wrong. As for cases of officials who were straightforward and courteous being murdered, I have never heard of such a case anywhere.

"Mr. Brockway's experience tells us just the opposite, and he gives many instances where the best behaved officials were killed quite young by the convicts, who had not even been ill-treated by them. It is quite possible that the independent character of the Americans cannot endure either restraint or control, and that, not being able to put up with either, they permit themselves to take a personal revenge; while the Russian criminals stand forward, in general, as avengers of the evils felt by their whole community, evils borne for a long time before being punished.

"In addition to this difference between our characters and way of behaving, we have yet another, not less clear and significant. Whereas Americans (like all Anglo-Saxons) are punctual in their business, and in all their conduct relating to their duties and their mutual relationships, we Slavs, and above all we Russians, suffer greatly from the fault of nonchalance. On the one hand, this fault makes us fall short (*manquer*) in many good things; makes us waste our time, our energy, even our knowledge, without deriving the necessary profit from them. On the other hand, in view of the severe laws, the rude manners, the despotism in all the corners of daily life, a rigid punctuality would make life, especially in the prisons, utterly unendurable. And it is in these cases that the Russian nonchalance permits the prisoners to breathe a little bit even in these frightful dungeons. In consequence, the Russian people abhor officials who are martinets, knowing that the rigidity of the régime carried out in all its severity would make life impossible. I venture to believe that the frequent murders mentioned by Mr. Brockway are in part the result of these incessant 'chicanes' which must be experienced by the individual subjected to a régime that deprives him of all liberty, even in relation to his smallest wishes and needs. It is possible also that the Russian people, knowing that they have by their side a constant and implacable enemy, an enemy that is complex and as it were *insaisissable*, may turn their eyes rather toward this complexity, wishing to get rid of it once for all. Hence individual cases of atrocities, horrible though they may be, are borne with patience, or rather with stoicism. We are accustomed to daily cruelties, and face them as inevitable facts.

"For instance, one day lately, an exile who was ill was obliged to leave the hospital before his strength was reëstablished. The doctor told him to stay in the city, so as to be able to make visits to the dispensary for some time longer. But the police had him arrested and taken to the place where he was to be exiled, 200 versts from here. The cold was intense, the invalid's clothes were too thin, and after two days of a miserable journey, the poor man was brought back again with his hands and head severely frozen. The doctor had to amputate his fingers, and both ears, leaving him maimed for life.

"To-day we have had the grief of burying another comrade, a very intelligent Jew, who, not being able to get a passport — Jews here are not allowed to have passports — not being able to go anywhere to find work, died almost of starvation. . . . You will understand that, having before me in the past and in the present an endless series of such pictures, it is not prison reform that I am thinking about, it is not to that object that I should like to direct the strength and attention of the public, although I venerate the beings who occupy themselves with it, but that I should like to see the whole *modus vivendi* changed so much that the population of the globe would not be subjected to sufferings from which they could be relieved with advantage to the whole world.

"I want to say a few words more about our friend Bullard's book, whose work arouses my lively curiosity (*m'intrigue vivement*), and this is why. Here again, perhaps, we have to do with the difference of racial characteristics. We prefer characters who are always in quest of the right and the true, under whatever form; whether God, or religion, or forms of social life, or scientific truths. A dogmatic form of thought is alien to us. While advancing for the present such or such a form as better than any other, our spirit, or rather our imagination, leaves us freedom to create for ourselves superior forms of life to that which in the present is placed as the aim of our aspirations. And here in Arthur Bullard's book I find a soul, a mind which is searching, which is feeling its way, which ends by understanding the imperfection of the very foundation where present society organizes its disfigured dwelling, where it introduces so many absurd customs, and, what is worse, so many deceptive principles. The character depicted in 'A Man's World' is likable on the one hand because of his disgust for evil, on the other because of his efforts to attain all the good permitted him by his nature, which is a little lymphatic, a little timid of the shocks which a bold and decided life risks encountering at every more or less decisive step. He is a conscientious and devoted pioneer, but a timorous spirit, not enlightened enough to go and fight the superstitions and evils of his century with an arm stretched out openly. It is people like that who take the first steps toward criticism, toward the renewal of the style of human life. I confess that in spite of the author's noble tendency, there were in his work pages that I had to skip, — not because they contained indecencies, there were none, but because I cannot bear scenes depicting the degradation of a human being, or moments of moral suffering, where the human heart is full of deadly fear. For, being sure of my own courage, of my strength, which enables me to endure long and unavoidable sufferings, it always seems to me that other people's afflictions are much heavier and more intolerable. That is a personal trait which I never could get rid of.

"Russians prefer works containing an idea, trying to develop it as far as possible, to make the reader understand and accept it. That is why I find a resemblance between 'A Man's World' and the writings of our favorite authors. Besides that, works of our avowed romanticists never contain scenes of seduction, scenes that are exotic or extraordinary, and for two reasons: 1. Our life, even the life of our great cities, is much less complex than that of American cities. 2. Our civilized public, and even our peasants, prefer works which lead us into regions of thought, of philosophy, of meditation, where one wishes to dwell without being interrupted by effects of a brutal or unbecoming kind. Our friend Arthur Bullard offers us his second book, 'Comrade Yetta,' which makes the continuation of a program of ideas and actions."

To Mrs. Barrows. November 30–December 13, 1912.

"My heart is full of you, for I am in distress thinking of your health. Why did you return from the sanitarium, where some months more would disfranchise you of your disease forever? What, am I more reasonable than you? I have never believed it. Think only of your husband, who watches over you day and night. His soul rejoices to see how much light is thrown on every one who has the happiness of knowing you."

To Miss Blackwell.   November 30–December 15, 1912.

"It is not true that the Socialists are opposed to culture and cultural work. It is absurd to affirm it. Yet I know that many people who understand the word 'culture' in a very narrow sense, as splendid and showy examples of different arts, believe it is premature to think about this before the things of vital necessity are obtained. Others say that, as despotism is forcibly holding back every effort to cultivate the country, one must apply one's strength to clear the way before entering upon it. But in your country, for instance, where no efforts are hindered or annulled, there is plenty of cultural work, and it is urgently necessary, for how can we expect to get the people ready to accept new forms of sociability, forms which demand a quite new and very accomplished conception of life and mutual relations, without preparing them for it? It is a great mistake to think that the human mind is ready to accept and to digest every new conception or idea, without having learned long in advance to understand it and to embody it.

"Culture, in its large sense, is a matter that involves in itself all the progress, with its functions, known from the beginning to the latest minutes of our existence. How can we allow ourselves to be deprived of this knowledge, which is the common treasure of mankind? How poor and naked our existence would be without those professions which give us the means of introducing into the minds and feelings, as well as the senses, of our brothers and sisters the best ideas, the best tastes, the best habits, best knowledge, and best sentiments! Are we not endeavoring to guarantee them all the means not only of conserving what has been acquired already, but of going forward with the improvement? This does not mean that we must forget the material side of the matter. It only means that, while establishing the material side on a durable foundation, we must by no means forget to arm the people with all the progress that history has made. Culture, so understood, is an inherent part of our activity and our endeavors."

To Miss Agnes E. Ryan.

"You are my weekly companion, too. I follow eagerly the progress of the *Woman's Journal;* it is the first thing I read after the mail is delivered. A great thing is the work of the suffragists; it is a big force to make the world better, and I am sure the women of all countries will improve the status of our planet's husbandry. Only we must not forget to do our best for the people who are now deprived of the possibility of enlarging the conditions of their welfare. I congratulate you on the fitness of your paper to maintain sympathy with all the most attractive sides of the general progress spread over all countries. China attracts my sympathy especially, and I am angry because the big governments are jealous of its success."

To Miss Dudley.   December 1-14, 1912.

"Helena! I am knocked down by the goodness of Wellesley College! I feel myself guilty, ungrateful. What can I do to show myself appreciative enough of such attention? I, who am ashamed even to write to persons who have no reason to be so indulgent as you are toward me. Nevertheless, I am very glad to get anything nice and new. For a long time, before it is sent or given away, I enjoy it myself, and so do all those who come to see me, and they are many. I am always proud to be able to show how good my friends are and how constant in their tenderness. Years and years coming and going away, times changing, and new cares and works overwhelming the busy heads and hearts — and yet the ties of friendship are strong, and do not yield to the temptations of the surrounding chaos of affairs, matters, feelings and duties, so multiplied and more and more complex. Oh! the American women contain a rich endowment of energy, of will, of sincerity and stability. Certainly I am proud, but I would not abuse, and take more than is due."

On the backs of three picture postcards, reproductions of pictures by famous Russian painters, Madame Breshkovsky wrote an explanation of each. The first shows a young man in student uniform, and a young woman, with smiling faces, stepping hand in hand into stormy surf. She writes:

"A student must wear a uniform, and many of our women students like to be 'fashionable.' The painter represents life as a sea. The young couple are ready to throw themselves into it, having faith in their strength and in the ideal they picture. Certainly only a part

of those radiant beings retain for long the thrillings of
their hearts, and most of them are lost in the depths of
common life, with its petty demands and cares. A
part of them become very superficial people, the boys
especially. Yet there are exceptions; we have had
them. I confess I do not like this genre, for I cannot
depend on people who are so light-hearted, so superficial. Profound natures make me happy."

The second shows a young peasant woman working
in the field with a horse. Madame Breshkovsky
says:

"Perhaps a young widow, perhaps the oldest of a
group of orphan children. She works hard, but she
will not desert her duty. When a girl, she will not
marry till all her brothers and sisters are conveniently
placed. She is a responsible being before God and her
community, and she will do all she ought, very seldom
complaining of her heavy fate. She is head of the house,
and all her pride and honor lie in performing the work
done by her late parents. Very often such girls remain
unmarried till the end, attached as they are to the welfare of the family. I am sure that if it were possible to
issue a call to the peasant women in order to have
nurses enough for the orphan children scattered through
the country, we should have plenty of 'mothers' ready
to bring up deserted families as tenderly and devotedly
as possible. I am sure it would be so with us, and no
doubt it would be so everywhere, for the woman soul
is the same."

The third card shows a young girl leaning against a
white birch tree in a thoughtful attitude. It is en-

titled "Fancies not to be fulfilled." Madame Bresh-kovsky says:

"Perhaps personal, perhaps altruistic fancies. We have many such types, but they are not quite Russian. It is a blend of Russian with some other blood. In England or America she would be a missionary. In Russia the intelligent people are not pious; they strive to be rational in the highest sense of the word. Yet to be so, one must be very strong and renounce one's own comfort; consequently those with less strong characters are vacillating, and muse too long on the path they ought to choose. I pity such girls much, for they are honest and sincere, and most of them remain unsatisfied all their lives. Even when they are married and have a family they feel as if they were guilty, as if they had thrown away some treasure that will never be found again. How happy are those who are sure of the way they have taken! This certainty makes one master of the world, which is only a stage, a beautiful one, for one's activity, and the object as well as the source of one's love."

To Lewis Herreshoff. (Undated)

"Your letter with the check reached me in safety, but I was embarrassed, not knowing what to do with it. We have no bank, no bankers in this wild country, and the money was so much needed before New Year's Day! I resolved to send the check to Irkutsk, where there is a branch of the Russian Asiatic Bank, asking them to return me the money by wire. So I did, and to my great pleasure, instead of 47 rubles I got 145 rubles. Some lady of my acquaintance learned the fact, and added the 100. I was so much surprised that I wired once more to know for sure, whether it was not a mistake. To my great joy it was not, and so your gift reached me in threefold size. Your promise to gratify me every year with $25 gives me great satisfaction, for I do not spend much for myself, and this sum will be my own. Thank you, Lewis, my friend, very good and chivalrous! You men cannot be otherwise in America, where you have such excellent women. I only wish the success that follows their energy may never make of them such business-like people as most of your men are. For nothing in the world is so lovable as a good heart, a sympathizing character. When a human creature sincerely smiles upon another, one feels one's self so well, more sure of one's safety. It is a horror to think that a human being can be a monster to his fellow creatures, a monster that is feared and hated. And yet there are so many educated Europeans who are pumping sweat and blood out of their neighbors' veins!

"I am deeply interested in the literary career of my friend Arthur Bullard, known by his pen name as Albert Edwards.

"As for the romances and novels that are so numerous in all the magazines which I get (and I get the best ones), they are tedious with scandals of every sort. We have among us also a lot of foolish writings, but they have their place apart; they are printed by the magazines destined for the street and for ignorant people. Our best magazines are careful in choosing the articles and novels to be put in. We do not prize so much art which does not contain any noble idea. Literature as well as painting, sculpture, music, and other arts must not only be perfectly performed, but must contain a meaning, or a majestic or noble idea, to be honored and admired.

"I am sure our nation is an enigma to all the rest. Having a sense of religion, of the holiness of human destiny, a love for all that is courageous and self-sacrificing, a taste for the beauty of earth and heaven — with all this our people endure a most miserable mode of life, always waiting for a miracle to get rid of it. We are not so lazy as the Italian lazzaroni, but we are slow, we contemplate instead of acting. It is our misfortune. Our peasants in Russia (not in Siberia) are like Diogenes; they can understand everything and reason about everything, and yet are capable of living like savages in cabins fit for cattle. . . .

"I could not continue yesterday, for there were 'boys' the whole evening. Some of them must have long talks with me, often on the subject of their mood, sadness, or longings that inhabit their minds and torment them. I am here like a priest, who must know all about his people, and have patience to hear all the details which my orphan boys have to confess. With me they are openhearted, being sure I love them and sympathize with all their griefs. Most of them are afraid to do anything wrong, for my sake; my severity as to principles is respected, and those who do not follow them as strictly as they ought are much embarrassed when they come to see me. I am not implacable, but I am sure that every man and woman must form the habit of careful self-control from their tender youth. And I am so much obliged to my parents for having taught me this duty."

To Miss Blackwell.   February 12–25, 1913.

"From my childhood I have never sympathized with the dualism of sentiments and devotion.   One may have a very complex character, one may admire the whole world and understand all the beauties contained in it; one may be happy to sympathize with every perfection of nature and art; and yet one must have along with all these riches an aim, a God, a virtue, or a principle, that will stand above all the rest.   And while enjoying the luxury of life, one must be ready at every moment to perform one's duty towards the aim that stands over all.   That is my ideal of a human being; and I must add that the more superior the aim chosen to stand highest is to other aims or ends of life, the more valuable is the person who has chosen it.

"My health is much better this winter, which seems to have no end.   All is right with me except my poor heart, which is always thrilling with sorrow for my starving boys, with no hopes for a better future for them; for we expect this summer more and more people who have served their terms in the hard labor prisons. What can we do?   One must endure the world's pain, and be satisfied to be able to do it."

To Arthur Bullard, with a photograph.   February
14–27.

"Here I am in my American overcoat, sitting at my large table, and sewing a shirt for one of our poor boys. Behind is a commode with my various possessions. My armchair being upholstered with light-colored stuff, I put my black skirt over the back of it, in order to have my white hair stand out from the furniture. And while sitting at my little work, I listen to the thoughts and fancies of my young friend, Arthur Bullard, as he creates the world of man's and woman's life, trying to bring them out of old traditions and corrupted morals, to enter a more human, more brotherly-constructed mode of life. It makes me very happy to see such a majestic commonwealth as the American States awakening to a more righteous and ethical life. This effort will stir the energy of other countries, not so quick to attain the end put before them. I bless you for doing your best for your people, for the growing youth, that before all must be human toward every one who needs care and bounty. Too selfish, too narrow is the human world, and cowardly subjugated to all the prejudices of mean spirits. Holding stiffly to all these prejudices, one cannot remain just toward the mass of the people that is struggling for the first necessities of life. Severe we ought to be towards ourselves and other intelligent and well-to-do individuals, but all the rest, all who are deprived of mental and material welfare, are to be helped only to come over the abyss ready to swallow them at every moment."

To Effie Danforth McAfee. March 15–28, 1913.

"Till now there has not been a mail that has not brought me something from America. This has not only made me a devoted friend of the United States, but has made me feel like a relation, especially to the American women, whom I praise as a beautiful species of the human race. Their energy and cleverness are equalled only by the women of Finland, who amazed me by their fitness for all that is worthy to be done.

That little country is a wonder of hard work and stability of character. The women there are the best part of the population.

"My opinion is that everywhere on earth the women are more exquisite creatures and much less corrupted than the men. But the difference between the two sexes is not the same in every country. I think, so far as I see, that all the northern countries have a most high contingent of women, because they have more time and chance to improve their minds, while the men are so busy with the material side of life. But in Russia, for instance, the opportunity to study and to perfect one's self is very hard for both sexes. Consequently the boys and girls are on an equal level of education, and so understand each other quite well. We should not have a 'woman question,' for the women would not ask but take their rights as a matter of course. Now every one is a slave, then everybody would be free."

To Miss Blackwell. March 15–28, 1913.

"My own experience seems to me a small matter compared with the sufferings of others, perhaps because of my strong constitution of body and spirit. And perhaps it has not happened to me to endure such tortures as were the case with others. Now, this very year, we have so many diseases, insanities and suicides, that sometimes my strong soul is going mad. I feel as if I were thrown into hell, where I cannot find an issue.

"In the first place, the longer the exiles remain in such wicked conditions, the less strength they have to resist them. Secondly, during the last two years we have had a lot of boys who were sent out from the prisons where they had finished their terms at hard labor. The conditions in these prisons are so atrocious that in three or four years a young, strong man becomes an invalid for life, and very often is deprived of his mental capacities. If he is not tortured himself, he becomes there a daily and nightly witness of the tortures of his comrades, who are beaten, starved, thrown into dungeons and humiliated. The more clever, the more energetic are sure to spend some years in these special prisons, and we receive them bruised, destroyed by consumption, and very often insane.

"And here, in Siberia, matters are going worse. Before the festivities took place, we were warned that after the 'Manifesto' new severities would be introduced. But they were enforced everywhere, in Russia and here, even before, and an innumerable quantity of people are arrested everywhere and sent into the more remote places. All this is horrible, but it is shameful too, for such a great country ought not to endure such calamities. Nobody can picture to himself all the horrors, all the miseries, all the disgraces the people endure. There, above, it cannot be seen, for the gentlefolk and bureaucrats are very nice towards free people. But all who are not 'gentle,' all who are captive, see well the underside of life, and cannot be happy. I beg your pardon for such an ugly letter."

To Miss Blackwell. March 30–April 2, 1913.

"Yes, all is well for some time, except the news about Arthur. In a hospital! Oh, dear and poor boy! What a pity for such a noble spirit! I am not an admirer of myself, for instance, but, being sure of my sincerity and good will, which make me ready to serve my neighbor, I wish to live as long as my mental capacities render me able to be of use.   There is not yet a very large lot of strong-minded and good-hearted people on our earth; therefore we must spare them, and do our utmost to retain their spirits with us longer and longer.

"Last night I was awakened by a terrible headache, which continued till now, 4 P.M. At first I could not explain my misfortune, but when I saw through the window a thick snow falling, I understood directly. Since I made acquaintance with prisons, my blood has not been so thick and so red, and it cannot resist the pressure of a condensed atmosphere, as it could before my imprisonment, when I was a very Cossack in strength and health.   But now that the heaven is not so heavy, I feel better, and can continue my affairs. It is the same with all my sorrows.   It is very hard to encounter each of the new ones.   But when you put your mind to action, to the search how to do your best, you have no time to spend on weeping, and you feel better, seeing that your efforts are not quite in vain.

"I am angry with myself for having written you my last letter, in which I deplored the horrors of the life of our exiles.   We must be accustomed to it, and none of us could expect a better lot.   And so you can be tranquil on my account, my shoulders being ready to bear every load.

" April 2–15, 1913.

"I find that, if my life had passed without the experiences I have had, it would be very poor and short-sighted.   Now, as the hard and wicked sides of life are familiar to me, I can judge what my people suffer, what every person in such or such a position suffers, and this makes me more indulgent, and better able to divine the sufferings of others, their inner life and feelings. Sometimes when I feel impatient with the crowd of visitors, I say to myself: 'For shame, old woman! You do not find it easy to bear the presence of good, unlucky people, while these people have to bear during the best part of their lives the rudest and most severe experiences that a black soul can imagine.' This thought makes me gentle and patient.

"Dear friend, it is vain for Aunt Isabel to believe in the possibility of some day seeing me at liberty. We must expect nothing good from a set of people who manufacture only dishonor for their country."

George Lazareff to Miss Blackwell. Clarens, Switzerland, March 31, 1913.

"Now the amnesty[1] has been proclaimed. It was not for the political offenders, but only for some criminal bureaucrats, who had robbed the State treasury. Even the exiles banished by administrative order have not been released. On the contrary, the persecutions have been intensified."

Mrs. Olive T. Dargan's book of plays, "Lords and Lovers", including her Russian play "The Shepherd", had been sent to Madame Breshkovsky by Miss Alice Lewissohn.

To Miss Blackwell. June 3–16, 1913.

"I have received a book containing three dramas, one of which aims to represent some types of our last

---

[1] It had been announced that the three hundredth anniversary of the Romanoff dynasty would be celebrated by granting an amnesty to many prisoners.

revolution, to give a glimpse of this original event. But one sees at once that the author is not acquainted with the real life of the people she speaks of, and all the entourage is taken from what she knows and sees in other countries. Nevertheless I am very glad to have this piece, for the foundation, the reasons for the troubles, are represented as they are in reality, truly."

To Mrs. Barrows. June 20–July 1, 1913.

"Your book, 'A Sunny Life,' is one of the everlasting writings. I mean it will be good always. It is of the same kind as the books that tell us about the lives of men like St. Francis of Assisi. Such books are not merely portraits of beautiful characters, but they are also historic documents of great value. As in a mirror one sees the moral capacities of the epoch described, and can judge the path and the progress toward the perfection of human nature. A thousand years will pass, and the book will be read with as much interest as now; perhaps with even more, for it gives a picture of moral welfare, of the happiness of a whole family, due only to its own perfection."

On a picture card. To June Barrows Mussey.

"How do you do, my dear grandson? This pretty girl wants to make acquaintance with you, and to show you the little dogs she is nursing with such pleasure. It is good that she loves every living thing, but you must remember to tell her that the largest share of our love and attention belongs to human beings. Children, women, and men, as having a more elevated spirit, must be attended, in order that they may become yet better, quite reasonable."

To Miss Blackwell.   July 31–August 13, 1913.

"What unexpected news! You were dangerously ill. You were operated on! Our dear Sophie will write me about your health. What does it mean, so many diseases? And I have been well all this time, notwithstanding the wet weather we have had this month. My lodging was undergoing repairs for more than two weeks. I spent them in a very disgusting cabin, and yet my health did not suffer. Now again I am comfortable in my palace, which is clean, bright and warm: excellent, indeed! So many pictures around, from America and Switzerland; many books, a gramophone and a sewing machine. My wardrobe is full, my dinners always good. And, what is most appreciated by me, I have some money to divide with my poor comrades."

(Madame Breshkovsky was provided by friends in Europe and America with a small fund with which to help the other exiles, to buy tools for them, etc.)

To Miss Dudley.   August 12–25, 1913.

"One good soul wrote me you are well and look quite flourishing and shining. God bless you! I can say the same of myself — blossoming!

"I rejoice that you were pleased with 'A Man's World.' I am even afraid I shall not be as well pleased with 'Comrade Yetta.' There was a character that questioned and searched, with all the earnestness of a noble soul. Here we shall have perhaps a character formed from the beginning of the world, I mean an integral force, which never doubted, never relinquished, was never weak. There are those diamonds amidst

mankind. I admire them; they are like stars to show
us our way, and to assure us of the possibility of such
perfection on earth; their march is beautiful and brilliant, their brow is serene and majestic, they never
stoop their heads, and the heads of others bow before
them. And yet such splendid characters are a result
of the work (historic work), which we cannot pursue nor
analyze; they are something ready, finished, not to be
studied and dissected. When we see such perfection
we can only guess, and we may mistake, not knowing
the sources of such an apparition. Another thing, —
when our attention is attracted to the process itself of
the construction of the psychology of a soul, it struggles
through life and is obliged to gain bit by bit the ground
where it resolves to stand, for which it resolves to fight.
I have seen many young people who envied characters
free from weaknesses and defects; they find it very
hard to struggle against the blamable habits inherited
or acquired; they would prefer to feel themselves
without failure. When young I wished it too, for I
was very much ashamed of my weaknesses, felt unhappy after every fault I committed. Now I prefer
characters that have had to do with many temptations
during their youth, and come out victors from a serious
struggle, fortified, with a strong will and understanding
of their own capacities and ability, and of human nature
in its consistence nowadays. Such people become more
exacting towards themselves and more indulgent
towards others, for they know how difficult it is to
overcome the passions implanted by nature in our being
before we are acquainted with it. The inheritance of
different weaknesses, as well as the undesired habits
acquired by an education full of prejudices, give us a

heavy task to clean ourselves all our life long, and, once diligent enough to fulfill this task, consciously, the work we put in makes us vigilant, develops our energy and enlarges our mind infinitely. The earnest desire to be as good as possible is a stimulant which influences the development of all our best qualities and capacities. The older we are, the wiser. And we do not cease to love the world that has given us the great happiness of mounting higher and higher.

"How charming it is that behind every one of my friends in America, there is another friend watching over my safety, and always alert to be there when needed! Sophie Siebker, Agnes E. Ryan, Miss Scudder, Ellen Starr, our dear Lillian, and many good souls are ready to inform me about what concerns my three angels before all, and about all that is so dear to me in your beautiful country. I am so happy as to see and to learn the best sides of American life, for I have to do with the best people, the best papers, and best magazines. I see from my distance so many splendid pleiades or sets of women and men that seem devoted exclusively to the welfare of the great problems of human life. The questions of ethics and eugenics are making great progress, and spirited minds are working with enthusiasm to forward them quickly, in their eagerness to see the world more and more conscious of the divine gifts with which nature has endowed it. Yes, it seems strange when we compare high-minded with low-thinking people. All the great questions are so simple to solve if one has passed one's time in studying about them, in thinking of them. And yet there are millions to whom the same questions are quite strange, a terra incognita, not worthy of belief.

"And now, if we see and know only the best part of humanity, the smallest part, we do not know the whole reality, and may be cheated in our ignorance. But also if we remain only with the other, the majority, made up of the ignorant and low-minded, we become pessimistic, and our energy in fighting the wilderness and the darkness is greatly diminished.

"Enclosed are two photos showing my *gemüsegarten* (cabbages, potatoes, etc.). Here I am with my two comrades (cultivators), and the two figures with little geese are the owners of the domain where my friends lodge, and where I have rented some beds for my plantings. They wished eagerly to be photographed in our company. Every one says I am not so old as the photos make me look. Perhaps it is because somehow in speaking and smiling one always seems younger and lively. But when alone and quiet, I must look as old as I do here, though my heart remains always young."

To Miss Blackwell. August 26–September 8, 1913.

"I feel so constrained when I write in English! This feeling of bashfulness has its root in the education I received from my childhood. My mother was never tired of repeating, 'Do well everything that you do. Never allow yourself to be inexact and negligent.' It was considered a shame to make mistakes when writing or speaking any language, and I feel so to this day. This has kept me from writing to so warm a friend as Arthur Bullard. I love him as well as the best boys of my own country, and God knows how much I love them, how proud I am of them.

"Aunt Isabel's illness kept me silent for a long time.

It was as if I spread my ears to catch the sounds of her respiration and the knocking of her heart. I watched her sleep; and, anxious to understand her thoughts, I examined with my imagination all her surroundings, running from one object to another, and from Mabel to Henry and little June. I feared the doctors, so serious and grave, and could never wholly understand their intentions. I said to myself: 'They have deprived our Isabel of all her teeth; what will they do next?' Now that I hear she is getting better, I do not suspect the great savants, but before that, I did not love them.

"Somebody has sent me 'The New Freedom,' by your President Wilson. Very interesting."

To Miss Blackwell. September 9–22, 1913.

"'Miss Caroline I. Reilly is spending a month with Miss Alice Stone Blackwell at her summer cottage at Chilmark, Mass.' This news has made me a sincere friend of the very noble Miss Caroline, whose hands I kiss; but I cannot conceal that I was jealous of her pleasure in remaining with you for so long a time. I am only afraid that my presence would be a burden, for we Russians are too expansive. I mean we show too often and too much caresses and tenderness, to which your people are not accustomed. It is very hard for me to refrain from pouring out my feelings towards one whom I love much. Nevertheless I understand how tired the person may feel, and object to everlasting tenderness.

"The same issue (No. 32) brought your articles. Your strong, experienced hand and mind are here like a hammer that strikes every question at its due place.

"All the money I get from your country is an enormous profit to us all. Certainly, in my position the comfort you have guaranteed is of great value to me; but all this is little compared with the value of the friendship, the moral support that my friends in America have granted me. Your love and esteem is a force which can never fail, which is with me always, and everywhere, even in my tomb. Unknown as I am in your country, I feel as if I were one of its members, never to be rejected or cast out.

"September 12–25.

"Soon I shall write to Ellen Starr about your President's book. I was agreeably surprised in reading it: but I am not sure how much will be done.

"My beloved daughter, take patiently all the kisses I send you, and pardon my obstinacy."

To Ellen Starr. September 26, 1913.

"Your face is as fresh as ever in my memory. If we met to-day we should perhaps find each other somewhat changed outwardly, but our spiritual state remains always the same, and we should know each other at once. I am sure our friendship would be even more familiar, because the long years of separation have given us ample proofs of the stability of our feelings and of our moral tastes. Yes, dear friend, you are a soul that I do not fear to approach, having learned in the course of years that the tendency toward everything beautiful and pure is the very essence of your noble heart.

"I look in vain for your name among the illustrious names of your American women; it is not there, nor that of Helena Dudley, that incomparable saint, always kneeling at the feet of her God of mercy. Once Helena was mentioned as about to take charge of a newly-established settlement outside of Boston. Alice's name is always there (nolens volens) as editor of her paper, which really constitutes an epoch in itself in the history of the woman movement of the whole world. Well, you three virgins who have devoted yourselves to serving the world without asking anything of it, without reaping any reward from it — you may remain unknown to the world, loved and appreciated only by those who know you personally, who have learned to cherish the memory of your characters, able to respond to the cries of those who are suffering far away from you. That is beautiful, it is immortal; but it does not always meet with its reward in this world. Nevertheless it is well to remain so to the end of our days, for nothing is so precious as a conscience sure of itself and tranquil as to the choice of the road that it has preferred to all others. The only thing that grieves me is the loss of persons who are the ornament of our race.

"I have just finished Woodrow Wilson's book, 'The New Freedom.' I am enchanted with it. He has exceptional talent as a speaker, and as a writer who knows how to set forth his thought as clearly as he carries it in his head. *Jamais de quiproquo, jamais de malentendu, et avec ça, logique et consequent tout le long du traité.* If that man set out from the standpoint of Socialism, he would be magnificent in his arguments, and his nation would be grateful to him throughout its whole history; for a sound idea, explained by so fine a talent, remains in the people's minds forever, even if at first it is not accepted in its entirety.

"At all events, if we take literally all the aspirations expressed by your present President, he would make a remarkable reformer if he should try with sincerity to make over a constitution which no longer harmonizes with the rights and the prosperity of the people whose ruler he is.

"Many, many of my old friends and comrades have been passing away of late years. I look upon myself as an old tree among a crowd of youths, and I try to be understood by my juniors, and to be indulgent towards them.

"I feel strong till now, but seeing how quickly my old friends are carried off by illness and death, I think sometimes everything is possible; one good cold might easily make an end of the matter.

"I have on my table one little picture representing Cornelia de Bey, 'the most active brain in Chicago,' as one magazine says. I remember so well this noble Hollandaise, who captured me at first sight. I passed a night at her house, and saw how much she has to do. There was with her a teacher, a different type, but very accomplished too. Cornelia is a figure distinguished from top to foot. I like her so dearly. Is she well now? The portrait of Miss Addams shows her much older, and I wonder how she can suffice to fulfill such a lot of different matters, to be everywhere at once. Active like an American; always ready for the need. Forgive me for my silence, and for my many mistakes. You might fancy me ungrateful from the fewness of my letters; yet my heart is full of thankfulness. Give my good wishes to all who will accept them."

To Miss Wald.   September 20, 1913.

"The snow already covers the mountainous borders of the superb Lena, and frost will soon fill the waters with masses of ice, which will interrupt all communications, leaving us isolated on our little island, entirely engulfed by cold, ill treated by the north wind.

"It is strange! Every time that I am asked to speak about myself, I am always confused, and find nothing to say. Very likely, if I had paid more attention to the outward circumstances of my life, there would be enough to talk about, that would fill more than a book. But, ever since my childhood, I have been in the habit of creating a spiritual life, an interior world, which corresponded better with my spiritual tastes. This imaginary world has had the upper hand over the real world in its details, over all that is transient.

"The aim of our existence, the perfecting of human nature, has always been present in my vision, in my mind. The route, the direction that we ought to take, in order to approach our ideal, was for me a problem, the solution of which absorbed the efforts of my entire life. I was implacable to myself for my weaknesses, knowing that to serve a divine cause, we must be at least honest in all things; we must sincerely love the object of our devotion, — that is to say, in this case, humanity.

"These meditations, this interior spiritual work, and a strong imagination, which always carried me far beyond the present, permitting me to inhabit the most longed-for regions, all combined to attract but very little of my attention to daily circumstances. With-

out doubt I have had suffering in my life, but I have
had moments of joy, even of happiness. It is also
true that the struggle with my failings, with my habits
engrafted by a worldly education, has cost me more or
less dear. The misery of those near to me has torn
my heart to the extreme. In a word, my life has
passed in the same way as a bark thrown on the mercy
of a sea often stormy. But, as the ideal was always
there, present in my heart and in my mind, it guided
me in my course, it absorbed me to such a degree that
I did not feel, in their fulness, the influence of passing
events. The duty to serve the divine cause of humanity in its entirety, that of my people in particular,
has been the law of my life — the supreme law, whose
voice quelled my passions, my desires, my weaknesses.

"This duty, cultivated from infancy by religious
sentiment, then fortified in its certitude by attentive
analysis of life in its entirety, formed the conviction
that there is nothing in the world so profitable for
certain happiness as to serve an impeccable cause, a
cause the noblest, the highest among all known to the
mind of man.

"For it is only in serving the cause that we inevi-
tably perfect ourselves, since it demands the most
uplifting transport of our souls; and that makes us
happy, our conscience being tranquil, our creative
spirit being sure of victory.

"I am sure that our Alice, as well as Aunt Isabel,
remembers how difficult it was for me to speak about
myself, when that was exacted of me. Since I live in
my thoughts more than by emotion, it is my thoughts
which I have to confess more than the facts of my life.
These facts, to tell the truth, are confused enough in

my memory, and often I should not be able to relate them in all their details. Also, in conversing with those who care to listen to me, I feel that I am monotonous, for it is always my ideals and my abstract observations that I want to communicate to my listeners. I have studied a great deal in order to understand even ever so little of the origin of the human soul, in order to understand more or less its complexity of today.

"There lies my only strength, so to speak, and I continue my study, knowing how complex my object of study is, and what an innumerable quantity of different combinations, of types, have been formed during the long history of the laboratory where is prepared the supreme fusion called the human soul.

"Respect for the individual of the human species, and adoration of the intellectual treasure of this individual, ought to form the centre of all knowledge, of all ideals. It is only in venerating the human being as the most beautiful creation of the world; it is only in understanding the beauty and the indestructible grandeur of an intelligence illuminated by love and knowledge, that the education of the young generation will bring the desired fruits.

"To be better understood, my dear Lillian, I turn to comparison: Suppose any one had devoted his whole life with enthusiasm to a science, which captivated all his energy, all his faculties; certainly he would remain indifferent (cold) to the details of his own existence, having his mind fixed on the object of his studies. A subject so interesting, so dear to me that I could scarcely ever detach my own self from the existence of humanity in its entirety, or from that of my people in particular — did I have time or de-

sire to stop and think about myself, or the particular-
ities of my personal life? All seem to me transient,
insignificant, in view of the happiness which, sooner
or later, must be the fate of the human world. I
myself have never experienced any disillusionment,
for, having in view the history of the past and the
present of our race, taking into consideration the
capacity of my soul to love without ceasing, and to
wish to go on instructing, I understand that the tendency of our nature towards good is a gift inseparable
from the character of man, and that all progress depends only upon seeing clearly, acquired by experience and knowledge. That which is dear to me above
all is that, notwithstanding my habit of living rather
in an abstract world, in the regions of my imagination,
I have in no way lost the ardor of my love for those
near me, and that all their misfortunes touch me much
more profoundly than my own. Probably I owe this
invaluable gift as much to my natural capacity as to
the continual practice of interesting myself in the fate
of those by whom I am surrounded.

"Lillian, my friend! I hope to be understood by
you, seeing that you pass your life in the same way that
I pass mine. It is not your personal happiness which
has been the object of your care, and if any one asked
you what your past has been, you would have to
reply: 'I worked for the happiness of others, and by
that means I forged my own.'"

To June Barrows Mussey. On picture card.
November 4, 1913.

"I know you are out of doors every day, like the
little girl here, who is enjoying herself with her parents

in a charming nook of a Russian forest. But I fear the cold, and my pelisse is heavy, so I cannot walk long or far. Sitting in my room I read many American papers and magazines, and then I think of our dearest Nonna. I have sent her book to a place where there are hundreds of our people that will profit by studying it."

November 17–30, 1913.

"She (Mrs. Barrows) was among us like an angel; and so she has passed away without trouble, never abusing her greatness of mind and feelings towards the masses that surrounded her with all their imperfections and meanness. She was above the world she inhabited, and, understanding the weakness which is yet familiar to the population of the earth, not only was she indulgent to it, but she worked her life long to improve, to comfort, to uplift. And she was beloved for her golden heart, for her friendship, for her delicate attention to the needs of each separate person. She was fit to be a mother, a wife, a sister, a friend; she never wished to be a benefactress, to impose, to be looked upon as an imperative being, that ought to be a model to be praised and marveled at. She was a good and wise spirit, that came to us to show how one can live and die, always ready to help and to improve. And now that people say she is gone, I see a blue star watching over our sorrowful heads, and pouring upon us such a soft and delightful light that we do not perceive the sadness and the darkness that surround us, for our hearts aspire to realize the light everywhere, to fill every heart with it. This desire makes us better and stronger, and this interior force develops the light of our own hearts, which in its turn continues the work begun by Isabel C. Barrows, and will never fail to do so, for the source of that light was and remains inexhaustible.

"A person who is not devoid of sense can never become a pessimist or a sceptic, after being acquainted with such a soul."

To Miss Blackwell.   November 20, 1913.

"It is wonderful and beautiful, such a friendship as ours.   Two souls found each other, and were bound by a sympathy that nothing can shake or disturb. What happiness to be sure of a treasure that is immortal!"

CHAPTER XVI

EAGER to resume her work for the revolution, and urged by her colleagues to rejoin them, Madame Breshkovsky made a daring attempt to escape, which very nearly succeeded.

George Lazareff to Miss Blackwell.   December 14, 1913

Clarens, Switzerland.

"Baboushka is captured!

"The account printed in all the Russian newspapers says she was accustomed to take her dinner daily at the house of her comrade exile Vladimiroff. Six spies, two at a time, regularly followed her to and fro. Across the road from her house a sentry-box had been built for the two spies who kept their eyes upon it day and night. On November 18 (Old Style) or December 1, she went out as usual to Vladimiroff's to dinner. As usual, the spies followed her. But in the evening one of the exiles, Andreeff, dressed in her clothes, came back to her house in company with some friends, followed by the spies. The latter did not perceive the trick. Meanwhile Baboushka had taken horses that were ready, and started away. For some days the spies were not disturbed, though she did not go out. Her dinner was sent regularly to her room,

as had happened before when she was not well. Every
night the light was shining as usual.[1]

"On November 21 (December 7) it was discovered
that she had fled. To escape she would have had to
get seven or eight days' start, in order to reach Irkutsk
on horseback (over 1000 kilometers). Madness followed. Telegrams were sent to the Governor of
Irkutsk, to the Minister of the Interior at St. Petersburg. The order was given to catch her at all costs.
One thousand rubles was the reward.

"November 23 (December 6) the Governor of Irkutsk with eight gendarmes and fifty policemen started
to meet her and intercept her on the way. And, to
everybody's astonishment, they met her only seven
miles from Irkutsk! How it was possible I cannot
understand. In two hours more she would have
reached a safe shelter in Irkutsk. The soldiers met a
coach with a passenger, who was a well-dressed gentleman. Unfortunately, it was discovered that this
gentleman was Baboushka, who was immediately
arrested and conveyed to the Irkutsk prison.

"It is a great blow to all her friends. But her
anxiety, I know, is not for herself, but for others.
She bade me in advance do my utmost to console you
and all her friends if the attempt was unsuccessful.

"I think the failure was due to some want of foresight. November 23 (the very day of her arrest) is
her birthday, and usually she received by post some
presents which required her personal receipt. Reg-
istered letters and parcels in such a remote place
would arrive before and after her birthday. She knew
all this. And I believe she found the circumstances
especially favorable if she determined to disregard it."

[1] See Appendix.

To her son Nicholas.   Central Prison, Irkutsk, Siberia.
November 30–December 12, 1913.

"My dear Kola : I write you from the Irkutsk prison, having been arrested on my way to this city.   The conditions of my life compelled me to leave the town without permission, and about my future fate I know nothing.   I have written my lawyer Prince Eristoff (of St. Petersburg) all the particulars of this affair.   I do not know whether I shall be allowed to receive an answer.

"But, as I know all my friends are anxious about my health, I ask you, my dear, to let them know that I am quite well, and for the rest everything is all right. I have everything necessary, and have money enough in hand.

"I have begun to read again, but I am sorry I have not so large a choice of reading matter as I had before. I kiss and bless you all.

"Your Mamma, Catherine Breshkovsky."

To Miss Blackwell.   January 13–26, 1914.

"I have been notified that I must not send or receive any letters in English, because none of the police here can read that language.   So I will try to write you in French to tell you that my health is still the same, and that neither you nor my other friends need have any fears for me.

"During my last months at Kirensk, my life was as disagreeable as it is here, so I am not suffering just now any more than I did there."

For this attempt to escape, she was kept in solitary confinement at Irkutsk for about two years, and then banished to the far north.

Her letters from Irkutsk prison continue cheerful.

To Ellen Starr, April 15–28, 1914.

"There is nothing more beautiful than to be trusted by our neighbors, to know that nothing can change the relations established between them and us. With this certainty, one feels strong, rich, superior to every misfortune.

"I look upon our life as a long journey, full of obstacles and difficulties of every kind. The traveler is always subject to the risk that he may not reach in his life-time the sacred mountain which he has chosen for his goal. But when once he is sure of his choice, and of the approval of those whom he respects, he marches on till his last breath, without growing discouraged. Beautiful Dame History, who accepts us as her companions, does not show us the general perspective in detail; all we can ask of her is that the direction shall be true for the whole time during which the life of humanity is to last."

Madame Breshkovsky once said to me, "My life has been like a long journey. If an opportunity of personal happiness came to me, I took it only as I might pick a flower by the way, or eat a bonbon."

To George Lazareff. May 12–25, 1914.

"May has come to Irkutsk, too. The Lena River is free from ice. I feel that the boats for the transportation of the exiles are ready for their work. I expect any minute to hear: 'Be ready! get up!' And, as before starting for the other world, I want to say: 'Good bye! good bye!' to all my friends, to all my dearest: 'Till a new place!' I do not fear the coming journey. Lately the good people in Irkutsk and in

Russia have nourished me abundantly, so as to make me gain not only in strength but in fat also. The cold winds of the Lena River do not frighten me any more. I have cakes, sweets of every kind; bird's milk alone is lacking. But I hope to get that when I reach the fabulous 'Isle of Bouyan, that lies in the Ocean' [expression from a Russian tale]. Oh, there are many birds there, the penguins and others! I hope to renew all my correspondence with my friends. Be sure that from every possible 'Isle of Bouyan' on the coming journey I shall try to write you. How glad I am! How many cakes I have! I am sorry I cannot treat you all. Do not forget me. The only food I need is good spirit.

> "Yours forever, Kitty."

A series of postcards brought loving messages to her friends, and said that she kept well. She spoke of receiving "a shower of cards" from America. Mr. Lazareff reported that she often wrote letters to him in Russian verses, and that he wondered at her talent.

To Miss Blackwell. June 8, 1914.

"Tulips, daffodils and other spring flowers rejoice my solitude and carry my thoughts to you. I shall be forced to spend the coming year alone, as I have the past six months. The lack of human society is hard for me to bear, certainly, but perhaps my health will not suffer from it as much as my spirits.

"Mabel has done me a great service in sending me the Book of Hymns. I am copying them out in order not to forget the English language, and I am studying them in order to see better how deeply the human heart is penetrated with ideal sentiments.

"I think that poetry, history, and even a magazine (of last year) might be sent to me in English."

May 13–26, 1914.

"In a few days the first party of convicts will start for the north. Whether I am to go with it or not they do not tell me. The summer is short here, but it rejuvenates me all the same, and if I can spend it in the open air, I shall be ready to meet the winter, however severe."

August 4–17, 1914.

"Remember me to all our mutual friends. Tell them I am bearing my hard lot bravely, and that if my physical strength should some day forsake me, it will not be the fault of my soul, which remains always calm, accustomed as it is to be surprised at nothing."

September 17–30, 1914.

"I am reading with great pleasure Dickens's 'A Child's History of England,' a gift from over the sea, sent in such stormy weather!

"Words freeze on the lips, the imagination refuses to picture the excesses with which the history of our days is filled. Without being resigned, one can only stand open-mouthed, as if struck by thunder. Nevertheless, in spite of all the countless misfortunes that accompany universal war, my heart, all bruised though it is, does not foresee a bad end for humanity. I have great hope that the minds as well as the hearts of our world will be purified and enlightened, after passing through such sinister trials.

"Already for many years the wisest and noblest voices have declared against all wars between the nations, and have foretold that militarism, when it has attained its highest point, must end by annihilating itself. And the sentiment of indignation which is invading all minds against the insolence of Germany proves that the people are for culture and not for destruction. The evil is horrible, for its depth as well as its intensity; but better days will come.

"All these years we have been losing the noblest hearts. Felix [Volkhovsky] is no more; brother Egor [Lazareff] feels weak, wearied with crushing toil, which has been his lot all his life. I feel well, despite the bars; and when weather permits, I go out for a few minutes to take the air and get the numbness out of my feet.

"I have just read 'De Profundis,' by Oscar Wilde; and what an immense difference I find between his psychology and mine! How much to be pitied are people who have never known the solidarity of human hearts and souls!

"I need postcards for children, and nobody sends me any. Into my letters to grown people I often slip pictures, which delight the little ones.

"In eight months I expect to be out of prison."

November 5–18, 1914.

"My health does not grow worse, and I believe that I shall get through the winter fairly well. I am becoming more and more prudent, for I would not for anything in the world disappoint my friends' hopes of seeing me safe and sound next spring.

"I often transport myself to Hull House, to greet its residents. The face of each of them lives in my remembrance. I must tell you that literature never leaves so strong an impression upon me as human presences; and I have never in my life quoted a phrase from any writer, while the words, the expressions, and the actions of human beings imprint themselves so deeply on my mind that they remain engraved there forever. It is because humanity is my passion; and the women are my hope of seeing it some day perfected.

"This winter I have reading matter enough, which ensures me against ennui, the more as the prisoners are allowed to read the cablegrams about the war, which, in turn, give rise to thought and meditation on many subjects."

To Miss Dudley.   January 17–30, 1915.

"Oh, how fortunate one is to have friends! There is a Russian proverb (very old) which says: 'Don't have a hundred rubles, but have a hundred friends.' In Russian it is in rhyme. That was said in times when rubles were very rare, and every ruble was considered a fortune. Now friends are looked upon as an invaluable gift, for each of them takes the place of thousands of rubles for an intelligent being. I always realize the truth of this proverb, for, having nothing of my own, I am provided with all necessities, even with luxuries. What would have become of me without all these kindnesses that the good Lord sends me!

"In four months I think I shall be sent to the north surely.

"Arthur Bullard is doubly close to me for having seen Russia, the Russian peasant, and for having carried away with him a souvenir which will make him always a friend of our country, entirely disorganized though it may be. I do not like to assure the world of the strength inherent in our people; it ought to be proved before speaking of it; but for myself, I believe in it with all the fervor of a soul that feels itself close to the soul of its people. Already the last ten years show the gigantic progress that is being made in the very entrails of our country. May the good God bless us all! And He will do it, since our spirit aspires to the good of all."

To Miss Blackwell. January 17–30, 1915.

"The victory (of woman suffrage) in Nevada and Montana is another proof of what well-directed energy can do; and it is for you, my daughter, to rejoice in it with pride — you who have followed so perfectly the course begun by your mother, who by her whole life proved the worth of a woman at the height of moral power. Honor to the American woman, since she leads her neighbors to the regions of a pure and noble life! Very certainly, the women of other countries will not delay to follow her, and the world will be rid of these horrible cataclysms, which destroy in a moment all that humanity has worked at for centuries.

"Brother George writes me long letters full of painful interest; but I feel that nothing can turn aside the movement of history toward a beautiful summer day. Is it not so?

"I want for nothing; my friends are untiringly kind, and I have ended by being ashamed of all the delicacies with which they surround me.

"The American postcards for children are often very comical. They furnish me themes for fables in verse which I compose for the little ones, and which make me laugh myself."

To Miss Blackwell.   March 10, 1915.

"I have 'Pioneer Work for Women', by Doctor Elizabeth Blackwell. I have read a few pages, and like it so much that I am saving it to read in case I should be sent into distant and solitary exile.

"I am suffering from the cold, and find it hard to breathe, but I hope to regain strength when out of prison."

George Lazareff to Miss Blackwell.   March 18, 1915.

"I have just received a long letter from Baboushka. She has entered upon her seventy-second year. She says she has decided to make a 'truck' with the Parcæ (the Fates). She has determined to throw off the seventy years of her life, and to begin her new era with her seventy years' jubilee. She is now to be about two years old. She says that perhaps the Fates will not perceive this 'truck', and will continue to spin her thread of life."

To Miss Blackwell.   April 2–15, 1915.

"The news that Miss Katherine B. Davis has been appointed superintendent of prisons is a great piece of good fortune in my eyes. It is high time that women should begin to have charge of the institutions that regulate the lives and fates of so many unfortunates. All the educational establishments for young people ought to be confided to them also.

"I am glad that alcohol has been suppressed in Russia, and I wish it may remain so forever. The war is going to open people's eyes to many defects, and this will be a stimulus to the population, and will compel it to regulate its living conditions better."

To Miss Blackwell. May 3, 1915.

"To-day I got the letter in which you speak of some day having the story of my life. Dear child, I tell you seriously that I do not know my own history. I have not felt it. It was always my soul that was in action, and the direction taken by it from my childhood has never changed, so that its history would be monotonous. The details of my material life interested me so little that I do not remember them clearly, and every time that it happens to me to read the memoirs of my old comrades, I am always surprised at what they say about me. It makes me smile. I have to make an effort of memory to recall the past, so far as it concerns myself. The only thing I can say with certainty about myself is that all my life I have wanted to be good and worthy, and that up to this moment I am correcting my faults and imperfections. In regard to others, it is their moral inclination, their psychology, which are the object of my observations, rather than anything else. Also I must say that it was always the future that especially preoccupied me. The past and the present touch me in so far as they lead up to, in so far as they give hope of such or such a degree of perfectionment of human life. The progress of my people — I think of it continually. I follow with eager interest the progress of other countries, knowing how interdependent they are. I am always absorbed in my ideas."

To Miss Blackwell.

"This is May 12. On May 13–18 I shall set out, probably for Kirensk. It is much better than to pass the summer in prison, where one feels the lack of air.

Just think, my friends have insisted upon my letting my mouth be filled with artificial teeth, which has already been done, and very skilfully, thanks to an able and attentive dentist. Now it is my eyes, which have served me so well hitherto, that are in need of repair, since I am getting cataract on both. The doctor says that they can be operated on in six months. It is growing hard for me to read, but I am sure of finding people to read to me as soon as I am reunited to my comrades. I can still sew for hours together, when the material is light-colored. The operation certainly could not be performed at Kirensk, but they may let me come to Irkutsk to have it done. At any rate, I am already accustomed to the idea of much privation, and my soul is ready to encounter anything. This must be enough to keep you from making a great outcry over my fate, which seems to me always an enviable one. Provided you keep well, I am sure to be cheerful."

To Miss Blackwell. May 22–June 2, 1915.

"I write to you still in front of my iron table and on my iron stool. How many days will pass before I leave them? They promise to apply to me — to me also — the new order which permits the exiles, after six months' residence in the place appointed by the government, to choose the place that suits them best, with the exception of the capital city. In my case it is Irkutsk that would be forbidden, but all the small cities would be open to me. The nearest one to Irkutsk is Balagansk, and that is where I am asking to be sent, since my health would be better protected. In case of serious illness, I should be only one hundred versts from the best medical help."

To Miss Dudley.   May 12–25, 1915.

"From patriotism as well as from indignation against the ferocity of the Germans, I am hoping for the victory of the Allies.   And then the whole world would be gainers, by getting back to a state of peace, and being able to continue its work of culture.   Our great country needs it badly."

June 2–15, 1915.

"Alas, the summer is passing, but I do not move. I am still ignorant as to what is to become of me.

"Thank heaven, after a month of terrible efforts, the war is resuming its normal course, and the hope of seeing it ended to the advantage of progress in general, strengthens the soul and makes one forget personal misfortunes."

To Miss Blackwell.   June 14–27, 1915.

"Now I can tell you what my address is to be: Yakutsk, Asia.   My friends' efforts to have me allowed to live in a more southerly place have failed, and I shall be two thousand versts further north than in Kirensk.   It does not much surprise me; and then, as I told you before, life at Kirensk was full of constant and intolerable persecutions; so that no change could affright me.   I am only sorry for my two extra months of prison, during our short summer; for the convoy will not start till July.

"The cold at Yakutsk rises above 55°; the winter lasts eight months; there is no spring, for the ground is still covered with snow in May, and in August the nights are freezing.   The two months of summer are sometimes very hot, and make it possible to grow a few vegetables.

"But, as it is the capital of the province of Yakutsk, which stretches for thousands of versts in every direction, there are some doctors there, and more people than in Kirensk. There are some political exiles, too, so you may be easy about me. I shall try not to lose what is left of my health, and it is not impossible, thanks to the care you all take of me.

"The longer I live, the more I realize that the foundation of my being is an ardent and invincible love for the human race, which, as I believe, has in itself all the germs of an endless intellectual 'perfectionment', an ascent to a moral life that will make it infinitely happy. This habit of living in human life as a whole has made me so associate myself with the universal psychology that I lose myself in it, and care little about my individual fate, which is not dear to me, once it is separated from the general course."

A political exile in Irkutsk saw Baboushka, at the moment of her setting off for Yakutsk. He wrote:

"She has become a little deaf; her shaggy hair is snow-white; but spiritually she is as strong as ever. On seeing her, at the first moment, I could not keep from weeping, hiding my face on her breast. 'Look up, let me see what is the matter with you, rascal!' she said. 'I don't like to see sad faces of my little children. Cheer up, my boy, and speak loud, like a good officer at the front. I am a little deaf.' I looked at her; her motherly mild eyes were full of tears; she was smiling. I was not able to utter a word. The other boys and girls were awaiting their turn."

To Miss Blackwell. Yakutsk, August 1–13, 1915.

"For two weeks I have been taking walks around the town of Yakutsk, visiting groves and meadows. I am happy to breathe a fresh air, very pure here, in the large deserts. It is cold enough, but cheering to the organism, eager for oxygen and ozone. I feel much better."

It was reported that Madame Breshkovsky would not be allowed to stay at Yakutsk, but would be sent still farther north, to Bulun, a tiny group of native huts, under the Arctic circle. Strong protests against her banishment to Yakutsk appeared in the American press, and a petition to the Russian government was started. Suddenly she was notified that she might return to Irkutsk. The winter was closing in, and it was not certain that she could get through, but she started immediately.

George Lazareff to Miss Dudley. November 15, 1915.

"Yesterday I received a new letter from Baboushka, written on the eve of her departure from Yakutsk. She had been glad and surprised when the authorities declared that she would not be sent further north, but she had not suspected that there was a possibility of her being allowed to return south. All the attempts made by many Socialist members of the Douma to get the government to leave her in the south of Siberia had been unsuccessful. So it was a surprise to everyone when she was unexpectedly allowed to turn back, after a tedious journey of three thousand miles.

"I cannot find any reasonable explanation of this

turn of affairs, except the impression made on the government by Mr. Lewis Herreshoff's letter, which I forwarded to Baboushka, and which was intercepted by the government, about the intention of the American friends to get up a petition in Baboushka's behalf. I believe the government resolved to let her come back to the south as though by their own will, and thus to prevent any agitation in America.

"In an earlier letter she had written:

"'I have been introduced into a good colony of the hearty men and women, the political exiles, a large number of whom have been sent here after spending many years at hard labor. They have married here, and have children. The destitution is great. My baggage has not arrived. I have no warm clothes, no money, and I am indebted to my friends of the colony. They are so kind, and touchingly attentive to me. A young man, after his work in some office, comes daily to me and Mrs. Lydia Yezersky, an old friend of mine, and spends the rest of the day in taking care of us both. In her youth Mrs. Yezersky was a good pianist. After so many long and hard adventures, she found herself in Yakutsk, and somehow procured a piano, and now I really enjoy her playing. . . . The touching care of my comrades gives me great concern; they are so poor, trying to earn their livelihood by all sorts of hard work. The war has an awful effect, living is dear, the products are rare; communication with Russia is long and difficult. Many of the exiles have lost their friends and relatives, who can no longer support the poor exiles. Everything is disorganized in Russia. At the first opportunity send me all the help you possibly can.'"

She went up the Lena on the last boat of the season, until the floating ice stopped navigation. She was halted at the little hamlet of Vitim.

To Miss Blackwell. Vitim, a little port on the Lena River. October 1–13, 1915.

"Amidst the ice of the Lena, 2000 miles from Yakutsk and 1400 miles from Irkutsk, waiting a practicable way to continue my travel, in a little home of my good friends I sit before a little table to inform you, my faithful friends in America, that there is no weather, no difficulty strong enough to crumble my health to pieces, to kill me to the ground. In a month there will be thick ice covering the Lena, and by that time I hope to find a companion with whom I shall reach Irkutsk."

To Miss Blackwell. Irkutsk, December 14–27, 1915.

"For two weeks I have been in Irkutsk, in the house of my excellent friends, surrounded by the most careful attention. I have now the opportunity to regain my health somewhat, for here we have many skilful doctors. But (there is always a but in our country) the government of the town has encircled me with such a régime that I cannot make a step alone, but every minute when out of doors am persecuted by a row of policemen, and one of them enters the house and even the apartment where I am staying, at home or anywhere else. Quite a prison régime. Such a state of things is little comfortable, yet I do not wonder, and will wait further.

"It is not difficult to wait, having so excellent moments in life as are part of my existence. Here I have received a large packet of letters and papers from America.

"Do not be sorry for my eyes. The four months that I spent out of doors, during the summer, were the best remedy I could have had. You see, I can write, and read all I get from you. I read books too, but little, for I have comrades ready to help me. The oculist says my eyes will serve me long enough if they are carefully used, and many years will pass before the cataracts are ripe. I am safe but for the persecution.

"Irkutsk is not a large town, only 150,000 inhabitants; yet, being the capital of Eastern Siberia, it is the centre of the intelligent forces of the country, and has many institutions of culture of various kinds. For my part, I am separated from people and institutions.

"How glad I am you are in communication with my brother [George Lazareff]. He helps me with money, and I pray God to secure him and his friends full safety; especially now, when everyone is laboring hard for the sake of millions of desolated people, deprived of all that is necessary for human life. The fugitives from all the frontiers encumber even the towns of Siberia, and provisions are growing dearer every day. It is the time when all the good elements and all the worse are working under a full head of steam. This war will be the proving stone of the capacities of all humanity, and especially of those of the cultured people and countries. A great show of the world's progress.

January 6–19, 1916.

"It has been my turn to be ill, ten days lying in bed and suffering seriously. But the efforts of my friends and a set of good scientists of medicine have worked real miracles. I now feel strong enough to read and write, and walk about the house, keeping a rigid régime. It was an inflammation of the liver, kidneys, stomach and bowels, followed by a persistent fever. The weather is awful. Notwithstanding the frost of 40°, it is only to-day that the beautiful Angora river has been frozen. Until now its streaming waves have filled the town with unwholesome vapors. Every nook in Siberia has its own poison. I am too sensitive to the cold. Yet there is no danger now. Your dear letters reach me, those of others, too, and I am happy."

To Miss Blackwell. February 9–22, 1916.

"You say that the women of the Westover School [1] mean to send me $50.00 a month. It will be a great relief, and my gratitude will be profound. You wrote me once that many persons said: 'She would receive much more help if she used the money for her own needs, but she gives it all away.'

"I think that if my sharing with the poor makes me happy, that is all any one can contribute to my welfare. I am not only happy when mending the naked needs of my comrades, but am seriously unhappy when, knowing those needs, I am not able to help. So every ruble, every dollar, is a joy, a hope, a possibility of rendering a service to those who lack the bare necessaries of life. Even when a prey to fierce inflammations, I never forget my obligations towards those to whom I have promised my help, and I cannot rest till my waiting comrades are provided for as arranged."

[1] At Middlebury, Connecticut.

(Undated)

"Knowing well the conditions in which I live, I destroy not only addresses, but even letters from relatives and friends, every time lamenting these sacrifices. Long experience has taught me to expect unfortunate occurrences where there is no reason for them whatever. Once I wrote to an old woman friend of mine asking her to send pumpkin seeds, which doctors say are a good remedy for tape-worms, which abound on the shores of the Lena and the Baikal. Owing to her correspondence with me, a search was made at the old woman's, and the gendarmes decided that 'tape-worms' meant 'gendarmes', and 'pumpkin seeds', 'explosive substances.' The old woman was sentenced to exile, and only after long and urgent solicitations and explanations was the 'penalty' reduced to two years' police surveillance.

"There have been many such cases. I do not begin a correspondence with anybody, do not become acquainted with anybody, knowing beforehand that it will do people no good.

"My whole present life, much like imprisonment, is a conclusive proof of how zealously the police are trying to compromise me and those coming in contact with me. It is not enough that a number of policemen and gendarmes are on guard, day and night, in the yard of the house where I live, examining and frightening with their electric lamps all who come and go in the evening (in the city people are free only in the evening — all are working); but in addition the police captain forces his way into the house at any time of day or night, to convince himself that I am here. Neither my illness nor the presence of doctors and nurses prevented him from 'verifying' me in bed.

"Once I said to him: 'You won't even let one die in peace,' but that did not keep him from breaking into the house at three A.M., when the policeman had reported that at two o'clock a woman had left this house for the maternity hospital.

"A soldier is in the habit of visiting my landlord's cook. A few days ago three of us were sitting in the evening, waiting for the samovar, but it did not come. It was already ten o'clock, half-past ten, and the samovar did not arrive. The kitchen here is across the hall, and our landlady went to find out what prevented us from having tea. Policemen and gendarmes were searching the kitchen, and right there were the cook and the unfortunate soldier. That was a search! They had not even thought of notifying the landlord. The cook was wanted at the police office. There she was questioned, reports were made out, and all the cook's love correspondence was retained, to examine into its meaning. Owing to my indisposition and my dislike for kitchen odors, I have not been in the kitchen since my arrival, and have not seen the soldier a single time. The policemen, who are always peeping in at the windows, particularly the cook's, know, of course, that I should neither see her guests nor speak with them; but if I had been in the kitchen at the time of the soldier's visit, what would have come of it? The police are obliged to bring information, even if they have to suck it out of their thumbs."

To Miss Dudley. March 19–31, 1916.

"Please do not send any petition on my account. In the first place, it will be of no use, and in the second, I am against such matters."

To Ellen Starr, with a picture card of a peasant woman.
(Undated)

"Nothing is so wonderfully majestic as a good sample of a peasant woman. She is robust, benevolent and condescending. Conscious of her vivid strength, she works and surveys like an energetic queen, fearing nothing, and acting for ten persons at once. All her dozen children do not embarrass her. Every one gets his place, his occupation, and she rules the house just by words and smiles. Such women are the benefit of every people, and the blessing of the world.

"Do not confuse the true Russians with others who belong to the Russian empire. The psychology of our people differs not only from that of other races, but even from that of other Slavonic tribes, such as Poles, Czechs, Bulgarians, etc. Our Russian women are not only brave, but endowed with a delicious tenderness of heart, and both these qualities make them unselfish, ready to help, and to take upon their shoulders every hard work.

"In general, I think women are the finest part of humanity. I respect and love them best of everything in the world. Almost all my correspondents are women; only the poor boys have the privilege of being answered richly, for they are little children, and ought to grow big men."

In a very grateful letter to the young women of the Westover School she wrote (April 22, 1916): "No vocation is so needed, so beneficent for the present and so fruitful for the future, as the rational and moral education of children."

In May she was transferred to the little city of Minussinsk in Eniseisk, about a hundred miles from the frontier of China. She was not sorry to have a change. "I always remember the saying of our peasants," she wrote, "'If worse, yet different.'" In Minussinsk the climate was warmer. She enjoyed much more freedom, and her health improved. "Really, my nature is like that of a wild man. Steppes, forests, air, river, sky, are the region where I grow young and strong. Without space I feel like a bird in a cage." She found herself in a congenial society of political exiles, and would have been happy but for her grief over the war.

To Miss Dudley. August 2, 1916.

"We must realize how dark the common brain still is. It needs thunder blows to be awakened and begin to think. Less than forty years ago, all the East, China, Russia, etc., were looked upon as dead, crystallized in their ancestors' prejudices. Now you see mighty China acquiring such ideas as are found in the van of European civilization; and that after five thousand years of slumber. During the last thirty years China has received heavy blows on her shoulders, back and head, and very hastily she understood that she can no longer exist if she does not prevent the new-coming blows. China began to think, to analyze, to compare, to find out issues, only after hard and costly experience.

"Now we never doubt the capacities of mind and the

progressive efficiency of the ocean of people that only yesterday were asleep. All the blows, however heavy and tyrannical, are so many lessons for the lazy brain of the world's population as a whole."

To Miss Blackwell.   October 1–13, 1916.

"I have read your article about me. It was too much. I feel myself a good soul, nothing more."

To Ernest Poole.   October 2, November 2, 1916.

"My very dear friend Ernest Poole! It was such a joyful surprise to me, your dear letter, with your and your little son's portraits!

"I judge that there has been a great change for the better in your country since I saw it eleven years ago. All right ideas and social reforms were in their beginning; they belonged to very few groups. But now they are so widespread that they influence even other countries. For instance, in 1905 there was not one paper like the 'New York Call',[1] which I get now. I am sure that to-day many cities have such papers.

"The large intervention of women in the prominent questions of State life is stimulating the progress of moral and physical culture in your country, as it has elsewhere. But what is more essential is the efforts of your intelligent people to establish connections with the people all over the world. The old world needs new impulses, and must be reminded of many questions already accepted by advanced minds, but not yet put in practice. All the visits made by delegates of the various International Congresses are of great value, and you must not weary of repeating them."

[1] The Socialist daily in New York.

To Lewis Herreshoff. July 24, 1916.

"I do not think there is any nationality quite innocent in the horrors we are witnessing. Yet I regard the conduct of the Germans as absurd, even unpardonable. From my childhood I disliked the disdain and roughness which characterized their behavior towards our Russian people, whom they regard as an inferior race. Our rich proprietors often engaged German agronomes as managers of their estates, and our peasants hated those managers for their systematic persecutions and roughness. The punishments were terrible; no mercy, no indulgence; very hard labors. I recognize that the Germans are skilful in every sort of manufacture, that they have energy and perseverance."

[In another letter she says: "When we were children my parents employed a German girl to teach us the language. I remember her rough voice and cold manners. Of course there are good souls among the Germans, too. But Russia has rather suffered from the German civilization."]

"The English and Americans are proud too, conscious of the dignity of their race; but, to my great joy, they have always recognized the good sides of our people. I have read many books by intelligent travelers in Russia, and I was always pleased with the authors' impartiality. Now too, when reading the opinions of the English papers on the bravery and honesty of the Russian soldiers, I am sure that they mean what they say, for they expressed the same opinions when witnessing our war with the Turks in 1877. Our young men fought like very lions.

"I do not desire the destruction of the German people,

not at all; but I wish with all my heart to see them, after this criminal war, humanized and respectful towards every other nation, white or black or yellow.

"The intelligence of our mind, our soul, is much more important than our skill in manufacturing and our outward culture; this last can be acquired with time and endeavor, but the religious tendencies are a donation of rare and happy chance. We have to develop them, and not to be ashamed of it. We shall always feel our God in our breast — a God of love and righteousness. That will give us strength to fight and to win the battle.

"I am not in the least a chauvinist. I respect the rights of every nationality. I desire full liberty for every people. Yet I have a large family of my compatriots that has its rights too, its own history and modes of life, its own philosophy and faith; and as long as my people wish to develop their capacities as they think best, they must be left alone and have time to use their innate energy and genius; on condition, of course, that they shall not meddle with the affairs of others. When ripe enough, it will make them able to live a common life with their neighbors, with all the world. Perhaps the time is not so remote as we might think."

To Miss Dudley. November 5, 1916.

"I am like a salted herring in a big but immovable hogshead, conserved nobody knows why, and waiting, waiting, without end. My straining and my activity are limited now so narrowly that I see myself like a sea urchin in its shell, only thinking and endeavoring to understand the meaning of what mankind as a whole is doing. I turn and re-turn the facts, the sayings and writings of different minds, of different people in different countries. As far as I know, it seems to me that we can agree with Mrs. Catt's speech, 'The Crisis.' This brave woman, of a bright and large mind, pleased me years ago, when, traveling over every country of the world, she described the situation of the suffrage amid the women of the various nations. She is born a leader.

"Now, I wonder, too, at the masterly way in which England does, with what genius she holds together the reins in her hands, wisely overlooking the affairs of the world. I wish only she may be as sincere and noble as she is wise and strong. But it would be a great mistake on her part to settle affairs selfishly and with partiality, for in that case nothing would be prevented. Yet a long, or, better, a continual peace is necessary; the desolation is too profound to be cured in a short time. The countries have lost all their best young forces, and we must wait till the young generations grow to be of use. We have thousands and thousands of orphans around us, and if we do not apply all our efforts and means to bring them up and teach them, we have no future.

"The child question is the most serious and continually pressing question of the age. I have a lot around me, the poorest. We are good friends, and the little I do is already a relief in their dull and needy life. Many of them visit the school, and need books and several pieces of clothes. I do my best to suffice, but they are so many! It is awful to see how the world is foolish. They are writing in every paper about food and fuel, and they forget that if the race dies out, there will be nobody to eat and to provide. For shame! I shall cry this question out in every letter to my many correspondents and urge them to do all they can to forward it."

To Miss Blackwell. December 1–14, 1916.

"If I worked as assiduously as you do, nothing would be left of me. Even here in my room, surrounded by comfort, I feel tired after I have been visited by a dozen persons, who want to hear or to be heard. Perhaps it is due to my excited feelings, that can't be quiet in the face of any need, or of the errors into which even goodhearted people often fall. From my youth I prayed the Creator to render my nature more cool and more quiet, but I succeed poorly, and it does not take much to inflame my heart, my passions — when the question does not concern myself. For myself I have worked out a philosophy that doesn't allow any sentimentalism, and holds me and my disposition in a good state of order and peace. I would not wish to disappear directly, without seeing the issue of the present world tragedy, yet, if the end came, I should not be afraid.

"To you alone I confess one thought that is of interest to me. Nearly every grand event in the life of my own country, also the solution of the moral and ethical questions of humanity, have been foreseen by me. In pursuing in my mind the present course of history (I have done it for more than half a century), in studying past history, I have acquired the power of forecast, and long before events take place or questions come to the front, I have had them in mind, and my imagination has worked out the ways and methods to follow. For instance, the war with Germany was not in the least a surprise to me. Five years before it happened, I had already plans made how to secure the integrity of our country, how to stop the invasion. My 'preparedness' was not an offensive one, but genuinely a defensive one. Moreover, all the institutions for the people's welfare have long ago been a reality in my imagination, and now I see that, nolens volens, some of them are to be realized in fact. The question of pedagogy was long ago discussed in my mind, eugenics, the perfection of the race. I could cite more examples; and it convinces me that the terrible war will have its positive sides, and that, notwithstanding the universal losses and disasters, the mind of all mankind will grow up, and many things and questions not understood till now will become clear, and will take a solid place in the minds that have so long been wandering in the dark."

To Arthur Bullard. November 30–December 13, 1916.

"The rigor of misery is spreading over all Europe, but Russia suffers the most, owing to her special conditions, internal and external, being a territory quite apart, surrounded on every side with enemies of all nationalities and creeds. Nobody is in fault except ourselves. But don't forget that the history of our people has been more cruel than that of other European countries. Very cruel it was, and we feel the consequences still. We shall feel them for a long time yet, if we do not change our indolence for a more active character. It is wonderful how much patience we have. We are not so devoid of reason as not to understand our position, our surroundings, the conditions that dominate us. We contemplate all this sighing and wondering, asking why it is. And we remain as pacific as if nothing changed.

"Sometimes the horror of the present is so awful that I need all my will not to sink into despair. You have witnessed the horrors of war, but perhaps you did not see the horrors of the countries lying behind the front. No soul is strong enough to bear the picture of the world's sufferings in all their details. The imagination halts, having no strength to continue the survey. Unless one is willing to go mad, one must not stand and inspect the facts. It is better to be occupied by some work which demands our attention.

"The best means to be diverted from the heart-rending spectacle is to have to do with children. These little creatures don't give us time or rest enough to be absorbed by the idea of the universal mischief. When they come six or ten into my room, we are full of activity, and all my attention is fixed on their welfare. Books, paper, pencils, scissors, chiffons, needle, thread and many other things are necessary to keep them busy and happy. Some milk and white bread are enough to satisfy their appetite. This little family is growing from week to week, for the orphans are so glad to have somebody whom they can call 'grandmother' and be sure to find a home on her bosom!"

To Miss Starr.   January 26–February 8, 1917.

"I do not know who sends me the *Public*,[1] but, reading this venerable paper, I always feel gratified at having the advantage of possessing it."

[1] A single-tax paper, published in New York.

To Miss Dudley.   January 28–February 10, 1917.

"I shall never forget the moment you took leave of me.   I do not think you have changed much since then, but sometimes I wonder if you would recognize me. My hair is not only white as snow, but very thin, my teeth are gone, my walking slow, with a stick in my right hand when out of doors.   Perhaps the eyes and the voice are the same, and I laugh often enough, which is a surprise to me.   It is the result of my faith that the great mischief of humanity will bring new ideas into the heads of the masses, and will make the heads more clear, the minds more strong.   A new era is coming, I feel it with all my soul.   Even if I die before the end of the war I shall die at peace, even for my country."

To Mr. Herreshoff.   February 4–17, 1917.

"Your sister is seriously ill!   Your best friend and companion!   I wonder that people living in good conditions, surrounded by their family and some comforts, can be ill, being not old enough for that.   The loss of good people is the greatest misfortune to which we are subjected.   When I hear that this or that old friend of mine has left us for another world, I feel lonely, for I know that by and by these brave old comrades will pass away one after another.

"Depressed!   it is an awful state of mind, and I wish I could send you, who have spent your life without constant misfortune, a part of my resignation.   Uncertainty is my constant condition.   In such a position one ought to be ready to meet bravely the worst that can happen.   Therefore I believe with the little nephew of your friend Miss Drury, who said to his nurse, 'Why do people look so stern when they say their prayers?'

All our sufferings are very small in comparison with the sea of sorrow that deluges the world with tears and wounds. Yet I hope that the moral courage of your country, for instance, and other efforts will bring about better results for the world, and teach a lesson for a long time to the wicked and to the best. The voice of the United States will be heard, if only that voice shall be on the side of right and impartiality. We can hear already the wishes all over the world that are asking for equality of interest and rights. In our misfortunes of to-day we can hope to see better times, with the help of rightminded people; and therefore we must agree with the child who remarked that we are wrong not to pray to God with serene faces, with love and hope in our eyes. I hope you will support the burden of life with a strong belief that your dear sister will never quit you. Two souls so closely bound together as yours were for so long a time can never be separated."

To Miss Julia C. Drury. February 24, 1917.

"My family is growing from day to day. We have orphans in such a quantity in every place and nook that we must be ready to see the whole country covered only with widows and children. What is absurd is that the rich people do very little to mitigate the wants and the misfortunes of the young people who are our only hope for a better future.

"Mankind is so short-sighted that it does not pay attention to what is the most precious thing the world over, children and youth.

"Animals, plants, bijouterie, furniture, all material things are of great value to them, and the best flower on earth, the best creature of the Creator, is only a burden, an undesired element that hinders them and disturbs their good humor.

"They forget that all our happiness depends on the welfare and good education of the country children, that must give us a strong, clever, and honest population.

"This furious war, as I hope, will teach the majority of mankind to understand its own interest, and to improve life throughout."

Writing in the *Neva* after the revolution, she said:

"There pulsed so much life in my heart that I could not imagine the end of my activities. Neither the long terms passed in jail nor my exile in Yakutsk had dimmed my spirit. 'I shall live through all this,' said an inner voice to me; 'I shall live through everything, and live to see the bright days of freedom.'

"In Irkutsk when I was very ill, I observed how carefully the physicians concealed from me the danger of my malady. It seemed so strange to me that people could think of my fatal end, when my soul was full of complete faith that time was bringing me nearer daily to a different kind of end, the triumph of the revolution!

"The longer the war continued, the more horrible its consequences grew, the more clearly the rascality of the government manifested itself, the more inevitable appeared the rise of democracy all over the world, the nearer advanced also our revolution.

"I waited for the sounds of the bell announcing freedom, and wondered why that sound delayed. When in November, 1916, explosions of indignation followed one another, I had already one foot in the Siberian sleigh, only feeling sorry that the snow road was beginning to thaw.

"March 4–17 a telegram reached me in Minussinsk announcing freedom. The same day I was on my way to Atchinsk, the nearest railroad station. From Atchinsk on began my uninterrupted communion with soldiers, peasants, workmen, railroad employes, students, and multitudes of beloved women, who to-day are all bearing the burdens of the normal and now also of the abnormal life of a great State."

CHAPTER XVII

ONE of the first acts of the Provisional Government was to declare an amnesty to all the political prisoners and exiles. There were said to be one hundred thousand in Siberia alone. All who could do so started at once for Russia.

The government sent Madame Breshkovsky a special invitation to return. The long homeward journey was one continuous ovation. The soldiers joined with the populace to carry her in triumph. When she reached Moscow, she was placed in the Czar's state coach, and taken amid a military escort to the hall where the Moscow Douma was sitting. There she was given an official welcome, with greetings and orations.

"Citizens," she said, "one thought is in my mind. Joy gives place to care. At every station and cross roads there is only one demand. It is the groan of the people for literature, books, teachers."

She went on to make an earnest plea for universal education. She had told her American friends that, instead of conscripting all the young men to serve a term in the army, as under the old régime, she would like to have every man and woman in Russia who could read and write conscripted to serve for a few years as a school teacher. In this way Russia's great illiteracy could all be wiped out in a very short time.

At Petrograd the whole city turned out to meet her. A vast crowd waving red flags and singing the Marseillaise extended down the west end of Nevsky Prospekt as far as the Nicolaievsk railway station. When the Associated Press correspondent arrived, he found the crowd trying to storm the station, to which none were admitted but veteran revolutionists and a deputation from the Ministry of Justice, headed by A. F. Kerensky, together with delegations of welcome from the Petrograd, Moscow and Dorpat Universities and high schools. A volunteer guard of soldiers and students was trying to hold back the crowd.

At Kerensky's suggestion, the welcome to Madame Breshkovsky took place in the gorgeous suite in the railway station called the Imperial Reception Rooms, which under the old régime were used only for the reception of royal personages. All the survivors of the "Old Guard" among the revolutionists were there. Around the large drawing room were scores of baskets and wreaths of flowers, the scarlet tulip predominating, with such inscriptions as "To Our Dear Grandmother", "To Russia's Martyr Heroine."

When the train arrived the crowd again attempted to storm the station, crying, "Let us see Grandmother!" The guards quieted them, explaining the danger of a crush, and assuring them that all would be allowed to take part in the welcome.

"I do not think that anywhere in the world there ever was a bride who received so many flowers," said the old heroine, smiling and pointing to her car in the train, filled with flowers given her on her way from Siberia. She had been met by enthusiastic crowds at every station on her long journey; she had seen all Russia, all her "grandchildren", workingmen, soldiers, peasants, and citizens of all ranks, greeting her as the symbol of the long struggle for freedom.

In her special car were several men, some of whom had gone to meet her in Moscow. Among them was the Secretary of Justice, Kerensky.

Secretary Kerensky handed "Grandmother" a bouquet of red roses, and they kissed three times. She addressed him with the familiar " thou", and described with enthusiasm her visit to Moscow.

Madame Breshkovsky appeared at the door, leaning on Kerensky's arm. Taking off his hat, the Secretary of Justice addressed the crowd: " Comrades, the Grandmother of the Russian Revolution has returned at last to a free country. She has been in dungeons, in the penal settlements of the Lena, has been tortured endlessly, yet here we have her with us, brave and happy. Let us shout 'Hurrah' for our dear Grandmother !"

The platform fairly shook with the thunder of acclamation that followed, and, to the accompaniment of rousing ovations, the beloved Grandmother, led by Kerensky, walked to the reception rooms, where numerous deputations were awaiting her.

A party of nurses came first, handing her flowers and waving a red flag with the inscription: "Long live the Grandmother of the Russian Revolution!" The spokeswoman said:

"We nurses are but an infinitesimal group of all those sisters who, in this happy day for Russia, send you their humble and worshipful greetings."

She was surrounded on all sides; women pushed

one another to kiss her hands, men doffed their hats and shouted "Hurrah!" as Madame Breshkovsky, accompanied by Kerensky, proceeded to the waiting automobile to be taken to the Congress of Workers' Delegates. A sitting of the Council of Soldiers' Deputies was in progress. When the news came that "Grandmother" had arrived, every one present rose and applauded. The ovation lasted a long time.

The first to speak was Kerensky. He said: "I am happy and proud to greet you, Grandmother, in the name of Russian democracy and the Provisional Government. I am happy to greet you, whom the old government had persecuted and whom we now meet with such honor."

"In the name of the Executive Committee of the Council of Soldiers' and Workers' Delegates," said N. S. Tcheidze, "I greet the woman who inspired the Russian Revolution. Let us hope that, with the same faith in the righteousness of the cause, she will continue to inspire us in our work of further conquests on the road of freeing Russia. Again I greet you humbly and salute you!"

One after another, representatives of various groups rose to greet the beloved Grandmother. Deeply moved, Madame Breshkovsky replied to these greetings. Every one rose. She said:

"I have come over a long road. I am old and cannot remember everything. As I came out on the platform I saw the people; all around I saw workingmen. I came into this temple of freedom, and see military organizations, workmen, Cossacks, sailors. Thus I have to-day had the happiness of seeing representatives of all organized Russia. Is not this complete happiness! It proves that we can work in unison, free and happy, without discord, as one man.

"Dear citizens! I have been fifty years in the ranks of the Russian Revolution, and without boast can say that there was never one more true to duty and discipline, or who appreciated more the meaning of obligations. Never has there been any wrangling or disputes in my party on my account. I have always respected the opinions of my comrades and the rulings of the party to such an extent that I have invariably stood for a friendly settlement of the most disputable questions.

"Do not I see that you are all children of the same cause? The soldier — isn't he the same as the workingman? You are all children of our one great mother, Russia, and why should you suddenly begin to quarrel with one another?"

A soldier approached close to the platform where "Grandmother" was speaking. She picked out a rose from her bouquet and handed it to her "grandson." The soldier kissed her hand tenderly. Madame Breshkovsky gently stroked the soldier's hair, and continued amidst thunderous applause:

"If we all aspire towards freedom and equality, what differences can there be between us? What is there to disagree about? Why put sticks in the spokes of one another's wheels? If we seek to overcome such an enemy, such a bitter foe of Russia as Wilhelm, can we not overcome our little differences? It would say very little for our wisdom if we could not combat those.

"All these greetings, on all sides, addressed to one and the same person — whom you call your Grandmother — prove that you are unanimous. Every one says, 'We will die for freedom.' In this I see solidarity. Everyone understands that if we do not overcome the foe, it will bring our country to grief; he, our bloody foe, will come and will dictate to us his laws. I am sure no one wants that. We do not desire any annexations, we have no wish to ruin others, but to allow yourselves to be trampled upon, to lose your self-respect, that would be unworthy of great Russia!

"My children, nothing is obtained gratis. No complete freedom can be obtained without hard work. You know perhaps better than I that nothing accomplishes itself — brain and spirit are necessary. For three years Russia has been suffering, as no one has suffered, and perhaps more suffering will have to be borne before we reach the goal. Then let us unite, and let us strive that no petty differences shall mar the way to our chief aim — the freedom and happiness of the whole nation."

Madame Breshkovsky ended amidst enthusiastic and continuous applause.

The chair into which she sank was lifted by Kerensky, Tcheidze, Secretary of Labor, Skobelev, and others, who placed it carefully on their shoulders, and accompanied by unprecedented acclamations carried it to the Ekaterininsk hall, where they were met with further applause and ovations. Flowers were carried in front of the chair. A ring was formed around to clear the passage, and the beloved Grandmother was carried to the entrance.

Here a large gathering of representatives of the army, from the trenches and reserves, awaited her.

"In the name of the old-Russian garrison of 25,000 men, allow me, Grandmother, to greet you!"

"Grandmother" patted the soldier gently and gave him a rose. "Go back," she said, "and tell them that Grandmother has sent them a rose and her greetings."

A Red Cross nurse approached. "In the name of the nurses on the northern front, allow me to kiss you." "Grandmother" kissed her and gave her a rose also.

"I have been wounded four times," said an officer near by. "My brother lost his life for freedom. My father has suffered. It was with difficulty that I obtained permission to don a uniform to stand in the ranks of the army. Allow me to greet you in the name of the invalided."

"Thank you, dear, thank you."

A. A. Nazarov, Cossack, member of the Douma, greeted her in the name of the members of the Douma :

"Long live the great Russian Grandmother! In your youth you spread the seed of freedom, and in your old age you have made Russia happy. Long live the bearers of peace; long live the Russian woman!"

An automobile carried away "Grandmother" and Kerensky.

The Guards' Economic Society was holding a meeting in the theatre of Musical Drama and invited her to honor them with her presence. Two other heroes of the Russian Revolution were present — Vera Figner and Herman Lopatin, both of whom had spent a quarter of a century in the Schlusselburg fortress. It is hard to describe the reception accorded "Grandmother" and the other veterans of the revolution. The audience hung on every word she said, on every gesture, and responded to everything with enthusiasm.

When she talked about the unity of the people, the power that is only obtained by unity, when she pointed to the other veterans of the old guard of the Russian Revolution, Vera Figner and Herman Lopatin, and told how they had replaced one another at the revolutionary front in the olden days, and emphasized that they were strong only because there had been no division among them; when she called upon all her friends and "children" to unite mind and heart in a single purpose, in the name of freedom — the crowd listened enraptured, and after a moment of dead silence, burst into applause.

Lopatin said: "There is no price too dear for that freedom which we now have. And I am happy that in the decline of my years before the end — I am growing deaf and blind — I am able to see the triumph of a freed Russia." Vera Figner was indisposed and tired, and did not speak.

The audience, as one man, stood up and applauded vociferously the old fighters for Russia's freedom. When the beloved Grandmother of the Revolution was carried from the hall to her automobile, to the strains of the Marseillaise played by the soldiers of the Volhyn regiment, hundreds of eyes followed this simple and quiet old woman, in whose face could be read the chronicle of a great struggle and the joy of the great triumph.

Cablegram.   Petrograd, April 13, 1917.

To Alice Stone Blackwell, the *Woman's Journal*,
Boston, U. S. A.

"Greetings from free Russia to the people of the
U. S. A.! Am enjoying happiness, with all the city,
and Russia and Siberia.

"Breshkovsky."

A like cablegram came to Miss Wald.

To Miss Dudley.   April 14–27, 1917.   On a picture
card.

"I have sent two telegrams to American friends,
but no letter until now. From the 4th of our March
till to-day, I have never been alone. All the way
through Siberia, the Urals and Russia, the people
came by thousands and wanted some words from
me; often even at night I spoke from my railroad
car, which is now my dwelling; for I go from one place
to another to see and speak and hear.

"I dare say with certainty that our people is a responsible and right-feeling one. The war will continue
till our friends will discontinue it without annexations.

"I was in Minussinsk when it happened. This
(picture) is the army of our people the first day of the
revolution in Moscow. We hope it will continue as
well as it has begun. I am quite well. Much to do,
very much: but it is my life."

To Miss Blackwell.   Moscow.   April 26–May 9, 1917.

"I am healthy, and strong, and happy — yes,
happy, though always thinking about the future.
How will the war end, and how soon? Will our peo-

ple be always as reasonable as they are now? I am sure they will: but certain foolish individuals hope to influence the masses badly. Yet there are more good events, and a quantity of good people.

"I had lived so long with my hope of seeing Russia free that I was not a bit astonished to see it realized, and the confidence of my fellow citizens makes me sure of a happy future, after the war. The losses are enormous, and every one is busy with some work to provide the army with food and all sorts of munitions."

We have had other glimpses of her through the press. At a great meeting in Moscow called by the League to Promote Equal Rights for Women, she said:

"You have received me as a heroine. As a matter of fact, you have never heard of anything heroic done by me, unless it be that all my life I have held my post like a faithful soldier and have done my work quietly. Even so, I could not do it all the time. Thirty-two years of prison and of Siberia kept me practically idle; only eleven years of 'underground' life gave me the opportunity to engage in the active work as dictated by my heart. And that was not heroic work; it was ordinary, everyday work, yet the kind of work the people need.

"There is no need of heroic deeds. Unfortunately, many inactive persons imagine that it is necessary to perform something wonderful, heroic — that one is either to sit in passive idleness, or else to ascend to the summit of a lofty mountain and there perform an act of such extraordinary heroism as shall reverberate throughout the world. As a result these people sit idly at home and do nothing.

"To be sure, there are times and emergencies demanding and producing great talents, prodigious powers of mind and action, heroic deeds. But I wish you to bear in mind that there is a great deal of work to be done in ordinary times — ordinary, not heroic work, that has to be done, that is of great importance and is much needed.

"My greatest treasure is my infinite love for the people. Many of those who worked and suffered with me shared that treasure. Only I have been more fortunate in that I happened to have a stronger constitution and survived, while the others succumbed. We all aimed to bring light and freedom to the people. Now it is the duty of those who survive to work harder for the realization of that aim.

"It is my desire now to organize a great publishing house for the purpose of producing and circulating among the plain people the sort of literature they need — the books to be written in the plainest language, so that any one can understand. It is likewise necessary to organize a corps of young people to engage in disseminating this literature throughout the length and breadth of the country. Within a few days I shall begin to work on these lines. I may, perhaps, be granted the use of a railroad car — I have no home — and travel from one end of Russia to the other, to meet and speak to those who need our word and deed."

To Miss Blackwell. May 3, 1917. My Railroad Car.

"This is only the second card I write you, since liberty made me a free citizen of a free country. You can't imagine how much there is to do now. Day and night the best people are busy with thousands of affairs, great and small. I am making a tour over our large country to see and to speak. The long years of sufferings have had their effect. Friendship is spread everywhere, and every one wants to have the old woman who loved so long and so heartily all who suffered and wished to be free. My voice does not suffice to express all I would say, and I have with me a young 'grandson' who continues the speeches I begin. Soldiers, peasants, workmen and all the youth is with us. Frenchmen and Englishmen wonder to see the solidarity of such a large country, with so many different nationalities. Alice, I am happy, but not quiet till the war is finished and all the forces occupied with the interior affairs."

To Miss Dudley. May 7–20, 1917. Petrograd.

"My travels will continue the whole summer, till we have the Réunion Legislative, when the voice of all our 170,000,000 people will be heard and the fundamental laws settled. We are having some trouble with a few bad minds, or foolish minds, but it is impossible to avoid some discomforts in such a large and new situation."

Moscow, May 13, 1917.

"To all my dear Friends: It goes better and better. The peasants are strong and well disposed, always ready to do their best. The army, too, for it is composed of peasants' boys. There are some people that have imbibed foreign ideas (from Germany), but they are few, and in a few days all the tempest they have awakened in the capital will disappear. Such a great revolution as we have here cannot be carried through without some troubles.

"We women have all the rights we wanted, quite such as the men. In short, the program is broad enough to make the people happy for centuries of ages. Yet we must work as never before; and the work would not be so hard if there were more people of experience.

"I have been expecting this time (of a great revolution) for many years. It gave me strength and courage, and I was prepared in my mind for the things I am doing now. But all the rest were so astonished, it was such a big surprise to them, that they are learning their task only now, when the events do not wait, and demand a resolute and strong conviction."

She was elected a member of the National Peasants' Congress, receiving the largest vote among all the nine hundred delegates, with one exception. She was with Kerensky when he reviewed the Black Sea fleet, and she has been standing with him during the recent troubles. She is reported as saying that the best thing the Americans can do for the Russians at present is to help them to vanquish Germany.

To Miss Blackwell. The Crimea. May 30–June 13, 1917.

"The old girl is busy, and often very preoccupied with the state of affairs throughout the country. Not the country, no, but the front, which has been going mad with the sole idea of liberty. Young people without education and knowledge imagine that the war must be abandoned, since the people were not asked to begin it. Some ignorant and some bad individuals inspired and enforced these ideas among the recruits, and it took time and efforts before the soldiers were convinced that they ought to begin again to do their duty. It is much better now.

"Thanks to Providence, our peasants, fathers and husbands, are reasonable enough to wait, and to maintain order in their villages. But the young workers and young soldiers are too inexperienced and ignorant to be mindful and patient. They imagine that all the old wrongs can be undone in some days, and therefore they demand new conditions of life that cannot be created in a few months, and with a war on our shoulders.

"Happily, we have now a board of Ministers very noble in all senses. Most of them are Socialists, old acquaintances of mine, too.

"After the war there will be a great deal of work to do, especially for the education of the whole people. I should be so happy to see this work begun and advanced before I am ready to go away!

"To-day I got a letter from some women who propose to form a regiment of women alone, to go to war and show how one must fight for the liberty and welfare of one's people. From another place I got the same proposition. If there are many women desirous to enlist, we will write to the Minister of War offering our services.

"Do not laugh. At this time every expedient that will serve to attain a good end will be welcome. Our women have never feared dangers, and if our example will promote the affairs of the war, we shall be glad to die for it. For Russia is bound hand and foot, resting as it is now.

"When the land of the republic becomes the commonwealth property of the whole people, it will make us rich, and able to attain many great advantages, not yet realized anywhere.

"My beloved child, there are moments when I would be so happy to lay my head upon your lap!"

She enclosed a photograph of herself surrounded by flowers, and said: "The young comrades cherish the grandmother, and wish to have her surrounded with flowers and red ribbons. The old woman is always ready to do the will of her little children. Sometimes she feels like a fool, but never mind.

"I am to install in many places printing presses to multiply pamphlets and newspapers for the peasants, soldiers and workmen. I collect the money and choose the most convenient places."

The Last Letter.

June 10–23, 1917.   The Crimea.

"My ever-dear and beloved friends, Alice S. Blackwell, Helena Dudley, Jane Addams, Ellen Starr, Arthur Bullard, friend Poole and so many others, faithful and brave!

"A new history of the world is beginning, and here we are at the first steps of a march always difficult, but promising the most desirable results.

"We are directing our steps toward Socialism, and the task is to make them secure, firm and real. We Socialists are working energetically for this, and the sympathy that we meet with from the people gives us courage and assurance.

"Certain disorders and some partial revolts, of which the newspapers speak, have taken place here and there, it is true. We are doing our utmost to combat the false ideas spread by stupid or malevolent persons, scoundrels who have nothing to lose, without conscience or honor, who have come from every part of the world. But the truth is that their propaganda affects only young, weak and ignorant minds. And as our army is made up mostly of such elements, it is the army that is the breeding place of all the disturbances which we have to overcome. As for the rest of the population — the men and women of the villages and of the faubourgs, — they constitute a peaceful and patriotic element, desirous to see the war brought to an end advantageous to Russia (without losses and without humiliations).

"But you can well conceive, my friends, that people most of whom (the women included) do not know how to read or write, cannot offer a foundation firm and durable enough, an audience intelligent enough to understand and remember everything that they hear from time to time from their Socialist friends, who, with all their efforts, cannot suffice to be everywhere and as often as would be needful.

"Vast distances, provinces situated at the farthest limits of this immense country, always remain plunged in darkness, and cannot take in, cannot form a correct idea of what is going on in the world.

"It is necessary to illuminate, to enlighten the minds of a nation that is ready to grasp knowledge; a nation that has been forcibly deprived of all teaching. For there are only a few thousand fortunate persons who were able to get an education in the small number of schools that did not in any way meet the needs of a population of 170,000,000.

"Yes, our past history has been a fatal one for Russia

in every respect. The finances utterly ruined, all the country's present wealth and resources devastated, the war which is absorbing the rest, increasing our debts at the rate of 40,000,000 rubles a day. Moreover, at present we lack everything necessary, such as machines, tools, paper, etc. We have everything to repair, not only to meet the present situation, but with a view to the future of our nation, which is capable of taking an active part in the upbuilding of the civilization of the world.

"The new history must make all the nations members of one family. The better these members are prepared for a reasonable and brotherly life, the better they understand the reciprocity of their mutual interests, the better they know each others' customs, history and civilization, the surer and deeper will be their friendship, the stronger will be the ties that unite them.

"The international interdependence of reciprocal interests (present and future) is a subject that must be thoroughly gone into in all its complexity; but an ignorant nation will have difficulty in understanding it unless it is introduced to it by some preliminary explanations and has some concrete ideas about it. We must teach them the causes of the present war, and set before them the consequences that may follow if the Russians do not behave properly towards their Allies.

"My friends and I are doing our utmost to furnish the country with the necessary literature, to organize groups of intelligent women and men ready to go among the masses to enlighten and instruct them — men, women, youths, even old people. In the hospitals,

in the barracks, wherever there is anybody to talk to,
they are explaining, giving lessons, readings, etc.

"But we are too few to meet this vast need for instruction. They snatch our pamphlets from us, they
ask for more and still more of them; from every corner,
near and far, they are begging us to send them teachers,
readers. But we cannot respond to more than a
tenth part of these demands. Time presses, questions
are piling up, the war is ruining the whole world; we
are nearer the brink of ruin than the rest.

"The bourgeoisie think only of themselves; they
are not helping us. We need many good newspapers,
capable of reaching the intelligence of all our ignorant people, and showing them the truth about the
present situation, the misfortune that awaits us if we
lose the esteem and confidence of our friends, the Allies.
For this we must have millions of copies of newspapers.
And in order to get them we need a printing office
with rotary presses, capable of running off a considerable number of copies every day. We have none such
in Russia, except those in the hands of the capitalists,
who will not part with them. We are receiving no
more since the breaking out of the war, since it has
become impracticable to import things.

"In our country rotary presses are not manufac-
tured. So we poor Socialists remain with empty hands,
limited to working with small machines, which give
us miserable thousands of copies, instead of the millions that are indispensable. That is why I address
myself to you, my friends. Get up a subscription to
raise a sum of money which will serve first to buy a
rotary printing press, and paper enough to furnish
reading matter for several months, until the meeting

of the General Assembly; the second part of the money as the capital necessary to begin the great affair of publishing the paper.

"Make the American public understand that this is not only a question of the salvation of the Russian people, but a question which concerns international relations and interests. The whole world would be a gainer by having as a member a country with ideas nobly and wisely directed toward the common good. This is in no sense a Utopia, for, as I have told you all along in our correspondence, 'The Russians are a capable people, and of a good disposition. All they need is civilization and education.'

"To be sure, after some years, and by great efforts, we should be able to accomplish it by our own strength, for in spite of the troubles and disorders that are manifesting themselves at present, common sense and good faith will get the upper hand. But it would be a great pity not to do the utmost possible to hasten the glad time of an order which would permit working with full power and speedy success, instead of letting the time drag along, at the risk of delaying the general well-being.

"Think of it, friends, and let me know your decision as soon as it is reached, whether favorable or unfavorable. I wish very much that it may be favorable. I urge you to decide as soon as possible, too, because my health is not as strong as it used to be. I should like much to see with my own eyes the installation of the whole affair. My experience has been great, and I have never had at my side persons unworthy of confidence. Now that all activities are carried on openly, I have every opportunity to make a good choice while I am alive to do it.

"So, in case you consent, I beg you to address the things (the machine, its equipment and the paper) as well as the money, to the address:

"'Russia, Moscow, Kusnezky Most 16.,

"'For Catherine Breshkovsky.'"

An Associated Press dispatch of September 21, 1917, speaks of her as lodged in the winter palace in Petrograd, and as finding the surroundings too gorgeous for her simple tastes. She reported that she and her friends had 140 printing presses[1] busy turning out literature for the peasants and workmen, and for the soldiers at the front.

Madame Breshkovsky was chosen a member of the Preliminary Parliament of Russia. When it assembled in Petrograd on October 20, 1917, Premier Kerensky, after his opening speech, called upon her to take the chair, as she was the senior member of the Parliament. She received a great ovation as temporary chairman.

As reported in the press despatches, she declared that the people ought to be masters of the soil they cultivate. A just solution of the agrarian question, she said, would enable the country to avoid dangerous collisions; therefore, if the council of the republic seriously wished to assist the country, it should solve this problem in conformity with the exigencies of Russian history, and she urged the intellectual classes not to oppose such a solution.

Madame Breshkovsky's whole life has fulfilled the words that she once wrote to an American friend:

"We ought to elevate the people's psychology by

[1] See Appendix.

our own example, and give them the idea of a purer life by making them acquainted with better morals and higher ideals; to call out their best feelings and strongest principles. We ought to tell the truth, not fearing to displease our hearers; and be always ready to confirm our words by our deeds."

APPENDIX

Dr. Gregory Gershuni (Page 107)

GERSHUNI was Madame Breshkovsky's closest col-
league in the work of the party. He was a Jew, and a
man of extraordinary force of character. His escape
from Siberia was remarkable. At the prison of Akatui,
the prisoners used to put up their own provisions for
the winter. These were then stored in the cellars of the
Governor's house, which stood outside the walls. Gershuni's fellow exiles put him in the bottom of a large
barrel, which had been furnished with breathing holes.
They spread a piece of leather over him, filled the top
of the barrel with pickled cabbage, and conveyed it to
the Governor's lowest cellar, where they left it. Comrades outside had dug a subterranean tunnel into the
cellar, and Gershuni got out of the barrel and went
away.

To keep his escape from being found out too soon,
the other exiles made a head out of cheese, and laid it
on the pillow in his cell. When the jailer made the
rounds in the evening to see that the prisoners were
all there, several of them stood around Gershuni's bed,
apparently holding an animated conversation with this
head.

Gershuni afterwards visited America. The great

reception given him on his arrival at the South Station by the Russians and Russian Jews of Boston was a wonderful sight. So was his funeral in Paris a few years later. He was as remarkable a character as Madame Breshkovsky herself.

The first number of *Free Russia* was published as a monthly in August, 1890, as the organ of the English Society of Friends of Russian Freedom, with "New York and London" in the date line. The November number of the same year appeared as an "American Edition", with the announcement that the Russian American National League of New York had united with the Society of Friends of Russian Freedom of England, and had organized the Free Russia Publishing Association "for the purpose of publishing this magazine in America." Thenceforward there was a special American edition of *Free Russia* issued every month in New York. The editing of it for American readers began with the number for July, 1891. This American edition ceased publication with the number for June–July, 1894.

American Friends of Russian Freedom (Page 124)

The call sent out in May of 1891 setting forth the objects of the association, and inviting membership, was headed by Colonel Thomas Wentworth Higginson, and signed by Julia Ward Howe, John G. Whittier, James Russell Lowell, George Kennan, William Lloyd Garrison, Henry I. Bowditch, Alice Freeman Palmer, Charles G. Ames, Edward L. Pierce, Phillips Brooks, Frank B. Sanborn, Annie Fields, Albert G. Browne, Edward Everett Hale, Minot J. Savage, R. Heber Newton, C. H. Eaton, Raymond S. Perrin, Mary

Putnam Jacobi, Titus Munson Coan, Marguerite
Merington, E. Winchester Donald, Lyman Abbott,
Hamilton W. Mabie, E. Benjamin Andrews, Lillie
B. Chace Wyman, Samuel L. Clemens, Joseph H.
Twichell, F. D. Huntington, William C. Gannett,
John W. Chadwick, John H. Vincent, W. H. Furness,
W. N. McVickar, and Joseph T. Duryea.

POEMS ON MADAME BRESHKOVSKY (PAGE 173)

The following are three of the many poems that
have been written to Catherine Breshkovsky:

BRESHKOVSKAYA

BY ELSA BARKER

(From the *New York Times*)

How narrow seems the round of ladies' lives
And ladies' duties in their smiling world,
The day this Titan woman, gray with years,
Goes out across the void to prove her soul!
Brief are the pains of motherhood, that end
In motherhood's long joy; but she has borne
The age-long travail of a cause that lies
Still-born at last on History's cold lap.
And yet she rests not; yet she will not drink
The cup of peace held to her parching lips
By smug Dishonor's hand. Nay, forth she fares,
Old and alone, on exile's rocky road —
That well-worn road with snows incarnadined
By blood drops from her feet long years agone.

Mother of power, my soul goes out to you
As a strong swimmer goes to meet the sea

Upon whose vastness he is like a leaf.
What are the ends and purposes of song,
Save as a bugle at the lips of life
To sound reveillé to a drowsing world
When some great deed is rising like the sun?

Where are those others whom your deed inspired
To deeds and words that were themselves a deed?
Those who believed in death have gone with death
To the gray crags of immortality;
Those who believed in life have gone with life
To the red halls of spiritual death.

And you?   But what is death or life to you?
Only a weapon in the hand of faith
To cleave a way for beings yet unborn
To a far freedom you will never share!
Freedom of body is an empty shell
Wherein men crawl whose souls are held with gyves;
For Freedom is a spirit, and she dwells
As often in a jail as on the hills.
In all the world this day there is no soul
Freer than you, Breshkovskaya, as you stand
Facing the future in your narrow cell.
For you are free of self and free of fear,
Those twin-born shades that lie in wait for man
When he steps out upon the wind-blown road
That leads to human greatness and to pain.

Take in your hand once more the pilgrim's staff —
Your delicate hand misshapen from the nights
In Kara's mines; bind on your unbent back,
That long has borne the burdens of the race,

The exile's bundle, and upon your feet
Strap the worn sandals of a tireless faith.

You are too great for pity.   After you
We send not sobs, but songs; and all our days
We shall walk bravelier knowing where you are.

TO CATHERINE BRESHKOVSKY

IN THE FORTRESS OF PETER AND PAUL

By Sophie Jewett

(Reprinted by permission of Thomas Y. Crowell.)

The liberal summer wind and sky and sea,
    For thy sake, narrow like a prison cell
    About the wistful hearts that love thee well
    And have no power to comfort nor set free.
They dare not ask what these hours mean to thee:
    Delays and silences intolerable?
    The joy that seemed so near, that soared, and fell,
    Become a patient, tragic memory?
From prison, exile, age, thy gray eyes won
    Their gladness, Mother, as of youth and sun,
    And love; and though thy hero heart, at length
Tortured past thought, break for thy children's tears,
    Thy mortal weariness shall be their strength,
    Thy martyred hope their vision through far years.

BABUSHKA

By Katharine Lee Bates

Thou whose sunny heart outglows
Arctic snows;
Russia's hearth-fire, cherishing
Courage almost perishing;
Torch that beacons oversea
Till a world is at thy knee;
Babushka the Belovéd,
What Czar can exile thee?

Sweet, serene, unswerving soul,
To thy goal
Pressing on such mighty pinions
Tyrants quake for their dominions,
And devise yet heavier key,
Deeper cell to prison thee,
Babushka the Belovéd,
Thyself art Liberty!

Though thy martyr body, old,
Chains may hold,
Clearer still thy voice goes ringing
Over steppe and mountain, bringing,
Holy mother of the free,
Millions more thy sons to be.
Babushka the Belovéd,
What death can silence thee?

Dates of Letters (Page 277)

Before her attempt at escape. Mme. Breshkovsky had written several letters to her friends, dating them in advance, and these were sent out to the post, day by day.

Printing Presses (Page 329)

These were probably the small presses that she had found so unsatisfactory. Her American friends had not been able to send a rotary press.

INDEX

DATE DUE

GAYLORD			PRINTED IN U.S.A.